Psychiatric Aspects of Terminal Illness

⟨Psychiatric Aspects of Terminal Illness⟩

Edited by

Samuel C. Klagsbrun, MD
Ivan K. Goldberg, MD
Marilyn M. Rawnsley, DNSc
Austin H. Kutscher, DDS
Eric R. Marcus, MD
Mary-Ellen Siegel, ACSW, MSW

The Charles Press, Publishers
Philadelphia

The Charles Press, Publishers
Post Office Box 15715
Philadelphia, Pennsylvania 19103

Library of Congress Catalog Card Number: 87-72173

ISBN 0-914783-21-1 (Cloth)
ISBN 0-914783-23-8 (Paper)

Sponsoring Editor: Sanford J. Robinson
Manuscript Editor: Lauren M. Meltzer
Production Manager: David L. Myers

Credits

Chapter 2, "Medical Care of the Dying Patient: Physicians Attitudes and Behavior," was adapted from I. Gerber, "The Making of a Physician: The Socialization Process and Medical Care of the Dying Patient," in *Education of the Medical Student in Thanatology,* New York: Arno Press, 1981

Chapter 3, "Physicians' Attitudes Toward Death and Bereavement: Comparison of Psychiatrists and Non-Psychiatrists," was adapted from D. Peretz, A. Carr, B. Schoenberg, and A. Kutscher, "A Survey of Physicians' Attitudes Toward Death and Bereavement: Comparison of Psychiatrists and Non-Psychiatrists," in *Perspectives on Bereavement,* New York: Arno Press, 1979

Chapter 4, "Caring for the Terminally Ill: Attitudes of the Housestaff," was adapted from J. Bruhn, M. Scurry, and H. Bunce, "The Care of Dying Patients: Attitudes and Experiences," in *The House Staff and Thanatology,* New York: Arno Press, 1982

Chapter 14, "Dilemma of the Dying — 'Why Won't People Listen to Me?'," was adapted from R. Stager in *Psychosocial Aspects of Radiation Therapy,* New York: Arno Press, 1981

Chapter 16, "Psychiatric Assessment and Management of the Dying Patient," was adapted from H. Muslin, "Training Medical Personnel for Terminal Care," in *Medical Care of the Dying Patient,* New York: Arno Press, 1982

Chapter 21, "Nursing Care and Terminal Illness," was adapted from J. Quint Benoliel, "General Principles of Nursing Care," in *Psychosocial Aspects of Radiation Therapy,* New York: Arno Press, 1981

Printed in the United States of America

Contents

PART II

THE IMPACT OF TERMINAL ILLNESS ON THE PATIENT AND FAMILY

PART III

PSYCHIATRY AND THE DYING PATIENT

PART IV

PSYCHIATRIC PATIENTS WITH TERMINAL ILLNESS

Editors

SAMUEL C. KLAGSBRUN, MD

Associate Clinical Professor of Psychiatry, College of Physicians and Surgeons, Columbia University, New York, New York; Director, Four Winds Hospital, Katonah, New York

IVAN K. GOLDBERG, MD

Associate in Clinical Psychiatry, College of Physicians and Surgeons, Columbia University, New York, New York

MARILYN M. RAWNSLEY, DNSc.

Associate Dean and Professor for Faculty and Academic Affairs, Pace University, Leinhard School of Nursing, Pleasantville, New York

AUSTIN H. KUTSCHER, DDS

President, The Foundation of Thanatology, New York, New York; Professor of Dentistry (in Psychiatry), Department of Psychiatry, College of Physicians and Surgeons, Columbia University, New York, New York

ERIC R. MARCUS, MD

Assistant Clinical Professor of Psychiatry, College of Physicians and Surgeons, Columbia University, New York, New York

MARY-ELLEN SIEGEL, ACSW, MSW

Senior Teaching Associate, Department of Community Medicine (Social Work), Mount Sinai School of Medicine, New York, New York

Contributors

JEANNE QUINT BENOLIEL, RN, PhD

Department of Community Health Care Services, University of Washington School of Nursing, Seattle, Washington

D. PETER BIRKETT, MD

Associate Research Scientist, Department of Psychiatry, Columbia University Center for Geriatrics and Gerontology, The Faculty of Medicine of Columbia University, New York State Office of Mental Health, New York, New York; Medical Director, Riverside Nursing Home, Haverstraw, New York

RICHARD S. BLACHER, MD

Professor of Psychiatry and Lecturer in Surgery, Tufts–New England Medical Center, Boston, Massachusetts

MARK BRODY, MD

Class of 1986, College of Physicians and Surgeons, Columbia University, New York, New York

JOHN G. BRUHN, PhD

Dean, School of Allied Health Sciences, University of Texas Medical Branch at Galveston, Galveston, Texas

HARVEY BUNCE III, PhD

Assistant Professor of Biometry, The University of Texas Medical Branch at Galveston, Galveston, Texas

ARTHUR C. CARR, PhD

Professor of Clinical Psychology in Psychiatry, Cornell University College of Medicine, New York, New York

DAVID F. CELLA, PhD

Instructor of Psychology in Psychiatry and Research Fellow, New York Hospital–Cornell Medical Center; Memorial Sloan–Kettering Cancer Center, New York, New York

VIRGINIA CRESPO, MSW

Department of Social Work Services, Neurological Institute, New York, New York

JODIE A. EMERY

Manager, Hospital/Home Care Temporaries, Inc., New York, New York

SUSAN EVANS, RN, MEd

Research Nurse, New York Hospital, Payne Whitney Psychiatric Center, New York, New York

ALLEN P. FERTZIGER, PhD

Independent Scholar, University of Maryland, College Park, Maryland

RICHARD FRIEDMAN, MD

Clinical Associate Professor of Psychiatry, Cornell University Medical College, Westchester Division, The New York Hospital, White Plains, New York

IRWIN GERBER, PhD

Administrator, Department of Neoplastic Diseases, Mount Sinai School of Medicine, New York, New York

JUDITH GIORGI-CIPRIANO, RN, MS

Nursing Care Coordinator, Department of Psychiatry, Cornell University Medical College, Westchester Division; The New York Hospital, White Plains, New York

MARGARET J. GREY, DrPH, RN

Assistant Professor of Nursing, University of Pennsylvania School of Nursing, Philadelphia, Pennsylvania

THERESA LADERO, EdD, RNC

Geo-Psychiatric Clinician, Bronx Municipal Hospital; Assistant Professor, Lienhard School of Nursing, Pace University, Pleasantville, New York

ROBERT S. LAMPKE, MD

Attending Psychiatrist, Consultation-Liaison Service, Kings County Hospital Center, State University Hospital, Brooklyn, New York; Clinical Assistant Professor of Psychiatry, State University of New York Health Sciences Center at Brooklyn, Brooklyn, New York

MARILYN LEWIS LANZA, RN, DNSc, CS

Associate Chief of Nursing Services for Research, Veterans Administration Hospital, Bedford, Massachusetts

LYNNA M. LESKO, MD, PhD

Assistant Attending Psychiatrist and Assistant Professor of Psychiatry, Memorial Sloan–Kettering Cancer Center and Cornell Medical Center, New York, New York

NORMAN B. LEVY, MD

Director, Liaison Psychiatry Division, Westchester County Medical Center; Professor of Psychiatry, Medicine and Surgery, New York Medical College, New York, New York

KENNETH R. LIEGNER, MD

Clinical Instructor of Medicine, New York Medical College/Westchester County Medical College; Private Practice, Internal Medicine/Critical Care Medicine, Armonk, New York; Emergency Room Attending (Part-Time), Northern Westchester Hospital Center, Mount Kisco, New York

LEONARD M. LIEGNER, MD

Associate Professor of Radiology, College of Physicians and Surgeons, Columbia University, New York, New York; Director of Radiation Therapy, St. Luke's Hospital Medical Center, New York, New York

KEN MAGRATH, PhD

Clinical Psychologist, Danbury Hospital, Danbury, Connecticut

HYMAN L. MUSLIN, MD

Professor of Psychiatry, University of Illinois College of Medicine, Chicago, Illinois

DAVID PERETZ, MD

Assistant Clinical Professor of Psychiatry, College of Physicians and Surgeons, Columbia University, New York, New York

CATHY RADUNS, MA

New York Hospital, Payne Whitney Psychiatric Cancer Center, New York, New York

PATRICIA M. REDDISH, MSN, CS

Psychiatric Clinical Specialist, Burn Unit, Westchester County Medical

JONATHAN SCHINDELHEIM, MD

Assistant Professor of Psychiatry, Tufts University School of Medicine, Boston, Massachusetts

BERNARD SCHOENBERG, MD

Associate Dean for Academic Affairs and Professor of Clinical Psychiatry, College of Physicians and Surgeons, Columbia University, New York, New York: Chairman of Executive Committee (Medical Affairs), Foundation of Thanatology, New York, New York; Deceased

MURPHY T. SCURRY, MD

Associate Professor of Internal Medicine, The University of Texas Medical Branch at Galveston, Galveston, Texas

IRENE B. SEELAND, MD

Assistant Clinical Professor of Psychiatry, New York University School of Medicine; Attending Psychiatrist, Goldwater Memorial Hospital, New York, New York

SALLY K. SEVERINO, MD

Assistant Professor of Psychiatry, New York Hospital-Cornell Medical Center, New York, New York; Collaborating Psychoanalyst, Columbia University Center for Psychoanalytic Training and Research, New York, New York

PETER A. SHAPIRO, MD

Liaison Psychiatrist (Head and Neck), Department of Psychiatry, College of Physicians and Surgeons, Columbia University, New York, New York

DONALD L. SHERAK, MD

Kings County Hospital Center, State University Hospital, Brooklyn, New York; SUNY Health Sciences Center at Brooklyn, Brooklyn, New York

RAE ELLEN S. STAGER, RN

Formerly Assistant Director of Nursing (Psychiatry and Pediatrics), Sheboygan Memorial Hospital, Sheboygan, Wisconsin

SANDRA SWIRSKEY, MSW

Staff Social Worker, Department of Psychiatry, Cornell University Medical College, Westchester Division, The New York Hospital, White Plains, New York

RAYMOND VICKERS, MD

Director, New York State Home for Veterans, New York State Department of Health, Oxford, New York; Associate Professor of Psychiatry, Albany Medical College of Union University, Albany, New York

MARCELLA BAKUR WEINER, EdD

Adjunct Professor, Fordham University Graduate School of Social Work at Lincoln Center, New York, New York

WILLIAM WEINER, ACSW

Psychotherapist, Private Practice; Department of Social Work Services, Bronx Veterans Administration Hospital, Bronx, New York

LYNN C. WINTHER, MD

Assistant Professor of Psychiatry, Cornell University Medical College, Westchester Division, The New York Hospital, White Plains, New York

MARY ANN ZUBLER, MD

Chief of Oncology, Veterans Administration Medical Center, Houston, Texas

Preface

This book brings together a variety of approaches and strategies for managing the mental distress that accompanies terminal illness.

Although the need for psychological help during the dying process is well appreciated in concept (and, certainly, instinctively) by physicians, nurses, and other professional staff, the actual implementation of emotional care in this circumstance is all too often wanting or inadequate. How to account for this lapse in care?

Part of the problem, especially among young physicians, is a personal uneasiness in dealing with the reality of death, coupled with a lack of training in care of the dying and an uncertainty of just what to do and say in this situation. Also, there is the unspoken thought that after all, the patient is dying, and does it really matter what is said at this stage? These attitudes undoubtedly explain the results of studies showing that doctors' visits to the terminally ill are much briefer and are conducted at greater distances from the bedside than with other patients. In his seminal work, *Dying,* John Hinton, discussing quality of care, observed:

> We emerge deserving little credit, we who are capable of ignoring the conditions which make muted people suffer. The dissatisfied dead cannot noise abroad the negligence they have experienced.*

It is universally acknowledged that, in order to provide optimal care to the dying and improve the quality of remaining life, the care team must recognize the emotional needs of the terminally ill and then be able to offer effective psychological care. But what is effective psychological care, and how is it achieved in this extraordinarily difficult situation?

---

*Hinton, J. 1972. *Dying,* Second edition. London: Penguin Press, p. 159.

Psychiatric Aspects of Terminal Illness focuses on this critical issue. Based primarily on the personal experiences and studies of 48 outstanding workers in the caring profession, the book examines the matter and manner of psychological care within four categories: the impact of terminal illness on the health care team; the impact of terminal illness on the patient and family; psychiatry and the dying patient; and psychiatric patients with terminal illness.

We believe that this book will be of genuine value to all those who provide emotional, social, and spiritual help to the seriously or terminally ill. This includes psychiatrists, nurses, psychologists, social workers, psychiatric nurse specialists, clergy, oncologists, and others who counsel the dying and their families. It is our hope that this work will contribute to making the dying process what Francis Bacon called "a fair and easy passage."

Acknowledgment

The editors wish to acknowledge the support and encouragement of the Foundation of Thanatology in the preparation of this volume. All royalties from the sale of this book are assigned to the Foundation of Thanatology, a tax exempt, not for profit, public scientific and educational foundation.

Thanatology, a new subspecialty of medicine, is involved in scientific and humanistic inquiries and the application of the knowledge derived therefrom to the subjects of the psychological aspects of dying; reactions to loss, death, and grief; and recovery from bereavement.

The Foundation of Thanatology is dedicated to advancing the cause of enlightened health care for the terminally ill patient and his family. The Foundation's orientation is a positive one based on the philosophy of fostering a more mature acceptance and understanding of death and the problems of grief and the more effective and humane management and treatment of the dying patient and his bereaved family members.

Part I

The Impact of Terminal Illness on the Health Care Team

1

Confronting Terminal Illness: The Training of a Physician

Donald Sherak

A chief medical resident, in his ongoing quest to stump his medical students, asked his current flock a question that had just been posed to him on his specialty boards: "In hypoxic shock, where is the site of the lesion?" He had forgotten that we were fresh from two years with our heads in the books, and that our thinking was pure and free from the vicissitudes of clinical experience. Almost in unison, we shot back, "The lesion is at the subcellular level—in the mitochondria."

Indeed, we had been well taught the biochemical mechanisms and histological changes involved in cell death. But how is a student trained to respond to that bedridden collection of cells and organs, the patient with a life-threatening illness?

Much of my medical education was devoted to elaborating the variety of interventions to which we students might subject those failing organ systems. Our goal was to bring the body's runaway parameters back to "laboratory values compatible with life"—to "lower the BUN," "raise the crit," "get the fluid out of the lungs," "get the heart back into sinus rhythm." I also recall a small set of lectures that mentioned that somewhere amid the group of failing organs, like dying trees, there existed a forest—the whole person.

The fact that this unique assemblage, the whole person, was in transit, passing from us, was not really addressed. The patient's feelings might be categorized by an external scale or analyzed for psychodynamic stressors by a consulting psychiatrist. But the loss of a whole person, if considered at all, was taken as something incidental. When a patient died, the case was closed after mention of the cause of death and how that might have been reversed or slowed until another organ system received the blame. There was never a mention of how the person died, the quality of the final events and how they might be handled differently in the future. Also, there was never a mention of how the dying and the death affected the staff. It was almost as if death were an incidental annoyance appended to the practice of medicine. The death of the patient fell outside of the quantification that defined medical treatment. There did not seem to be anything the physician could medically "do" in that situation. Furthermore, for the medical intern, by the next morning there would always be another patient in that bed, waiting to be examined and worked up.

CASE HISTORY

During my fourth year of medical school, I studied with Dr. Bernie Siegel, an attending surgeon at Yale–New Haven Hospital. While with Dr. Siegel, I came to know one patient, whom I refer to as Terry. She was a strikingly beautiful, dynamic woman from the Southwest, in her late thirties and the mother of two young children.

Terry had worked with her husband in the production of television documentaries until five years earlier, when he died of pancreatic cancer—a disease that has virtually no long-term survival rate. Fourteen months earlier, Terry had been diagnosed as having this same disease. A year ago, she had started coming to one of the Exceptional Cancer Patient support groups that Bernie Siegel led. At the same time she went to a massage therapist for help in alleviating some of her pain. Daniel, the massage therapist, was 15 years younger than Terry. With full knowledge of her prognosis, he became her lover. This, I learned later, was typical of Terry's charisma.

I knew none of this when I first followed Bernie into Terry's dark, monitor-jammed room in the intensive care unit. My prior experience in the intensive care unit was only as a member of a team that "did things" to patients—adjusted beds, drew blood gases, checked monitors—and then left. Bernie gently woke Terry up by calling her name, sat on the edge of her bed, and began talking to her in a soft voice, his hand resting on her thin, waxen arm. Not knowing what to do, I stood in the doorway. My feelings ranged from empathetic tenderness to outright terror. More important, I felt terribly out of place, embarrassed and intrusive. After a while, Bernie mentioned that he had a new medical student with him. Terry briefly acknowledged my presence and they then continued their discussion.

She had terminal, inoperable pancreatic cancer. She was on a variety of medications, and was receiving intravenous nutrition. Her heart was being monitored around the clock and nurses were taking her vital signs hourly. Her concerns, however, were directed elsewhere. Should she stay in the hospital, find a hospice, or arrange for nursing care at home? How often should her two young children visit? How would she deal with her mother and sister, who were flying north shortly? Her questions, then, were how to live and how to die.

I think I stood open-mouthed as Bernie told Terry that she could die whenever she was ready to let go, that her children would be all right and would draw strength from her memory. Furthermore, she could decide where she would be most comfortable—home, hospital, or hospice.

Bernie made arrangements with the staff for Terry to be moved to a general medical-surgical floor and for her vital signs to be taken only once during each nursing shift. He went to the nursing station and began charting his note with the thick, purple lines of the discarded surgical marking pens that he favors. He wrote a brief summary of Terry's physical status and then began committing to paper what everyone knew, but no member of the health care team was acknowledging: that Terry was dying and that nothing could stop or even slow that process. Furthermore, any consideration of medical or surgical intervention should be secondary to her needs for comfort and support.

As I stood at his side reading this note, which was unlike any other I had ever seen in a chart, I began to cry uncontrollably. I have since come to know and be comfortable with the fact that there are many varieties of crying and that mine at that moment was the crying of one who is moved and shaken but, at the same time, self-conscious and apprehensive about losing control, the crying of one who has had light but genuine contact with the massive force of death's inevitability. She was young, beautiful, and talented, and she had small, angelic children. If she died, anyone could die. I cried for myself. Bernie looked up at me. "I still cry," he said, "but it is different now. Every so often, when I'm watching a sad movie with my wife or seeing a sunset, it all comes out. Then I cry for my patients, my family and myself. It all comes out together and I feel cleansed, until it builds up again."

The next time I saw Terry, she was in a large room on a medical-surgical floor. The room had several appliances to enable her to move her bowels and to shower with minimal assistance. There were pictures of and by her children on the walls, cards and flowers on the windowsill. I pulled up a chair this time, and sat down beside Bernie. Talk was now focused on practical issues. She wanted her children to spend the rest of the school year living with Daniel and then, during the summer, move south to live with her sister, even though she was at odds with her brother-in-law. Furthermore, she wanted everyone in the family to accept it her way. At a certain point, she stopped going over and over the details and dropped her head onto Bernie's shoulder and collapsed into sleep. I did not understand what was happening. I was not accustomed to such intensity between doctor and patient, and I had not previously considered how it might be handled.

Later, we went to the nursing station and read from the chart the medical resident's note from the previous day. It began, "The patient is an unfortunate

39-year-old woman with pancreatic cancer ..." "That's just it," Bernie said, "that's where doctors get caught and feel like failures. You saw Terry. She's not unfortunate. She has a disease."

Futher in the chart we noted that she was still receiving Synthroid, a hormone supplement given for a low-grade chronic thyroid condition, not something that would be a factor for a terminally ill patient. In his note, Bernie wrote, "Patient is trying to die. In accordance with her wishes, I suggest holding all medications except for pain relief." Initially, I felt discomfort with this—I remember repeatedly asking Bernie if this was indeed all right. Eventually, I was able to trust what I was seeing.

Several days later, we went to see Terry during rounds. Her mother and sister were standing outside her closed door, looking at a loss about what to do. Upon entering, we found Terry, propped up, furiously smoking, a habit she had stopped when her cancer was diagnosed. She stubbed out her cigarette and said, "Bernie, dying is hard. Why isn't it working? When am I going to die?" At that point, I remember thinking, "Hey, this isn't like the way the books said it would be. We're in trouble." While I vacillated between frozen panic and an inner search for a good reason why I should leave the room, Bernie advanced to Terry's bed. She seemed genuinely glad to see him. He said, "You can die next Thursday at three p.m. Do you have any other questions?" After she stopped laughing, he got serious. "What is it you need to do so you can die? What do you need to know before you can let go?" In fact, she had great concern about her children and was trying to squeeze the work of a full lifetime of mothering into her remaining time.

While she used the toilet, we went out into the hall and I learned from her mother and sister that we were seeing a partial return of the old Terry—feisty, colorful, and strong-headed. Her family felt both appreciation for the re-emergence of her spirited personality and a desire to help her. When we went back inside, Bernie began talking to her in a new way: "O.K. Terry, you're the director again, finishing another show. You tell me, what does it need for a good ending?"

Was it all right, I wondered, to talk this way to a dying patient? It was more than all right. Her features softened and she smiled. She said she would try to think things through that way and see what came up.

One of the most important lessons of my month's rotation came several days later. I had clearly become involved in the daily developments of Bernie's patients. Now we were ending the fourteenth or fifteenth hour of his day of office visits, surgery, and consulting. Another member of his team was on call that night. He began debating out loud about whether or not he should return to the hospital and make his own rounds anyway. He then turned to me and said, "There are some people we really love in the hospital tonight. But they are in good care.

We should go home, rest, and see them tomorrow."

I saw Terry on the last day of my rotation. Her lover, Daniel, was partially living in her room. He had a small mattress folded up on the floor where he slept at night and sat quietly while she slept during the day. He left for a few hours each day to work some jobs. Terry's children were staying with neighbors and came to visit every other day. Her family had gone south again.

When we walked in, Daniel was manicuring Terry's nails. She was frail and more cachectic, now receiving only fluids and morphine sulfate. Bernie had plans to begin his vacation in two days. They talked briefly and acknowledged what might happen. When it was time to leave, I found myself thanking her for what she had shared with me. Her response was straight from what I had come to know as "the old Terry." She took my hand and said, "Life is a roller coaster ride, my friend, grab your ticket and get on board." She kissed each of us and we left. She died a week later.

Terry's living and dying was important to me. So many issues clustered around that one relationship. I believe that if every medical student were to spend one month with a skilled doctor, social worker, or psychologist at the bedside of a dying patient, the experience would permanently enhance each one's ability to approach life-threatened patients. Such exposure would make medical students less likely to be consumed by the routine of hospital expediency and would help them to remain open to the transforming potential of simply knowing patients in all of their manifestations. In addition, the students would come to know that there are many varied occasions for letting go, not simply one.

In having the opportunity to shadow a member of the health care team who has already done much work on himself or herself and developed these skills, a student encounters an important role model. Here is an opportunity to set aside questions of theory and technique and to experience directly how another, with years of experience, handles these issues. It is one thing to read of Kubler-Ross' (1969, 1981) explanations of the value of open communication with those who are dying. It is something else to be sensitive to this value and to do the work necessary to fulfill it.

Although I felt overwhelmed and confused in meeting Bernie's life-threatened patients, I also felt permission to engage myself, to open up. I found that I was not facing potential mistakes, but opportunities for growth. I was introduced to the concept of dying as a task to be fulfilled; I saw a physician shift from the role of lifesaver to that of facilitator in an appropriate death. Directly out of this experience, I began to sense a way of being that would be consistent with my strengths and weaknesses and that could help patients address their unfinished business. The patient and the process became my teacher.

Privileged Listener

Bernie has recently written about how the receptive professional can become a "privileged listener," one who begins to hear things "too emotional or too weird to tell other doctors" (Siegel 1966). My experience has been that this material is usually passed off as rationalization or grasping at straws. But this is the organism at work, using literal and symbolic language to come to terms with disease and dying. When the receptive healer begins to enter into this language, the patient begins to teach the doctor. This so-called "weird stuff" is truly significant to the person. To help the patient in appropriate dying it is necessary first to demonstrate familiarity with and acceptance of the contents of the patient's inner world. My experiences with two patients whom I cared for during my medicine clerkship help illustrate this.

Mrs. Eaton was a frail, 92-year-old great-grandmother from the Carribean. She was like the good grandmother from an old story—petite, genteel, delightful, and quite literally from another century and culture. She had diabetes and her kidneys were failing. Several times she became overwhelmed and frightened by hospital procedures and withdrew with a baby-like grimace of fear. It was my task to draw blood from her daily, and I quickly came to dread it, knowing that despite her best efforts she would flinch, and might, as she often did, break into tears. One day, in an effort to soothe my own nerves, I began talking about my experiences in Jamaica years ago. Eventually, I started talking about the food I had enjoyed. It turned out that her daughter had been preparing her favorite, pepper pot soup, the night she fell ill, and she was homesick for her soup, codfish, and curry. Now we shared something that was more pleasurable for both of us. I still drew her blood, but I always talked about our favorite foods or at least made reference to our first lengthy discussion of the spicy delights of Caribbean cooking. I kept it up because it made my unavoidable task easier and because it allowed me to share some good memories. Only when she came up to me on her day of discharge to let me know, with a wide, warm smile, that she was on her way home to a good bowl of pepper pot soup, did I realize how much it had meant to her.

Archibald Spree was another sort of patient. He was 33 years old. He had an 18-year drinking history and a 12-year history of intravenous drug use; he had neuropathies, stasis ulcers, active tuberculosis, neurosyphilis, and AIDS. In some combination, these problems were coming together to kill him soon. My first thought was, "This guy is going to be a lot of work," and my second was, "Extra precautions, kiddo!" I mention these thoughts because I think they are near the top of the list of every clinician who works with AIDS patients.

Two things led me to touch the entire person. Mr. Spree, in fact, broke the ice. The night he spiked a high fever I was poring over his tortured circulatory system, looking for an inlet from which to draw a series of blood cultures. He called out from his delerium, "Ouch! What'd you go and do that for, boy?" He immediately became embarrassed and apologetic. "Hey, you know I've got to be badly messed up if I just called my white doctor, 'boy.' " It was all I could do to keep from laughing at his wackiness. Then I became deeply touched: this was probably the one time in my life that I would be called "boy," but I could only imagine the number of times he had been subjected to that indignity. My laughter dissolved his fear of retribution.

Mr. Spree had a mother who came daily and read the Bible at his bedside. I think it was the day after the "boy" incident that I asked Mrs. Spree what passage of the Bible gave her strength. At that point we became real to each other.

Lest you think it was smooth sailing with Mr. Spree, I want to tell you that he soon developed a very shaky mental status, fading in and out of various degrees of stupor and delirium. Once when I was in his room concentrating on something else and his mother was praying, he abruptly awoke and shouted at me, "Hey, Doc, one thing I got to know. Am I going to die?" I can still hear that voice. I don't think I ever had an answer that satisfied either of us.

I dwell on my affectionate, if uneasy portrait of this patient for good reasons. As the neurological sequelae of AIDS become more widely known, such patients may become a new class, life-threatened patients with severe organic mental disturbance. Even we who now find that we can work with the more typical dying patient may find ourselves overwhelmed by the intensity of these patients' escalated demands. The serene, cachectic patient we leave one evening may transform into a delirious, violent source of danger to himself and others before morning.

DEATH EDUCATION

Medical students can only learn through experience that their base of professional knowledge is not the only vehicle for treating patients who have life-threatening illnesses. Their capacities in these situations will grow out of their encounters with patients, if they are able to sustain compassionate and open hearts. To do this, medical students must have at least begun to grapple with their own unfinished business and with the meanings of the deaths in their own lives. Working with life-threatened patients under the guidance of more experienced professionals with skills in this area provides a safe place in which students can begin to examine and free their responses to dying. They will also then be able to begin to appreciate how this greater receptivity contributes to the healing, supportive relationship that is so central to the needs of life-threatened patients.

The transition to this approach is difficult for those doctors in training who have not had the exposure or life experience to develop in this direction. It contradicts the superficial but pervasive expectations of a physician's emotional makeup that often become internalized as the doctor in training's own projected performance. In recounting his personal development, Bernie Siegel (1986) notes,

I used to think that a certain amount of [this] distancing was essential, but for most doctors, I think it goes too far. Too often the pressure squeezes out our native compassion. The so-called detached concern we're taught is an absurdity. Instead, we need to be taught a rational caring, which allows the expression of feelings without impairing the ability to make decisions.

Lectures, videotapes, and discussion groups are excellent preparation. They can be analogous to the other preclinical courses. However, the integrative learning of how to approach the dying patient is only fully done at the bedside, where the skills that make a physician converge, and where most of the role modeling process takes place.

Young interns make a harsh discovery when they must confront the family of a patient who has died. They have received a death education, of sorts, "on the street corner" and they often find that feelings of incapacity and unpreparedness leave them full of anger, emptiness, and a sense of failure. Having previously avoided the topic, if for no other reason than because it was accepted policy, they now find it too late to bridge the gap. The result is often even earlier distancing and greater denial the next time. To inculcate different and medically significant skills, those responsible for the education of physicians must arrange for the medical student to learn about death and dying at the bedside. It must be done before students become interns and their concern for the whole person is at the bottom of a tremendously long list of house officers' daily duties.

Much has been written about the medical student's first encounter with death, dissecting a cadaver in the gross anatomy laboratory. Yet this is death without the person; denial goes unnoticed. Much later, when patients are alive and dependent on the doctor's care, there is the shock of clinical responsibility. Between this recognition of death and the recognition of life, we can interpose a recognition of dying and move future physicians away from a unilateral focus. The extent of this need becomes more evident when we take into consideration the fact that at this time more than half of all deaths in the United States occur in hospitals.

What is the state of death education in American medical schools in 1986? Dickinson's (1981, 1985) ongoing assessment of this area of the medical curriculum shows that as of 1985, only 14 medical schools offered full-term courses in death education. However, a full 82% of American medical schools integrate short courses and lectures into the curriculum. The number of schools that offer no formal death education is decreasing (14 in 1975, 10 in 1980, and six in 1985). It is hoped that this embarassing statistic will continue its linear path to oblivion. Although more than half of the schools offering death education employ a team approach, thus allowing students to appreciate the perspectives of nurses, social workers, philosophers, and attorneys, Dickinson reported that the most frequent format continues to be a combination of lecture and discussion, with the seminar approach less frequently used.

In a theoretical paper, Olin (1972) observed that "often it would seem that [medical school] faculties assume that the development of attitudes and skills necessary to work with the dying patient will somehow be acquired without direct instruction." He proposed that medical students be paired with dying patients in the same manner in which some medical schools pair first-year medical students to a family with an expectant mother. Olin structured his proposal in three parts. Students in small group tutorials would examine appropriate topics, such as the students' conceptions of death and the physician's role with the dying patient, as well as such practical matters as the care of small problems (bed sores and constipation) that loom large in the reality experienced by dying patients. The small groups would also provide students with opportunities to explore their own experiences and reactions. In the second part of this educational effort, the students would conduct ongoing interviews with the dying patient throughout the course of medical training. Finally, in an innovation, he proposed follow-up interviews with a family member for a while after the patient's death in order that the student involved might gain an understanding of the dynamics and medical complications that can be associated with the mourning process.

Nelson (1980) reported a particularly promising development at Dartmouth Medical School where, "as part of a broader conception of patient care," there is a death and dying component to the psychiatry clerkship. This course, unlike many offerings, but like death itself, is mandatory. The exposure to dying patients for one-and-a-half to three hours a week is "not an attempt to convince medical students to become psychiatrists or experts in death and dying, but rather to facilitate the medical student's understanding of the patient as a bio-social-psychological being." And, one might add, it is a means of preventing some of the mismanagement and pain that is often perpetuated by the unprepared physician.

In this program, the initial focus is on the student's exploration of patient's coping processes and learning how to give support. The student visits the patient alone and, once weekly, with a supervisor. The supervisor also meets with the student to discuss the relationship between the patient and the student-doctor and to explore relevant issues, including therapeutic relationships, communication skills, and the student's own reactions. Students also meet with other members of the health care team, both to learn of their plans for the patient and to appreciate their perspectives. Three meetings are scheduled for a group of students with a supervisor for presentations on coping styles and basic support therapies, as well as exploration of their own experiences. Nelson reports that students frequently request a fourth meeting for the discussion of ethical dilemmas.

A summary of verbal and written evaluations indicates that most students report greater ease in dealing with these issues and an increased ability to hear what the patients are actually saying. The students come to know the supportive potential in their role. Furthermore, "students discover . . . that most . . . patients with cancer are much stronger than many staff members tend to believe." Overall, it is a well-structured, time-effective way to achieve a significant advance in medical students' supportive and communication skills with the dying patient.

Dickinson and Pearson (1980-81) have also done a study of 1,093 physicians, which suggests that death education is not wasted time siphoned from other areas. Medical students who are given the opportunity and guidance to focus on the needs of dying patients and their families find that their clinical approach is inevitably colored. In summary, bedside teaching of the clinical approach to the dying patient has several unique advantages:

1. Supervisor–patient contact provides a necessary role model. I feel that appropriately trained psychologists, social workers, nurses, or members of the clergy might provide some of the role modeling.
2. The students may benefit from a halo effect and find the patients more willing to open up here than in an unstructured situation, thus giving the students a sense of the potential inherent in all doctor-patient relationships.
3. The students can take emotional risks, knowing that an experienced hand is standing by as they are facing some of the most difficult questions and emotions in medicine.
4. The students have an opportunity, almost unique in medical training, to explore their own intrapersonal conflicts, and if they are lucky, those of their advisors, perhaps giving the students an appreciation of the value of understanding their reactions to the medicine they practice.

Now I return to my original line of questioning. When the whole person dies, where is the lesion? I propose that it is at the site of that person's relationships. It is at that level that students need to work. A student who has worked under a professional who is skilled in the needs and language of patients whose lives are threatened will be able to be faithful both to the clinical tasks and to the patients' deeper agendas.

2

Medical Care of the Dying Patient: Physicians' Attitudes and Behavior

Irwin Gerber

In recent years the medical profession has experienced much criticism from within its ranks as well as from outside sources. One major area of attack has been the medical care of the dying patient. With the increased interest in thanatology, mainly through the efforts of practitioners such as Kutscher (1969), Parkes (1972), Ross (1969), and Saunders (1959), the existing problems physicians encounter with dying patients can no longer be exclusively discussed within the medical profession. The medical care of the dying patient has expanded beyond pure medical technology into the realm of psychosocial considerations. On face value, this reformulation of the physician's role should be welcomed and pursued by the medical profession. Physicians' intense anxiety, indecision, and withdrawal from the dying patient could be reduced if the knowledge and expertise of "thanatologists" are taken seriously. Unfortunately, the acceptance and practical use of this knowledge has been minimal. By glancing through *Index Medicus* one notes a paucity of articles dealing with the question of the dying patient. To go one step further, reading the existing articles leaves one with the impression that what is desired by physicians are two or three pages of quick and easy solutions to difficult problems such as how to communicate with a dying patient, to inform or not to tell a patient he has a terminal illness, and, of course, the most sensitive question of euthanasia. These are important problem areas. However, the advice given in the published material is often contradictory and clearly implies that medical education has been delinquent in meaningful instruction regarding the dying patient. Therefore, almost all written material by physicians seems to be presented as a "crash course" in thanatology.

The above comments represent a somewhat bleak picture of medicine's concern about the dying patient. This is not a false impression. Although attempts are being made to change this situation, the existing programs in thanatology are, in the main, too limited in scope and effects do not appear to be very encouraging. In addition, except for isolated cases (see for example, Barton, 1972) the logical starting point for such training has been totally ignored. The medical profession is not fully responding to the problem of the dying patient when it offers seminars and lectures after the period of formal medical education. Training in medical school must include the area of thanatology. This training can have a positive impact only if it is considered important enough to warrant equal time with the basic clinical courses, and if the future physician is exposed to dying patients very early in the formal curriculum. The medical student should be made aware that the "process of dying" is not only terrible for the patient and close family members, but equally traumatic for him as a physician. Because of changes in medical technology, physicians will be treating more terminally ill patients and for a longer period of time than in the past. The result of this situation is physician exposure to problems that go beyond traditional medical management. Levine and Scotch (1970) urge medical educators to give more emphasis to the dying patient because "...the new medical technology has provided more options and alternatives and, at the same time, more conflicts and dilemmas for the physician in the management of the dying patient, that dying now as never before approaches the dimensions of a medical social problem." Individuals who have the opportunity to observe the present-day management of the dying patient will find it difficult to argue against the point that the dying patient *is* a contemporary medical social problem.

Physician Attitude And Behavior

The literature pertaining to physicians' handling of the dying patient reveals a disturbing pattern. The attitudes and actions of most physicians appear to be as painful for the practitioner as they are for the dying patient, concerned family members and friends and other health professionals (e.g., nurses). The most typical behavior of the physician is to withdraw from the terminally ill patient. This disassociation may take many forms. Depending on the physician's estimate of how long the patient will live one observes almost complete physical and emotional withdrawal from the patient (Glaser and Strauss, 1968). The closer the patient is to death the more likely most physicians will decrease the number of times they "stop by to see the patient," each visit will be shorter, and attempts to communicate will decrease. At this point, it must be emphasized that we are not referring only to a patient who is comatose with a certainty of death within the next twenty-four hours. Physician withdrawal starts well before this stage of the dying process. It has been noted by Lippincott (1972) that this withdrawal is a "conspiracy of silence" between physician and patient, each having needs to deny the inevitable. The moving away from the dying patient has been observed to produce unnecessary discomfort for the patient at a time when such contact and comfort is most needed. As Feifel (1963) suggests, some patients have more pain from sudden emotional isolation and rejection than from the illness itself. Furthermore, the patient begins to have more contact with personnel, other than physicians, who are themselves in a bind because of certain professional restrictions on what they can say to the patient. In addition to her own anxieties about death the nurse, for example, is placed in an extremely difficult situation when dying patients begin to probe about their conditions, changes in medicaitons and, of course, whether or not they are dying. The combination of physician withdrawal and the nurse's professional limitations create a vacuum in this area of patient need.

By virtue of having specialized skills and knowledge, and professional dominance, the physician is the leader of the health team. Withdrawal from the patient may make the doctor less of a leader in the eyes of other staff members and they may follow his lead. In addition, withdrawal does not necessarily reduce the anxiety the physician has about death. Crane (1970) points out that physicians as other "mortals" see death as an event that holds no more than passing concern. However, continued interaction with dying patients brings forth latent fears about death, and, therefore, makes contact with dying patients extremely difficult. Yes, the physician is human with personal feelings and emotions. But, can we justify the physician's withdrawal from patients simply because he is human? I think not. We must remember that his role-functioning in other areas of medical care is not justified because he is human, but rather because the role of physician has certain rights, obligations, and responsibilities that are not observed for other professional roles. These role expectations create a "god-like" aura sufficient enough to warrant others to anticipate a more human approach in treating the dying patients, e.g., to actively participate in the medical care of the dying patient, as opposed to withdrawal.

Lasagna (1969) has been particularly pointed in his comments about the relationship between physicians' attitudes toward death and the care of the dying patient. Lasagna is of the opinion that physicians avoid telling patients about the terminal nature of their illness in order to satisfy personal needs. Lasagna concludes, "The physician's ego and peace of soul are apt to be assaulted by the knowledge that he is unable to alter the downhill course. He may feel uncomfortable and ill at ease; he may also be so busy that he is reluctant to take the time required to get to know the patient and family well enough to do the job properly." To tell or not to tell the dying patient is probably the most sensitive and controversial issue in the medical care of the dying patient. We recognize that this issue may never be resolved, but what is of interest is that during the period of formal medical education this question is rarely discussed. If it is a topic of discussion, the physician in training is rarely made aware of its importance and the impact it will have on his future medical practice. A possible relationship exists between informing a patient that he will die and the observed withdrawal from the patient. Physicians who either strongly believe that a patient should not be informed or are uncertain how to approach the individual are more likely to withdraw physically and emotionally from the dying patient than physicians who believe in and actually tell the patient. The potential effects for physicians who inform patients are less personal anxiety, more confidence when a case is discussed with colleagues, and increased emotional strength to communicate with dying patients. Patients, of course, will probably feel less isolated, have more confidence in their physicians, and be thankful for the opportunity to share personal feelings and discuss ways to "put their house in order."

It can be argued that the above discussion represents a gross generalization of the situation because the decision to inform terminally ill patients of their impending death is dependent upon the uniqueness of each case. There is some validity in this argument; however, the exisitng research on patients' and physicians' attitudes about being informed and informing seem to indicate that patients are more likely to want to be informed, while physicians have less of a desire to inform. Kasper (1959) found that from 77 to 89 percent of patients say they would prefer to be told that they are dying. Feifel (1963) reported that 82% of patients favored complete knowledge of terminal illness. Pursuing this area of inquiry, Feifel and his colleagues (1967) found that most physicians were in favor of being informed that they had an incurable illness, but were less willing to inform others in the same situation. Of direct importance to the relationship between the "making of a physician" and the subsequent handling of dying patients is Feifel's hypothesis that many physicians enter the medical field in order to control their own fears of death. Questioning of 40 physicians by Feifel (1963) indicated that while physicians *thought less* about death when compared to patients and nonprofessionals, they were *more afraid* of death than any of the control groups. In a follow-up study, Feifel (1967) reported that 63% of physicians were less fearful of death than before they became physicians. In response to how one would react to the death of another person, "feeling bad" and "sorry" were most often mentioned by physically ill and healthy non-medical respondents, while, "Would make me reflect on my own mortality" was the most common reaction of physicians. Feifel's work suggests that medical schools are training individuals with a high level of death anxiety which is reduced during the course of medical training. Nevertheless, the final product of medical education, the physician, is still *unusually* anxious about death.

It may be interesting to note that a substantial number of patients know at some point in time that they have a terminal illness (Glaser and Strauss, 1968). This knowledge is gained not by what is told, but by what *is not* told. The physician recognizes that his own behavior such as withdrawal represents "death clues" for the dying patient. Therefore, it is not an unlikely assumption that physicians have some awareness of the patient's knowledge. If this is true, then we can futher assume that this awareness increases the physician's anxiety regarding contact and communication with the patient. The increased anxiety solidifies the need to withdraw from the death scene. Lasagna (1970) presents three additional reasons for the reluctance of physicians to tell dying patients the nature of their illnesses: the physician may consider it both pointless and cruel to tell the truth; to have such a discussion is likely to be both awkward and abrasive to the doctor's ego, conceding as it does his helplessness as well as his relative ignorance about just when death will take place; and the doctor may know his patient less well today than in the past and, therefore, will be in a less satisfactory position to know how best to handle the total situation.

In review, we have concentrated on three prevalent attitudes and behavior of physicians in the medical care of the dying patient: the tendency to withdraw physically and emotionally from the patient at a time when the patient needs support; the related hesitancy of physicians to tell patients the nature and finality of their illnesses; and physicians' anxiety about death which in part accounts for the above behavior. Several explanatory schemes for the above attitudes and behavior can be offered. This chapter will only concentrate on one scheme which is sociological in orientation and is universal inasmuch as all physicians are exposed to its influence. Our working hypothesis is that the process labelled "the making of a physician," which is the period of formal education, directly influences the present-day medical care of the dying patient.

THE MAKING OF A PHYSICIAN: THE SOCIALIZATION PROCESS

Medical education is a period of socialization into a specifically defined role called "physician." The process of socialization is the means by which individuals acquire knowledge, skills, and dispositions that make them more or less able members of society (Brim, 1966). Basically, socialization trains and motivates individuals so that specific roles which are functional for a society are performed in a proper and continuous manner. Because of the unique role the physician plays in our society, medical sociologists have extensively researched the process of shaping an individual into a physician. Specifically, the process of socialization in medical school is referred to as "professionalization" — "A process of socialization, which involves a matrix of social relations in which the (medical) student internalizes and makes his own the attitudes and values which will largely determine his future professional role" (Bloom, 1958).

The socialization of an individual into the role of doctor mainly occurs during the formal years of medical school. Experiences during internship and residency polish the final product. We must emphasize that medical education not only teaches the student basic medical skills but of equal importance formulates a set of values and attitudes which influence the way these skills are applied. These values and attitudes constitute the physician's professional orientation. In general, the socialization process has emphasized technical skills with a proportionate de-emphasis of social and emotional skills. This situation is exemplified by the lack of training in and discussion of death and dying. The effect of this lack of training is best described by Artiss and Levine (1973): "…it is apparent that physicians, particularly those in training, have great difficulty in maintaining their equanimity when they must care for and relate intimately to terminal patients for many months. Most young doctors in this setting discover themselves engaging in such unusual defensive measures that they are at the least puzzled, usually dismayed, and not infrequently depressed. In all cases, anxiety is around, and the physician's manner of dealing with it becomes the major question in considering the relation between doctor and patient."

Very few physicians believe that how they approach the dying patient is related to medical training (Lasagna, 1968). This is not an accurate judgment. When we consider those aspects of the socialization process that encompass formal and informal learning of professional values and attitudes, medical training unwittingly influences how physicians care for the dying patient. Bloom (1958) believes that medical education has three effects on the future physician which reduce the importance of the emotional and social aspects of medical care. First, "dehumanization" which is the arbitrary separation of students in laboratory, library and lecture hall for the first two years of medical school. The intensive experience of medical students with cadaver, specimen, and elaborate pathology, unrelieved by contact with the whole living patient for two years, often produces an "emotional callus" which impairs the development of attitudes toward patients. The second effect is "compartmentalization." The emphasis in the laboratory is on dissection and other forms of reduction of the whole into component parts. This reductive process is reinforced by didactic presentations by experts who dramatize the extent to which knowledge about each part has been developed. The effect is to overwhelm students with the scope of knowledge about disease processes and heighten their sense of the need for specialization. Moreover, and of extreme importance, the student's image of the patient is fractionated and a frame of reference is learned for the perception of a "segmented" rather than a "whole" patient. Finally, Bloom introduces the "institutionalization" effect. This is a learned tendency to see patients as isolated individuals, as "hospital cases" rather than as human beings. If a student learns his clinical skills in the hospital only, his perception of the patient is limited to an institutional context. The student, therefore, lacks first-hand experience with the social and emotional background of the patient. The institutionalization effect is solidified when the medical student enters the period of internship, and beyond. Although a few hospitals attempt to emphasize the social and emotional needs of patients, most do not and continue to give high priority to the technical goals of medical care.

The general inference from the above discussion is that physicians have little or no training in how, and why, social and emotional factors influence medical care. As Bloom strongly suggests, the fault lies in the structure of medical education. Medical education tends to encourage physicians to define a patient as a "case," which has a diseased part that can be healed with the use of appropriate medical technology. The medical skill is present, the illness is located and defined, and technical care is offered. But where is the patient? The learned orientation of treating the part rather than the whole is directly related to the medical care of the dying patient. If a physician has limited interest in the social and emotional aspects of patient care, this learned orientation will be very evident when the physician is confronted with a terminally ill patient. The proper medical care of the dying patient necessitates that the physician functions beyond his learned technical skills. The question is, how can the physician be a comforter, as well as healer, when his training discourages social and emotional skills? By maintaining the present trend of de-humanization, compartmentalization, and institutionalization, the medical school will keep producing physicians who find it difficult to contemplate the feelings and needs of the dying patient. Therefore, future physicians will still show signs of anxiety and withdrawal when treating terminally ill patients.

One may argue that since medical students either have already experienced a personal loss through death or will be bereaved in the future, this nonprofessional exposure is sufficient to negate the effects of thanatological omissions in medical school. This is a poor argument for two reasons: our society teaches a "death orientation" which does not substantially differ from that observed in medical schools; and we cannot equate the impact of a personal loss with feelings associated with caring for a terminally ill patient. In effect, the socialization process in medical school must fill the gap that society has created. Unfortunately, the medical profession which constantly encounters death during the normal performance of its goals has been dilatory in preparing its recruits to handle death situations beyond purely technical and administrative responsibilities (e.g., preparing autopsy reports). As a physician, Rabin (1970) is quite open on this point: "In fact, discussion of death is conspicuous by its absence. Death is not even to be found in the indexes of most medical and surgical textbooks, nor can I recall any discussion in medical school concerning the consequences of death for the physician."

One of the major role-orientations medical educators convey to students is that the physician's role is primarily healer to the sick. The student is not always lectured on this point, but internalizes the healer syndrome on the basis of his readings, discussions within the student "subculture" (Becker et al, 1961; Merton et al, 1957) and his perceptions of society's expectations. Therefore, when graduating from medical school the neophyte perceives himself in a role that heals or cures, but does not necessarily comfort. To comfort or care for is viewed as a task for the nursing staff. With this strong focus on the healing roles, the inability to cure is often considered a failure. Hence, a death is a personal failure as well as professional defeat. The extent to which a death is so defined will vary by factors such as the age of a patient and the stage of malignancy (as an example of a lethal disease entity) when it was first discovered. The orientation of considering death a failure was succinctly expressed to me by a physician during a conversation on the meaning of an autopsy. This physician indicated that for many house staff members the job of obtaining consent for an autopsy was "punishment" for his failure. This may sound slightly dramatic; however, it suggests that the orientation within medicine that a physician has control over life and death, the healer role, is still evident during internship and residency. One aspect of the student's socialization into the physician role is the understanding that the doctor–patient relationship must be controlled by the physician. Having control over who directs (the physician) and who is subordinate (the patient) is considered beneficial for patient care, and in addition fortifies the physician's prestigious position. A dying patient is a potential threat to this role expectation. The usual means of doctor–patient control are no longer appropriate, and the total situation does not fit into the scheme of things which were taught in medical school. Looking at this frustrating situation from the physician's own self-definition, Cappon (1967) notes, "The physician's professional role as a healer is important to his own self-esteem, and someone who relies unduly on success in this regard can be made to feel intensely frustrated and impotent by the patient whom he cannot cure and for whom he mistakenly feels that he can do nothing." We are proposing that physicians withdraw from dying patients, prefer not to inform terminally ill patients of the facts and exhibit personal anxiety because the "doctor–dying patient" interaction system is never discussed in most medical schools as a legitimate part of the doctor's role. In effect, the doctor–dying patient system becomes unique and is looked upon as a threat to the traditional role of healer.

A final example of how the making of a physician influences future attitudes and behavior toward the dying patient is the professional value labeled "detached concern" (Coe, 1970). As in the case with the business executive who must make decisions based on objective criteria, the physician must not become emotionally attached to a patient in order to make objective medical decisions. The physician is trained to be emotionally detached for the benefit of the patient as well as to protect his own professional status. However, life is not so simple. An additional aspect of his role requires that he be sympathetic and understanding of his patients' needs. Therefore, a delicate balance exists between objective role performance and being concerned. When confronted with a dying patient, many physicians have difficulty in maintaining this balance and weigh their behavior in favor of the detached, objective value system. To the outsider this takes the form of emotional callousness. There has been some interest in medical sociology in the relationship between training for detached concern and the well-documented change in medical student outlook from "humanitarianism" or "idealism," during the early years of schooling, to "cynicism" at the time of graduation. The pioneering study in this area of medical education was completed by Eron (1955), who reported that medical students become increasingly cynical as they progress through medical school. In addition, when compared to nursing students and law students, the physician in training reveals a higher level of cynicism at the point of graduation. Of interest, Eron noted that law students are typically cynical at the beginning of their formal training, while medical students are more likely to be humanitarian; yet, both groups are cynical after four years of professional socialization. It appears that medical training produces a more dramatic change in professional outlook than is noted for other professions.

The change from idealism to cynicism has been analyzed by Becker and his colleagues in their "Boys in White" investigation (Becker, 1961). The researchers feel that the "fate of idealism" or humanitarianism is similar to what occurs in other professional fields. Medical students adjust their youthful and naive values toward a more realistic and specific set of orientations. What appears to be a harmful change of attitudes is part of a functional learning process. The medical student reduces his idealism in favor of cynicism in order to be effective as a physician and to meet the requirements of medical school. During the freshman year students begin to lose their idealism when they realize that they will not be near patients at all. Also, students quickly learn that they cannot absorb all the information they are taught and, therefore, decide to select those facts that will pull them through exams. This technique to "get through" exams increases the newly-found cynicism. Becker emphasizes that for the observer this type of outlook is cynical, but in reality it is a logical result of certain forces inherent in formal education. During the third and fourth years of medical training students have patients assigned to them for examination and follow-up. One would assume that this exposure would regenerate idealistic thinking. Not so, claims Becker, because students tend to talk about the problems certain patients create for the student. Of interest, Becker uses as an example patients with terminal illnesses. These cases are more likely to be talked about as producing extra work without "compensation in knowledge" or the opportunity to practice new skills, rather than as cases which raise questions about the doctor–dying patient relationship.

Such patients require students to spend time checking on the progress which he feels will not take place and to write long progress notes in patients' charts although little progress has occurred. Cynicism is still maintained because the student does not feel that he is having the type of patient contact he expects that a physician should have. However, as the end of school approaches, the original medial idealism reasserts itself. This is attributed to the fact that students see their immediate future role (e.g., as interns) free of exams, involving reading material they consider relevant and having contact with patients from whom they can gain experience.

In the study of physicians' outlooks, Grey (1966) suggested that while attitudes of cynicism are functional to the medical student role (similar to Becker's observation), they are not for certain medical specialities. Grey compared two groups of physicians on cynical-attitude scores prior to and after entrance into what he called "high"- and "low"-interaction specialties. High-interaction specialties such as general practice, psychiatry, internal medicine, and pediatrics offer a great deal of doctor–patient interaction. This is in contrast to low-interaction specialties such as surgery, radiology, anesthesiology, and pathology. Sixty-four physicians were given the Eron Scale of Cynicism following graduation and again four years later when they were in actual practice. The findings revealed no differences between the two groups of physicians immediately after graduation, but did differ after several years in practice. Physicians in low-interaction specialties had significantly higher cynicism scores than those physicians who had high rates of patient interaction. Grey concludes that medical specialties which are structured on the basis of high levels of affective mutual responses between doctor and patient necessitate, for the physician, a low cynical profile; while physicians in comparatively low-interaction specialties maintain a level of cynicism or detached concern which is similar to that observed in medical school. Although medical training produces a cynical, low humanitarian outlook for all physicians, the degree of detached concern varies by type of medical practice.

Both detached concern and cynicism are internalized by the physician during the period of formal medical education. Detached concern is a learned professional outlook considered essential for the physician's role. Either through informal discussions with medical educators or during peer group conversation, the medical student slowly takes on the objective, detached approach to patient care with only token concern for social and emotional patient considerations. The change from an initial humanitarian approach to one of cynicism seems to be more of a result of formal educational requirements, such as passing exams, than a planned attempt on the part of the faculty and fellow students. Becker (1961) claims that at the point of graduation medical students show less cynicism than during the initial years of medical school. Nevertheless, he does not deny that cynicism is still evident after four years of training. Whatever the reasons for detached concern and cynicism the fact is that they exist and are incorporated by the medical student as a highly valued part of the physician's role. Taken together these two outlooks present a picture of a quasi-sympathetic health professional. What is important is that detached concern and cynicism help solidify the medical student's acceptance of his future role as a healer who diagnoses, offers treatment, and hopefully cures. To be comforter and source of emotional support is ludicrous when one has a professional orientation which emphasizes technical skills. Detached concern and cynicism make the physiology of death more appealing for the future physician than the social and emotional needs of patients and close family members. The results of this role definition are withdrawal from terminally ill patients when they are in need of support and comfort, possible inter-staff tension (e.g., between physicians and nurses), and unnecessary anxiety for the physician.

DISCUSSION

Medical educators and physicians cannot ignore the present-day care of the dying patient. The basic problem is found in the definition of medical care. This is a traditional definition emphasizing technical skills and life-saving apparatus with a concomitant de-emphasis of the target of all this activity — the dying patient. It would be interesting to ask medical educators and physicians what activities on the part of physicians constitute medical care of the dying patient. In all likelihood very few respondents would mention the social and emotional aspects of medical care. This is understandable, because the physician has not been properly socialized into a professional role that *should* emphasize such attitudes and behavior. As we have attempted to show, in a limited fashion, one cannot justify the way physicians are presently handling terminally ill patients simply because they are human, and therefore have personal values. Society has placed the physician in a highly-valued position with expectations that go beyond omnipotent technical skills. To function in his position the physician must meet patients' affective needs.

If we accept the hypothesis that attitudes and behavior of physicians when confronted with a dying patient are partially the result of medical training, then we must also accept the challenge to create changes within the medical school. To be a comforter to the dying patient and the family and to function as a concerned leader should not be considered demeaning to the medical role. These activities should be proudfully judged as a vital and necessary part of the physician's status. We agree with Ross (1969) that the training of specialists for dying patients is not the answer to the problem. The objective is to train, within the medical school, future physicians to feel comfortable in facing the dying patient and actively participate in the doctor–dying patient system rather than withdraw from it. This can be accomplished only through professional socialization into a broader set of role obligations than is presently the case. To avoid this challenge will produce more physicians who are totally unprepared to care for the dying patient.

REFERENCES

ARTISS, K. L. and A. S. LEVINE. 1973, "Doctor-patient Relation in Severe Illness." *New England Journal of Medicine* 288:1210-1214.

BARTON, D. 1972. "Death and Dying: A Course for Medical Students," *Journal of Medical Education* 47:945-951.

BECKER, H. S. et al. 1961. *Boys in White: Student Culture in Medical School*. Chicago: University of Chicago Press.

BLOOM, S. W. 1958. "Some Implications of Studies in the Professionalization of the Physician." In E. G. Jaco (ed.), *Patients, Physicians and Illness*. New York: The Free Press, pp. 313-321.

BRIM, O. G. Jr. and S. WHEELER. 1966. *Socialization after Childhood: Two Essays*. New York: John Wiley & Sons.

CAPPON, D. 1967. "What Some People Say about Death." Paper presented before the American Psychological Association (September), mimeographed.

COE, R. M. 1970. *Sociology of Medicine*. New York: McGraw-Hill.

CRANE, D. 1970. "Dying and Its Dilemmas as a Field of Research." In O. G. Brim, Jr. et al. (eds.), *The Dying Patient*. New York: Russell Sage Foundation, pp. 303-325.

ERON, L. 1955. "Effect of Medical Education on Medical Students' Attitudes." *Journal of Medical Education* 30:559-566.

FEIFEL, H. et al. 1967. *Physicians Consider Death Proceedings* 75th Annual Convention, American Psychological Association, pp. 201-202.

————— 1963. "Death." In N. L. Farberow (ed.), *Taboo Topics*. New York: Atherton Press, Chapter 2.

FREIDSON, E. 1961. *Patients' Views of Medical Practice*. New York: Russell Sage Foundation.

GLASER B. G. and A. K. STRAUSS. 1968. *Time for Dying*. Chicago: Aldine Press.

GREY, R. M. et al. 1966. "The Effect of Medical Specialization on Physicians' Attitudes." *Journal of Health and Human Behavior* 7:128-132.

KASPER, A. M. 1959. " The Doctor and Death." In H. Feifel (ed.), *The Meaning of Death*. New York: McGraw-Hill, pp. 259-270.

KUBLER-ROSS, E. 1969. *On Death and Dying*. New York: Macmillan Company.

KUTSCHER, A. H. (ed.). 1969. *Death and Bereavement*. Springfield, Illinois: C. C. Thomas.

LASAGNA, L. 1970. "The Prognosis of Death." In O. G. Brim, Jr. et al. (eds.). *The Dying Patient*. New York: Russell Sage Foundation, pp. 67-82.

————— 1969. "The Doctor and the Dying Patient." *Journal of Chronic Diseases,* 22:65-68.

————— 1968. *Life, Death, and the Doctor*. New York: Knopf.

LEVINE, S. and N. A. SCOTCH. 1970. "Dying as an Emerging Social Problem." In O. G. Brim, Jr. et al. (eds.). *The Dying Patient*. New York: Russell Sage Foundation, 211-224.

LIPPINCOTT, R. C. 1972. "The Physician's Responsibility to the Dying Patient." *The Medical Clinics of North America* 56:677-680.

MERTON, R. K. et al. 1957. *The Student Physician*. Cambridge, Mass.: Harvard University Press.

PARKES, C. M. 1972. *Bereavement*. New York: International Universities Press.

RABIN, D. L. and L. H. RABIN. 1970. "Consequences of Death for Physicians, Nurses, and Hospitals." In O. G. Brim, Jr. et al. (eds.). *The Dying Patient*. New York: Russell Sage Foundation, pp. 171-190.

SAUNDERS, C. 1959. *Care of the Dying*. London: Macmillan Company.

3

Physicians' Attitudes Toward Death and Bereavement: Comparison of Psychiatrists and Non-Psychiatrists*

David Peretz, Arthur C. Carr, Bernard B. Schoenberg, and Austin H. Kutscher

In the past decade, increasing interest in the investigation of attitudes and practices concerning dying, grief, bereavement states and other issues related to death has developed. Though death has been a "taboo" topic, the accumulating literature indicates important breakthroughs in an awareness of this hitherto neglected area of essential human experience. The necessity for elucidation of the subject of death and bereavement becomes highlighted by recent findings (Carr and Schoenberg, 1970) suggesting important relationships between loss by separation or death and the onset of certain diseases. One report (Rees and Lutkins, 1967) indicates that bereaved spouses in particular age groups are more likely to die in the six months following their loss than controls of similar age and circumstance. Other recent studies include those of the dying patient (Hinton, 1967; Glaser and Strauss, 1965), the investigation of the psychosocial events surrounding the phenomenon of death (the "psychological autopsy" — Weisman and Kastenbaum, 1968), and clinical examination and follow-up study of reactions in the bereaved (Clayton, 1969; Maddison and Maddison, 1968).

*This study was supported by the Foundation of Thanatology, 630 West 168th Street, New York, New York; acknowledgment is made of the assistance of Austin H. Kutscher, Jr., and Alan Rosell.

The present report presents the results of a survey of physicians' attitudes toward the bereavement state. For this purpose a multiple-choice survey was constructed as indicated below.

Groups sampled included physicians, clergy, social scientists and the widowed. The physicians polled throughout the country included 150 members of the Academy of General Practice, 100 Board certified general surgeons, 50 Board certified practitioners of Internal Medicine, 175 Board certified psychiatrists and 116 medical psychoanalysts. Of the 591 physicians surveyed, 14.6% (86) replied. While other published reports have described physicians' views (Schoenberg et al., 1969), the views of the widowed group and a comparison of the clergy with physicians (Reeves et al., unpublished), the present report is based on a comparison of the internist-surgeon-general practitioner group with the psychiatrist-medical psychoanalyst group. Hereafter, for the purposes of discussion, we will refer to the latter as the psychiatric physician group and the former as the non-psychiatric physician group.

Devised to elicit attitudes related to dying, death, grief and bereavement, the questionnaire covered five categories:

 I.   Signs and symptoms of bereavement.
 II. Guilt and bereavement.
 III. What the bereaved should be told by the physician.
 IV. What the bereaved should be encouraged to do.
 V.   Advice concerning remarriage.

Results are presented below for questions in each subcategory, showing percentages of agreement for each of the two groups. A brief discussion of general trends follows each section.

I. OCCURRENCE OF SIGNS AND SYMPTOMS

At least 75% of both groups (psychiatrists and non-psychiatric physicians) predict the appearance of anticipatory grief *always* or *frequently* for the "bereaved-to-be" prior to the death of the patient. More than one half of both groups anticipate dreams of the deceased *always* or *frequently* (psychiatrists 76%, non-psychiatrists 57.7%). Illusions of the presence of the deceased are expected to occur *always* or *frequently* by 34.8% of psychiatrists and 22.5% of non-psychiatric physicians, while 13% of psychiatrists and 40.5% of non-psychiatric physicians expect this to occur *rarely* or *never*.

Physical symptoms such as anorexia, weight loss and sleeplessness are expected to occur *always* or *frequently* by at least one half of both groups of physicians — as are feelings of despair, emptiness, hopelessness, and helplessness. Although more than one half of both groups *sometimes* expect subjective symptoms similar to those of the deceased, the non-psychiatric physicians anticipate more frequently than psychiatrists that this will occur *rarely* or *never* (37% and 13% respectively).

More than 85% of both groups predict diminished sexual desire and sexual impotence by the bereaved at least sometimes. Greater inclination toward masturbation is expected to occur at least sometimes by at least one half of both groups with the non-psychiatric physician anticipating it *rarely* or *never* more often than the psychiatrists (42.5% to 23.0%).

At least 75% of both groups anticipate feelings of infidelity in relation to the deceased to occur at least *sometimes* with the non-psychiatric physician expecting it to occur *rarely* or *never* more frequently than the psychiatrist (24.5% to 4.0%). Angry thoughts concerning the deceased are predicted with greater frequency by the psychiatric group, 41.3% expecting it to occur at least frequently (in contrast to 10% of the non-psychiatrists), while 32% of the latter group predict that it will occur rarely (in contrast to 6% of the psychiatric group).

At least 90% of both groups expect guilt feelings towards the deceased to occur at least *sometimes,* with the psychiatrist anticipating its occurrence *always* or *frequently* more often than the non-psychiatric physician (69.6% to 40.0%).

II. GUILT AND BEREAVEMENT

Both psychiatrists and non-psychiatric physicians (78.2% and 75% respectively) expressed the belief that guilt is *frequently* or *always* less likely when there has been free expression of feelings between the dying person and the "bereaved-to-be."

Fifty percent of each physician group expects guilt to be experienced *sometimes* when pictures of the deceased are put away and the bereaved begins to function on his or her own. In fact, from almost one-third to over one-half of each group expects guilt *sometimes* under various circumstances of mobilization in or after the bereavement period.

On the other hand, about half of the non-psychiatric physicians expect guilt to *rarely* or *never* be experienced by the bereaved when he or she begins to function independently, experiences pleasure once again, accepts the inevitability of the deceased's death and takes up old or new interests again. The psychiatrists, in contrast to their non-psychiatric colleagues, expected guilt more often to occur either *sometimes* or *frequently.* This can be noted where psychiatrists (28.3%, 39.1% and 23.4% respectively) expect guilt frequently when the bereaved functions on his own, begins to find pleasure once again and accepts the inevitability of the loss.

When questions are asked concerning renewed interest in the opposite sex and the decision to remarry, psychiatrists and non-psychiatric physicians are in greater agreement on the expectation of experiences of guilt, 73.8% and 67.5% respectively expecting guilt at least *sometimes* and 34.7% and 27.5% respectively expecting it at least *frequently.*

There is also considerable agreement between the two groups of physicians as to when it is normal for the bereaved to experience some pleasure again. Fifty-seven and one-half percent of non-psychiatric physicians and 65.2% of psychiatrists expect such an occurrence from a few weeks to three months after the loss. Twenty-seven percent of non-psychiatric physicians and 16% of psychiatrists expect pleasure to be normally experienced a few days to a week or so after the funeral.

III. WHAT THE BEREAVED SHOULD BE TOLD BY THE PHYSICIAN

There is close agreement between the non-psychiatric physician group and the psychiatrist group regarding what the bereaved should be told. Over half of each group (57.5% and 62.0% respectively) feel that it is *always* or *frequently* important that the bereaved be advised how often death is faced by the dying with serenity. Both groups strongly feel that the "bereaved-to-be" should *frequently* be made aware of the patient's right to die without prolonged but futile efforts. There is similar strong support by both groups for the non-psychiatric physicians' advising the bereaved in detail that everything was done. Surprisingly, the non-psychiatric physician group would recommend no more pressure regarding autopsy permits than the psychiatrist group. Greater reservation is expressed by both groups concerning what the bereaved should be told regarding his own status; e.g., that he has "no place to go but up." Both groups approximate a "bell-shaped curve" distribution regarding whether the bereaved should be encouraged to appreciate that following his loss he may well experience lessened fear of future sorrow, tragedy and death. On the other hand, emphasizing the fact that fortunately the bereaved has a child by the departed spouse seems relatively more acceptable with almost three-fourths of each group (75% and 73.9% respectively) indicating that this is at least *sometimes* desirable.

IV. WHAT THE BEREAVED SHOULD BE ENCOURAGED TO DO

On the subject of seeking care and advice, at least two-thirds of each group agreed that psychiatric advice would be of benefit at least *sometimes* for the "bereaved-to-be." While 39.1% of psychiatrists indicate it as *always* or *frequently* desirable, 32.5% of the non-psychiatric physicians deem it *rarely* or *never* so. While a majority of both non-psychiatric physicians and psychiatrists (62% and 77.8% respectively) feel that regular visits by the bereaved to the physician during the first year should be encouraged at least *sometimes,* a substantial minority of non-psychiatric physicians (37.5%) feel this should *rarely* or *never* be encouraged.

There is fundamental agreement between the two groups that the bereaved should preferably not be hospitalized for an elective procedure soon after or during the course of bereavement. Most non-psychiatric physicians (63.7%) and psychiatrists (36.9%) suggest that the bereaved seek advice at least soon after the funeral and the majority also believe that the advice should be considerable in extent. Non-psychiatric physicians suggest turning to the clergy, the physician and the lawyer; psychiatrists suggest the physician, the clergy and the psychiatrist as sources of this advice. When the bereaved is religiously inclined, the great majority of each group suggests that, at least *sometimes,* the bereaved should be urged to attend religious services on the day(s) which have special significance with regard to the deceased. A majority of non-psychiatric physicians and psychiatrists (67.5% and 56.6% respectively) also agree that vocational guidance would be of benefit at least *sometimes,* but about 30% of each group feels this should *rarely* be encouraged during bereavement.

Both groups appear to favor expression rather than repression of feelings. While a majority of the psychiatric group would *frequently* encourage crying, discussion of suicidal thoughts and feelings and the discussion of bereavement with old friends or someone with similar experience, the non-psychiatric physicians show more division of opinion. Thus, while a majority of non-psychiatric physicians would encourage crying and expression of suicidal thoughts and feelings at least *sometimes,* approximately 20% would *rarely* or *never* do so. While almost half of each group feels that repression of distressing memories should *rarely* or *never* be encouraged, 35.0% of non-psychiatric physicians favored such repressions *always* or *frequently* as opposed to only 13.0% of psychiatrists. In regard to speaking with old friends, 67.0% of non-psychiatric physicians answered that such encouragement should *rarely* or *never* be given, in contrast to 23.3% of the psychiatric group. Talking with someone who has had a similar experience is encouraged at least *sometimes* by both groups.

Over half of both groups favor keeping the deceased's wedding ring permanently. As to various other personal belongings of the deceased, there seems to be general agreement: keep some, give some to family or friends, give some to a charity. A majority of non-psychiatric physicians and psychiatrists (76.0% and 67.3% respectively) agree that promises made by the bereaved to the deceased during life should be followed if practical and reasonable, but few indicated that such promises should be followed if not practical. The majority of each group offers the opinion that the bereaved should *always* or *frequently* be encouraged to relinquish excessive attachments to the deceased.

Both groups feel predominantly that at least *sometimes* the person in grief should be encouraged to obtain a pet, seek a companion (if elderly), travel, shop, change jobs (if he had long wanted to do so), or move to a new living location. About half of each group would encourage the bereaved to resume work within a week (three-quarters within two weeks); however, some non-psychiatric physicians and psychiatrists (15% and 21.7% respectively) would encourage a return to work only when the bereaved feels up to it. Non-psychiatric physicians (80.0%) and psychiatrists (62.9%) both indicate that at least *sometimes* this might be a time to encourage the bereaved to change jobs, if this had been his long-time desire. More than 85% of both groups see working as being good for the bereaved *frequently* or *always*, with the non-psychiatric physicians (45.0%) indicating greater emphasis on work as *always* being good in contrast to the psychiatric group (30.4%). There was greater support from non-psychiatric physicians (47.5%) for the bereaved *always* or *frequently* to make major decisions as early as possible, in contrast to the psychiatric group (28.2%).

V. Advice Concerning Remarriage

There is general agreement between the non-psychiatric physicians and the psychiatrists with respect to advice to the bereaved concerning remarriage. For example, among those who responded to the question, there is near complete agreeeement that the bereaved should be encouraged to remarry. The majority of respondents in both groups believe that remarriage is the major long-range problem to be dealt with by a relatively young bereaved spouse, and both groups indicate that the bereaved should generally be encouraged to believe that he has much to offer in such a relationship. Over two-thirds of each group (75% and 69.6% respectively) believe that at least *sometimes* the bereaved should be encouraged towards remarriage for the sake of any young children. Over 40% of each group feel this should *always* or *frequently* be the case. Both groups showed approximately equal reservation about whether it is desirable to encourage the bereaved to make the decision regarding remarriage before a particular person is considered, with approximately equal but even great reservation about the desirability of informing relatives and in-laws of this decision before a specific person is considered. Perhaps of greatest interest, however, is the evidence suggesting that the psychiatric group consistently has greater reservation about their wisdom concerning advice regarding remarriage, reflected in their more frequent failure to answer such questions.

Discussion

On the whole, there appears to be general agreement between psychiatric and non-psychiatric physicians in their attitudes, expectations and practices concerning death and bereavement, although some important differences can be noted.

In all cases, the psychiatric physician anticipates that signs and symptoms of bereavement will occur more frequently than does the non-psychiatric physician.

Similarly, while from one-third to one-half of both groups expect guilt to occur *sometimes* during or after the bereavement period as the bereaved returns to various functions, about half of the non-psychiatric physicians expect guilt *rarely* or *never*. As the bereaved begins to function independently, experiences pleasure, accepts the inevitability of the loss, takes up old or new interests, psychiatrists expect guilt to occur more frequently than do their non-psychiatric colleagues.

The fact that psychiatric physicians tend to expect symptoms and signs of bereavement to occur more frequently than do non-psychiatric physicians may be related to the selected nature of their patient sample. This interpretation is supplied in two studies (Clayton, 1969; Schoenberg et al., 1969). In contrast with the results of a survey of widows and widowers utilizing the above question-naire, both physician groups anticipated signs and symptoms more frequently than the widow and widower (Schoenberg et al., 1969). Only feelings of despair, emptiness, hopelessness and sleeplessness were expected to occur frequently or always by more than a majority of the bereaved. Forty percent expect loss of appetite and/or weight to occur *frequently* or *always*.

In another study, 40 relatives of patients who had died in a hospital were interviewed from 2 to 26 days after the death and re-interviewed from one to four months later (Clayton, 1969). Only these symptoms had occurred in more than 50% of the relatives: sadness or depressive mood, crying, and difficulty in sleeping. Loss of appetite and weight, loss of interest in television, current events and/or friends and difficulty in concentrating were frequent, but occurred in less than half the relatives. Severe psychiatric symptoms such as self-condemnation, guilt, suicidal thoughts, etc., were rare. Improvement dated from six to ten weeks after the death. Symptoms that improved most strikingly were depressed mood, sleep disturbance and crying.

This progression in the frequency of anticipation or experience of symptoms, from lowest incidence in the bereaved themselves to a higher incidence in the non-psychiatric physician group to the highest in the psychiatric physician group, suggests that the bereaved are a heterogeneous group, some of whom have little symptomatology; that the physician will see from this group those who seek help for their suffering, and that in turn an additional relevant factor could be that those with the most severe or prolonged symptoms go to the psychiatrist.

Regarding what the bereaved may wish to be told by the physician, both groups tend to support the concept of the physician at least sometimes providing support to the bereaved through information about the dying patient and his death. Both groups are inclined to either encourage consent for autopsy or suggest ascertainment by the bereaved of the significance of the findings so that they may make their decision accordingly. Comforting and reassuring the bereaved with "there's no place to go but up," and similarly oriented appeals are not often seen as helpful by either group. Over 40% of each group, however, would emphasize that the bereaved fortunately has children by the departed spouse. Apparently, both groups of physicians favor those forms of support which turn the bereaved's attention outward and tend to avoid statements which remind the bereaved of their good fortune in being a survivor. This may be a response to their concern with "survivor's guilt."

Non-psychiatric physicians (about one-third) are more likely to believe that psychiatric advice for the "bereaved-to-be" or visits to physicians during the first year of bereavement are rarely or never desirable. About 50% of each group believes that psychiatric advice sometimes is desirable, with 30% of psychiatrists indicating it would frequently be desirable for the bereaved-to-be. This could be consistent with the psychiatrists' expectation of more extensive symptoms in the bereavement state. Interestingly, while the bereaved's responses resemble those of the non-psychiatric physician concerning psychiatric advice for the bereaved-to-be, almost 30% of widows and widowers anticipate the desirability of regular visits to the physician during the first year of bereavement, in contrast to 15% of non-psychiatric physicians. Indeed, 44% of those subjects re-interviewed in one study (Clayton, 1969) had visited their physician by the time of follow-up. Six recognized their symptoms as related to grief, four had symptoms of depression, and two had excerbations of previous physical complaints that flared up "because of nerves."

The majority of each group believes that the bereaved should seek considerable advice and soon after the funeral. Non-psychiatric physicians suggest the clergy, physicians and lawyers as sources of such advice. While psychiatrists agree with reference to the clergy and physician, they prefer psychiatrists to lawyers.

While the majority of each group favors experession rather than repression of feelings, this is more often true of psychiatrists than non-psychiatric physicians. Thus, psychiatrists would encourage crying, discussion of suicidal thoughts and feelings, acceptance of distressing memories, talking about bereavement with old friends, etc. A substantial minority of non-psychiatric physicians would rarely or never encourage the above. This may reflect greater experience with or a greater acceptance by the psychiatrist of intense feelings.

While generally favoring relinquishing of excessive attachments to the deceased, both groups favor keeping the wedding ring permanently. Each group substantially believes that moving back into old and possibly trying new situations should be encouraged. Travel and shopping are more often encouraged by non-psychiatric physicians than by psychiatrists. Resumption of work is favored by the large majority of one group, usually within two weeks.

While each group favors encouraging remarriage with support of the idea that the bereaved has much to offer in a new marital relationship and that those who have loved deeply and satisfyingly tend to remarry more quickly, non-psychiatric physicians more frequently feel that remarriage is the major long-range problem to be dealt with than do psychiatrists. The bereaved, in their response to this same question, feel to a greater extent that this is their major problem. While over 40% of each group believes that the bereaved should be encouraged to remarry for the sake of young children, about one-fourth of each group believes this should rarely or never be the case. With regard to remarriage, a majority of each group expects guilt at least sometimes, although a larger percentage of psychiatrists expect it to occur frequently. The great majority of each group expects experiences of pleasure to occur within three months after loss, with a few weeks to three months as the median range.

About 20% of the psychiatrist group tended to have no answer for a number of the questions concerning remarriage. It would seem probable that this reflects reservations about giving advice in matters of such crucial and unique personal significance. This is borne out by the fact that there is less reluctance evidenced by the psychiatrist respondents to give advice about shopping, return to work, travel, etc.

In summary, there is considerable agreement among non-psychiatric physicians and psychiatric physicians with regard to the signs and symptoms of bereavement as well as the physician's role in the management of the bereaved person. In those instances of substantial disagreement, an attempt has been made to explore the possible sources of difference. For some questions there were substantial minorities within each group that help explain different opinions. The differences may testify to a need for further education concerning what occurs during bereavement. More open recognition of the bereavement state as a crisis which faces individuals with difficulties and decisions at a time when they are experiencing intense, often disruptive feelings, might pave the way for clearer delineation of both the needs of the bereaved and the appropriate role of physicians in helping to meet these needs. It is hoped that the results of this survey will contribute data in this direction.

REFERENCES

CARR, A. C. and B. SCHOENBERG. 1970. "Object Loss (Separation) and Somatic Symptom Formation," in B. B. Schoenberg, A. C. Carr, D. Peretz, and A. H. Kutscher, *Loss and Grief: Psychological Management in Medical Practice*. New York: Columbia University Press.

CLAYTON, P. 1969. "Evidence of Normal Grief," in A. H. KUTSCHER (ed.). *Death and Bereavement*. Springfield, Illinois: Charles C. Thomas.

GLASER, B. G. and A. L. STRAUSS. 1965. *Awareness of Dying*. Chicago: Aldine Publishing Company.

HINTON, J. 1967. *Dying*. Baltimore, Maryland: Penguin Books.

MADDISON, D. and A. V. MADDISON. 1968. "The Health of Widows in the Year Following Bereavement," *Journal of Psychosomatic Research* 12:297.

REES, W. D. and S. G. LUTKINS. 1967. "Mortality of Bereavement," *British Medical Journal* 4:13.

REEVES, R. B., Jr., B. B. SCHOENBERG, A. C. CARR, D. PERETZ, and A. H. KUTSCHER. "A Survey of Attitudes Toward Death and Bereavement: Physicians, Psychiatrists, and Clergymen." Unpublished data.

SCHOENBERG, B. B., A. C. CARR, D. PERETZ, and A. H. KUTSCHER. 1969. A Survey of the Advice of Physicians for the Bereaved," *G. P.* 40:105.

WEISMAN, A. D. and R. KASTENBAUM. 1968. *The Psychological Autopsy: A Study of the Terminal Phase of Life, Community Mental Health Journal*, Monograph Number 4. New York: Behavioral Publications, Inc.

4

Caring for the Terminally Ill: Attitudes of the Housestaff

John G. Bruhn, Murphy T. Scurry, and Harvey Bunce, III

Little education is offered in medical school about the care of dying patients, nor is much opportunity provided to understand how personal attitudes and feelings about death influence patient care (Dickinson, 1976; Liston, 1973; Dickson and Pearson, 1977). Ways of coping with death in medicine are learned first in anatomy laboratory. In this setting, many students learn that to deny or repress their feelings about death is acceptable. As they enter the clinical years of medical school and come into contact with severely ill, terminal, and dying patients, their anxiety about death increases (Livingston and Zimet, 1965). During these years, students learn how to care for dying patients and how to express their feelings by observing the behavior of the faculty and housestaff. Although little attention or study has been given to this behavior, some evidence indicates that denial or repression of feelings about death is common (Friedman, 1970; Rich and Kalmanson, 1966). This is often evidenced by the physician's avoidance of a direct discussion of death with a dying patient.

Our purposes here are to describe the attitudes of housestaff toward dying patients and their medical care; to determine if housestaff attitudes differ by sex, level of postgraduate training, and medical specialty; and to ascertain the needs of housestaff concerning the topics of death and dying.

METHODS

Subjects

After pretesting and modification, a self-administered, precoded questionnaire was mailed to the 315 housestaff members at The University of Texas Medical Branch at Galveston with a cover letter written by the authors. The letter expressed our intent to learn about the experiences of housestaff in caring for dying patients, their individual attitudes toward death and dying, and their current needs as physicians concerning the topic. We requested no name on the questionnaires and explained that they would be coded for computer processing. About three weeks after the initial mailing, a follow-up card was sent to all housestaff members to encourage those who had not yet responded to do so.

A total of 136 (43%) of the housestaff responded. When the characteristics of those who returned the questionnaires were compared to the characteristics of the entire housestaff, the sample proved to be representative of the population by postgraduate year and by specialty, except that no housestaff members in pathology and only about one-fourth of those in anesthesiology returned the questionnaires. Also, slightly fewer of the female housestaff returned questionnaires. With these exceptions, the respondents appeared to be representative.

Questionnaire

The questionnaire asked the respondents to supply only sex, year of postgraduate training, and specialty (Table 1). The substance of the questionnaire consisted of 19 attitude statements expressing feelings and reactions toward death and toward dying patients. The respondents were asked to react to the statements by selecting the degree to which they agreed or disagreed with each on a six-point scale, ranging from strongly agree to strongly disagree. Several of these attitude statements had been used by Dickinson and Pearson (1977) and were modified slightly for our study.

In addition to the attitude statements, the respondents were asked to indicate from a list of suggestions any needs they had as a physician with respect to the care of dying patients and their families.

RESULTS

Distribution of Attitudes of Housestaff

The attitude statements numbered 1 through 5 were agreed with by 83 to 96% of the housestaff and attitude statements numbered 16 through 19 were disagreed with by 68 to 89% of the housestaff (Table 2). The remainder of the statements (numbered 6 through 15) elicited a mixed pattern of agreement/disagreement.

TABLE 1
Characteristics of Housestaff Population and Sample

Sex	Total Population		Sample	
	Number	Percent	Number	Percent
Male	260	83	119	87
Female	55	17	17	13
Total	315		136	(43% response rate)

Mean Age 29.1 years
Age Range 25-51 years

Postgraduate Year				
1 (internship)	89	28	34	25
2	76	24	35	26
3	78	25	33	24
4	41	13	19	14
5	21	7	7	5
6	6	2	5	4
7	2	.006	2	1
8	2	.006	1	.007

Specialty				
Surgery	64	20	27	20
Internal Med/Dermatology*	58	18	26	19
Anesthesiology	39	12	10	7
Pediatrics	32	10	20	15
Radiology	26	8	12	9
Obstetrics/Gynecology	25	8	11	8
Family Medicine	24	8	8	6
Otolaryngology/Ophthalmology*	21	7	11	8
Psychiatry	13	4	6	4
Pathology	7	2	0	—
Neurology	6	2	5	4

*Dermatology was combined with Internal Medicine, and Otolaryngology and Ophthalmology were combined because of small numbers.

Attitude Clusters

A factor analysis was carried out with the 19 attitude statements to determine if any of the statements to determine if any of the statements clustered. Three attitude statements did not correlate with other statements; however, 16 of the 19 statements clustered into 5 groups or factors (Table 3). A label was derived for each factor by the authors on the basis of the apparent theme of the statements in each group. The factor loadings beside each statement indicates the correlation between the statement and the factor group, and whether the correlation was positive or negative.

TABLE 2
Distribution of Responses to Attitude Statements (N = 136)

Attitude Statement	Percent Agreeing* with Statement	Percent Disagreeing** with Statement
1. In caring for dying patients some physicians decide at some point that cardiopulmonary resuscitation and other unusual life-maintaining procedures are no longer indicated in an individual patient. This practice is morally and ethically correct.	96	4
2. When a patient of mine dies, I always wonder if something could have been done to save him.	94	6
3. Clergymen are quite helpful to dying patients.	89	11
4. Telling a person he is going to die is difficult for me.	84	16
5. I think it is essential that a dying patient be told of his progress.	83	17
6. I find it more difficult to deal with the family of a dying patient than with families of my other patients.	59	41
7. I believe physicians refer terminal patients to other physicians more often than nonterminal patients in order to avoid having to deal with their dying.	57	43
8. A patient's death does not depress me when I know there was nothing I could do to save him.	51	49
9. On the basis of my experience with dying patients, I would say that most of them are afraid of death.	51	49
10. On the basis of my experience with dying patients, I would say that most of them did not want to talk about death.	49	51
11. On the basis of my experience with dying patients, I would say that most of them had a painful death.	46	54
12. I do not think about death very much.	45	55
13. I try to avoid telling a patient directly that he is dying.	43	57
14. Treating a dying patient is one of the most unpleasant aspects of my profession.	42	58
15. On the basis of my experience with dying patients, I would say that most of them had a quiet, peaceful death.	41	59
16. On the basis of my experience with dying patients, I would say that most of them looked at death as a comfort.	32	68
17. I feel as comfortable with a dying patient as I do with any other patient.	24	76
18. On the basis of my experience with dying patients, I would say that most of them talked openly about dying.	18	82
19. Whenever possible I avoid a person who is dying from an irreversible condition.	11	89

*The three categories of strongly, moderately, and mildly agree were combined here.
**The three categories of strongly, moderately, and mildly disagree were combined here.

TABLE 3

Clusters of Attitude Statements Resulting From Factor Analysis

Factors	Factor Loadings
Factor 1	
Housestaff Feelings About Relating to Dying Patients and Families	
Telling a person he is going to die is difficult for me.	.77
I find it more difficult to deal with the family of a dying patient than with families of my other patients.	.70
I feel as comfortable with a dying patient as I do with any other patient.	−.57
I try to avoid telling a patient directly that he is dying.	.55
Treating a dying patient is one of the most unpleasant aspects of my profession.	.49
Factor 2	
Housestaff Perceptions of Patient's Feelings and Openness About Dying	
On the basis of my experience with dying patients, I would say that most of them talk openly about dying.	−.72
On the basis of my experience with dying patients, I would say that most of them looked at death as a comfort.	−.71
On the basis of my experience with dying patients, I would say that most of them are afraid of death.	.65
On the basis of my experience with dying patients, I would say that most of them didn't want to talk about death.	.62
Factor 3	
Housestaff Perceptions of the Nature of Death for Patients	
On the basis of my experience with dying patients, I would say that most of them had a painful death.	.89
On the basis of my experience with dying patients, I would say that most of them had a quiet, peaceful death.	−.89
Factor 4	
Housestaff Feelings About Death and Caring for Dying Patients	
I do not think about death very much.	−.69
A patient's death does not depress me when I know there was nothing I could do to save him.	−.69
When a patient of mine dies, I always wonder if something could have been done to save him.	.48
Factor 5	
Housestaff Attitudes about Prognosis	
In caring for dying patients, some physicians decide at some point that cardiopulmonary resuscitation and other unusual life-maintaining procedures are no longer indicated in an individual patient. This practice is morally and ethically correct.	.69
Whenever possible, I avoid a person who is dying from an irreversible condition.	−.67

Factor 1 consists of five statements. These statements all relate to housestaff feelings about their relationship to dying patients and families. Four of the five statements are positively correlated with Factor 1, and the fifth, the statement "I feel as comfortable with a dying patient as I do with any other patient," shows a negative (-.57) correlation.

Factor 2 is composed of four statements that convey housestaff perceptions of patients' feelings and openness about dying. Two of the statements are negatively correlated with Factor 2, and two are positively correlated.

Factor 3 consists of two statements that appear to relate to housestaff perceptions of the nature of death for most patients. One statement is positively correlated with the Factor and the other is negatively correlated.

Factor 4 is made up of three attitude statements that relate to housestaff feelings about death and caring for dying patients. Two of the statements are negatively correlated with Factor 4, and one statement is positively correlated.

Factor 5 contains two attitude statements that convey housestaff attitudes about prognosis. One statement is positively correlated with Factor 5, and the other is negatively correlated.

Correlates of Housestaff Attitudes

We examined the relationships between sex, level of postgraduate training, and medical specialty, and the 19 attitude statements. We found a few statistically significant differences in housestaff attitudes related to these factors. The small number of differences and lack of any pattern, however, led us to conclude that these statistical differences were due to chance. Housestaff attitudes appear to be quite homogeneous.

TABLE 4

Housestaff Needs With Respect to the Care of Dying Patients and Families

	Respondents	
	Number	Percent
None	49	36
An elective seminar	21	15
Personal consultation with a resource person experienced with dying patients	17	13
Informal group discussion	12	9
Case conferences on dying patients	11	8
Death and dying are already overemphasized	3	2
Combinations of above	23	17
Totals	136	100

Housestaff Needs

The housestaff were asked to indicate what their present needs were as a physician with respect to the care of dying patients and their families. Thirty-six percent of the housestaff said that they had no current needs with respect to the topic of death and dying (Table 4). Only 2% of the housestaff said that too much emphasis is already given to death and dying. The remaining 62% said that they had a need for information, consultation, or discussion regarding death and dying.

DISCUSSION

The results of our survey indicate that relating to dying patients and their families is difficult for most housestaff. A majority of the housestaff disagreed with the statements that they avoided patients who are dying and avoid telling patients directly that they are dying. At the same time, most of the housestaff agreed that they felt uncomfortable with dying patients. Perhaps this discomfort exists because most housestaff did not perceive that their patients viewed death as a comfort, and because of their own lingering thoughts about what more could have been done to save a dying patient. While clinical knowledge and experience are helpful in relating to dying patients, these cannot generally substitute for the personal attributes of the physician used in meeting the unique needs of each dying patient and his/her family.

In the earlier study that most resembles ours, Dickinson and Pearson (1977) surveyed recent medical school graduates regarding their attitudes toward dying patients and found that those physicians who had had a medical school course on death and dying tended to feel more comfortable with dying patients than physicians who had not had such a course. Only 20% of the physicians in their sample had an entire course devoted exclusively to death and dying, but an additional 30% had taken portions of a course devoted to the topic. In our study, 25% of the respondents had completed a course on death and dying.

A single-course exposure to the topic of death and dying, even if it were required of all students, should not be expected to bring about pronounced changes in attitude. Such a course can establish the foundations for open discussion in the medical school environment, but how the faculty treat dying patients and their degree of openness about the topic of death and dying are probably a more potent influence on housestaff attitudes than formal courses.

We thought it was significant that the majority of housestaff (about 62%) in our study indicated a need for seminars, discussion groups, case conferences, or personal consultation on the subject of the care of dying patients. Artiss and Levine (1973) conducted a five-month seminar for oncology fellows on the subject of death and dying. They identified the major defenses used by the participants as anger and denial. The major problem discussed, however, was the formation of dependency relations between doctors and patients. Examining this phenomenon encouraged the participants to confront basic issues in their own lives; and after such a confrontation, the oncology fellows became increasingly effective with patients. Such seminars for housestaff seem welcome in other specialties as indicated by the needs expressed by housestaff in response to our questionnaire.

Most housestaff have had little opportunity to learn about death and dying or to talk openly about the topic. When housestaff do discuss their dying patients, they do so among their peers or faculty. There was little indication that they talked with or worked with the clergy, social workers, psychologists, or psychiatrists in the care of dying patients. In summary, there is an unmet need to help prepare future physicians for the care of dying patients by providing educational and personal opportunities to learn about and discuss death and dying. To make death and dying an acceptable topic for learning and discussion in a medical school is essential for both faculty and students if the total care of patients is to be the best available.

REFERENCES

ARTISS, K. L. and A. S. LEVINE. 1973. "Doctor-Patient Relation in Severe Illness: A Seminar for Onocology Fellows." *New England Journal of Medicine*, 288:1210-1214.

DICKINSON, G. E. 1976. "Death Education in U. S. Medical Schools." *Journal of Medical Education*, 51:134-136.

DICKINSON, G. E. and A. A. PEARSON. 1977. "Death Education in Selected Medical Schools as Related to Physicians' Attitudes and Reactions Toward Dying Patients." *Annual Conference on Research in Medical Education*, 16:31-36

FRIEDMAN, H. J. 1970. "Physician Management of Dying Patients: An Explanation." *Psychiatry in Medicine*, 1:295-305.

LISTON, E. H. 1973. "Education on Death and Dying: A Survey of American Medical Schools." *Journal of Medical Education*, 48:577-578.

LIVINGSTON, P. B. and C. N. ZIMET. 1965. "Death Anxiety, Authoritarianism and Choice of Specialty in Medical Students." *Journal of Nervous and Mental Disease*, 140:222-230.

RICH, T. and G. M. KALMANSON 1966."Attitudes of Medical Residents Toward the Dying Patient in a General Hospital." *Postgraduate Medicine*, 40:A127-A130.

5

Fatal Illness:
What Should the Patient Be Told?

Norman B. Levy

What a physician tells or does not tell a patient who has a fatal illness is crucial (Blumenfield and Blumenfield 1982). The most widely accepted premise is that patients should be told only what is in their best interest to know. Accordingly, one should respect the defense mechanism of denial in those people who are afraid to be confronted with their fatal illnesses. In these cases, a relative of the patient should be informed of the truth. By the same token, people whose best interest is served by knowing about their illness should be told of their fatal diagnoses. Although this method seems relatively uncontroversial, it is generally not what is done in medical practice.

Interesting paradoxes become evident if one examines the practices in the United States over the past 20 years with respect to informing or not informing patients of their fatal diagnoses. The same holds true if one compares practices concerning these attitudes in the United States to those in other industrial countries. In this country, the practice of informing patients about fatal illnesses has changed radically since the early 1970s; before then, there was a tendency not to tell patients their diagnoses. Fitts and Ravdin (1953) questioned 444 Philadelphia physicians concerning their attitudes toward being forthright with their patients regarding their fatal illness and found that only 37% of them usually informed patients of their diagnoses. In a classic study of 219 physicians at Michael Reese Hospital in Chicago (Oken 1961), only 12% stated that their usual policy was to tell patients that they had cancer. Feifel (1965) reported that between 10% and 31% of physicians favored letting patients know that they were dying.

Just a few years later, attitudes and practices seem to have changed. In a study

42

published in 1974, Mount, Jones, and Patterson found that 78% of physicians usually told patients their diagnoses. In the same year it was reported that 53% of physicians and 51% of third- and fouth-year medical students surveyed favored informing patients of their fatal diagnoses (Travis, Noyes, and Brightwell 1974). In a study done at the Strong Memorial Hospital (Novack 1979), 97% of all staff physicians reported that they were honest with their patients. These studies not only show a marked change in physicians' attitudes and practices within just a few years, but also reveal a polarization between physicians who are honest and those that are not.

How does the United States compare to other nations with respect to this issue? Currently, patients in this country have to try hard *not* to be told their diagnoses. Frequently they are informed of their fatal illness, with little consideration of their feelings and in most situations of this sort, the patients don't have someone who can speak up for them and essentially say, "Don't tell." In Western Europe it appears that the percentage of people who are told or not told is about equal. In Eastern Europe patients usually are not told their fatal diagnoses, and in Asia, patients are almost never told. I discovered how pervasive this policy is when, a few years ago, I visited a friend who is the chairman of the Department of Medicine in a hospital in his native Japan. We talked about the practice of telling patients their fatal diagnoses. I learned that even *physicians* in Japan are rarely told that they have a fatal illness, and that others are virtually never told. Since Japan is a wealthy, highly industrialized country, the practice of informing or not informing patients, at least in this instance, seems not to be dependent on literacy, economic considerations, or the level of medical care.

Both the rapid change in attitude in this country and the wide difference in practice in other parts of the world indicate that social custom is a major determinant of whether or not people are informed of their fatal diagnoses. One must ask where the needs of the patient enter into all of this. Although these needs are affected to some degree by social factors, the danger is that when social custom is strong (as the policy of honesty between patient and physician is now strong in the United States), then the individual needs of each patient tend not to be considered adequately.

A few years ago I participated in a study of all medical students and house staff at the Downstate Medical Center/Kings County Hospital in Brooklyn to determine their attitudes toward this issue. Specifically, the study asked the subjects the following: a) if they themselves had a fatal illness, would they want to know or not, and b) what were their attitudes about informing their current or future patients of terminal illness (Blumenfield, Levy, and Kaufman 1979a). We gave each subject a five-page questionnaire containing statements to which they responded by selecting from a list of possible answers. For example, in response to the statement, "If I had a terminal illness I would want to be told about it," subjects could indicate that they strongly favored that statement, somewhat favored it, were uncertain, somewhat disfavored it, or strongly disfavored it.

The results showed that 81% of the medical students, 80% of the interns, and 90% of the residents believed that patients have a right to be told about their fatal illnesses. Of this group only 3%, 7% and 2%, respectively, felt that patients should be protected from the truth. In response to a question regarding the need for more discussion of death and dying in medical school, 97% of the psychiatry residents, 92% of the medical residents, and 52% of the surgical residents indicated that more discussion was needed. The proportions of residents in these specialties who thought there was too much discussion were 0%, 8%, and 29% respectively.

Eighty-nine percent of the medical students, 93% of the interns, and 90% of the residents said that they would want to be told if they had a fatal illness. Although the loss of a parent or sibling was not reported as a factor in determining their attitudes, 58% of the students and house staff who had lost a parent or sibling during childhood said that they would want a close family member to be informed of a fatal disease. Seventy-two percent of those who had not suffered a loss said that they would want a family member to be informed, a difference that was significant at $p < 0.05$. An interesting aspect of this study was that medical students who identified themselves as already being interested in a specialty tended to express attitudes that were similar to the attitudes of resident physicians in the same specialties. Its importance speaks to the question of the medical school educational process.

We wanted to find out how our data concerning a medical physician population compares with the general population (Blumenfield, Levy, and Kaufman 1979b). To do this, we turned to the Gallup Organization, the well known polling company in Princeton, New Jersey that studies the attitudes of the United States population. To accomplish this, they replicate in miniature the United States population by periodically polling representative samples of non-institutionalized Americans. At the time of our study, they questioned 1,518 people in 300 different communities who shared the same basic demographic characteristics as the general population of the U.S.

One question they asked was: "If you had a fatal illness, would you want to be told about it or not?" It is important to keep in mind that the attitudes of healthy people may be different from those of the sick, and the group questioned here was healthy. In studies comparing populations of cancer patients and healthy individuals, it has been shown that a lower proportion of patients than of healthy people express the wish to know their diagnoses. Since our medical population was presumably a healthy group, the comparison to a larger healthy population seemed appropriate for this study.

The Gallup data showed that 90% of the people wanted to be informed of a fatal diagnosis, 8% did not, and 2% did not know. Interestingly, there was a statistical difference between men and women. Eighty percent of women and 92% of men wanted to know, a difference that was significant at p<0.05. In white versus nonwhite people, 91% of the whites wanted to know their diagnoses compared to 82% of nonwhites. Regarding educational differences, 85% of those who were unschooled or who had completed only grade school wanted to know, as compared to 93% of college-educated people. Thus, education as well as other socioeconomic measures affected whether or not people wanted to be told a fatal diagnosis. A greater percentage of those at a higher socioeconomic level wanted to be told. For example, 83% of those with an income of $6,000 or less wanted to be told their diagnoses, as compared to 92% of people with an income of $12,000 or more per year.

Our medical study showed that students enter medical education with a pre-existing attitude concerning telling people about their diagnoses, even though they commonly stated that clinical experience is the most significant factor affecting their attitude, followed by their reading. The reality is that neither of these factors seem to affect them greatly, since the attitude of medical students who were attracted to the same specialty throughout their education remained throughout their education essentially unchanged from first year to senior residency. The data further shows the medical population and the general population in this country are similar; the overwhelming majority do wish to be told their diagnoses.

The rapid change in attitudes in this country with respect to informing patients of their fatal illness, the world-wide differences in attitudes on this issue, and our two studies present us with interesting data. They suggest that national, regional, and perhaps personal style play more important roles than do clinical experience and reading in the formation of the attitudes of physicians (and of their patients). Education may not be as important in shaping these attitudes as we have believed and wish it to be.

Medical students and students of other health professions need to recognize that their own attitudes may be fixed and, if so, that the needs of their patients may suffer. It is therefore essential that medical professionals make a distinction between their own feelings and the needs of their patients. What must be cultivated is the ability to reach conclusions about individual patients that are not predetermined by a sense of what they might want to know if they were in the patient's place.

REFERENCES

BLUMENFIELD, M., N. B. LEVY, and D. KAUFMAN. 1979a. "The Wish to Be Informed of a Fatal Illness." *Omega* 9(4):323-326.

BLUMENFIELD, M., N. B. LEVY, and D. KAUFMAN. 1979b. "Current Attitudes of Medical Students and House Staff Toward Terminal Illness." *General Hospital Psychiatry* 1:306-310.

BLUMENFIELD, M. and S. BLUMENFIELD. 1982. "Talking to the Patient with a Terminal Illness." *Medical Times* 110(5)73-76.

FEIFEL, H. 1965. "The Function of Attitudes Toward Death." *Group for the Advancement of Psychiatry Report, Death and Dying: Attitudes of Patient and Doctor. V Symposium* 11:632-641.

FITTS, N. and I. RAVDIN. 1953. "What Philadelphia Physicians Tell Patients with Cancer." *Journal of the American Medical Association* 153:901-904.

MOUNTS, B. M., A. JONES, and A. PATTERSON 1974. "Death and Dying. Attitudes in Teaching Hospital." *Urology* 4:741-748.

NOVACK, D. H., R. PLUMER, R. L. SMITY, H. OCHITILL, G. R. MORROW, and J. M. BENNETT. 1979. "Changes in Physicians' Attitudes Toward Telling the Cancer Patient." *Journal of the American Medical Association* 241:897-900.

OKEN, D. 1961. "What to Tell Cancer Patients: A Study of Medical Attitudes." *Journal of the American Medical Association* 175:1120-1128.

TRAVIS, T., R. NOYES, and D. BRIGHTWELL. 1974. "The Attitudes of Physicians Towards Prolonging Life." *International Journal of Psychiatry in Medicine* 5:17-26.

6

Death in the Hospital:
Some Thoughts on Mrs. E.

Mark Brody

Our patient died today. She died. She died. She's dead. How many times must I repeat it before it sinks in, or will it ever? She was our patient. Well, what am I supposed to do — cry, scream, be depressed, say over and over, "Oh, how awful!," say a prayer, forget it?

We all go through the motions of seeming upset. We know how to look — wistfully regretful, bothered, concerned, eager to know where we went wrong. But nothing can disguise our utter confusion about how to behave. Mother and father didn't teach us the proper etiquette to follow when our patient dies. And in medical school no one tells us whether or not we should be caring and comforting to the patient's family or how to do this. No one tells us what we will feel, what we should feel, and how to deal with our feelings. No, for most medical students, medical school is not about that kind of learning; it is about symptoms and diagnoses and treatments and pharmacology and pathophysiology and pathology.

The nurses cleaned up the syringes, tubes, needles, gauze, and other medical paraphernalia strewn on the dead one's bed, left there by the wild tornado of the resuscitation crew that had furiously but unsuccessfully attempted to revive the woman during her final moments. I watched them move around her with the purposefulness of an ant colony, slowly and surely removing all of the superfluous supplies and gadgets from her bed — the pacemaker, the Swan-Ganz catheter, the intravenous line, the bag ventilator — until all that was left was the silent figure on the bed, in her scanty hospital gown. The nurses went about their business quietly and efficiently except, occasionally, when one of them would

47

stop in a mysterious moment of empathy and curiosity and stare at the strangely still thing that had once been a person. When calamity comes suddenly, we become oddly pragmatic; as Robert Frost (1962) said, "And they, since they were not the one dead, turned to their affairs." When one doesn't know what to do or how to be, one simply carries on with the mudane matters of living.

There is something disturbing about this sort of behavior. After all, a person has just died. It is not as if a piece of machinery has broken down. No, if that were the case we would all become overtly upset and would express our sense of loss. "What, the computer is down? Oh, damn, how I'm going to miss using that computer! I hope it's not too long until it's fixed." We can allow ourselves to feel the loss of the computer because it is only a machine, but to feel the loss of a person — that is too dangerous to expose ourselves to. But there are feelings there. No one who has been involved in the care of a patient — bringing food, giving medicine, answering questions, attending to personal needs — can escape having some feelings about the patient's death. What happens to those feelings? How are they expressed, or do they just disappear as we allow the memory of the patient to slip from our minds?

In the aftermath of a patient's unexpected death, we reflexively seek permission for an autopsy so that we can find out what killed the patient so that, perhaps, we can avoid making the same mistake again. We discuss whether or not the patient received the best treatment and how the treatment might have been improved. But these are merely ways we have of relieving the guilt we feel about our patient's death, not expressions of our grief at the termination of a human life. By dying, our patient has pointed an accusatory finger at us, which we cannot ignore. But allaying our guilt does nothing for our grief, or for the awe and fear we feel about the mystery of death. How do we cope with them? Perhaps by talking about them with friends, family, or co-workers. Still, something is missing.

Death in the hospital is ignominious; it is not acknowledged as a significant event, but is regarded as simply another routine event in a typical day. Inside of us, there is nothing routine about death: it has a powerful effect on us, which we suppress with great effort so that we may continue to carry out our responsibilities. Outwardly, we behave as if death were routine, isolating our grief by focusing on the clinical issues of the patient's death or intellectualizing our grief by listing the patient for discussion at the next "Mortality and Morbidity" rounds. But by not giving in to our feelings, or at least acknowledging them — by ignoring the importance of the patient's death — we belittle the value of the patient's life. If the patient is just a lump of flesh to be removed by the transport crew so that a new patient may come in to use the bed, then the patient is made into something insignificant and meaningless.

I don't say that we should all go into mourning and spend long hours bemoaning the passage of life. But when our patients have died, not to express any of the feelings we had for them when they were alive seems equivalent to saying that they did not mean anything to us, that we have no feelings for our patients. I do not accuse doctors of not having feelings for their patients, but only point out that when we fail to express these feelings we do a disservice to ourselves and to our patients. By expressing our feelings about our patients' deaths, we elevate the importance of our work and our own lives. In essence, we affirm that life has meaning. By neglecting to affirm life, we implicitly deny it.

REFERENCES

FROST, R. 1962. "'Out, Out —.'" *Complete Poems of Robert Frost.* New York: Holt, Rinehart and Winston.

Part II

The Impact of Terminal Illness on the Patient and Family

7

The Importance of
Discussing Death with the Dying

Irene B. Seeland

A doctor is obligated to talk about impending death with terminally ill patients and with the patients' families. Patients need and want to take care of unfinished business in preparation for their death. When patients are not informed about their condition, they have every reason to be angry and resentful. They have a right to use the time before they die as they wish.

For example, a patient with leukemia suddenly came to the realization that he was dying. "Why didn't they tell me?" he asked the young medical student sitting with him. He had been told that he had a simple form of anemia. "Why didn't they tell me? My wife and I saved all our lives to have the money to travel when we retired. Now, I know her, she'll never go, and if I had known I had this illness I could have traveled for the last four or five years and we could have used the money together."

Another patient, an 82-year-old Irishman, had begun to beat his wife even though he did not have a history of violence toward anyone. He finally admitted that he was very angry. He said, "You know, all my life I've saved money and I made a nice will, but now I realize I'm going to die before my wife and, of course, she gets everything. She's going to make such a mess of things because she doesn't know how to handle anything." His anger toward his wife reflected his frustration at the disruption of his orderly estate plans. A talk with his doctor resulted in his seeing that he couldn't take the money with him, that perhaps he could talk with his wife about what he would like to see done with his property, and so on. He stopped beating his wife.

In a recent informal experiment, a group of medical professionals were asked to imagine that they were terminally ill and had just been told they had six months to live. What would they do with their time? They were all fairly sophisticated young people. Every one of them wanted to clear up all financial responsibilities first. They wanted to straighten out the property issue and give away the things they wanted distributed, personally. Then they wanted to forget about this issue so that they could focus on people meaningful to them. Some wanted to travel; some wanted simply to spend time with their children.

This sounds sensible, but we have a problem. We have been allowed to believe that somehow we will not die. We place enormous trust in our sophisticated medical advancements and we continuously believe that there will be one more treatment that will rescue us. Confidence in medical miracles, such as resuscitating people who have been dead for a few minutes, just feeds the belief that "it's not going to happen, at least not now." We can allow ourselves to postpone things for a very long time, so it becomes a difficult and even courageous task for a doctor to confront a patient and say, "You've run out of options." This is hard to do and few physicians do it well, in a way that patients do not feel abandoned. A good physician will say, "I can't cure you but I will live through this with you." This is a very important statement. It allows the person to say, "Okay, I have things I have to finish."

Much has been said about the conspiracy of silence surrounding a dying person. It is not the patient who wants this silence; the people around the patient perpetuate it. Just as people know when they have a bad cold, so, too, do they know when they are terminally ill. When patients who deny their condition are asked directly if they know why they are in the hospital and whether they are worried that they are going to die, they inevitably say, "Yes." Where is the denial? The denial is in the surrounding silence. The patients themselves know that death is not a pleasant subject and that people do not want to hear about it because it reminds them of their own mortality.

Patients want the option to talk about their death, not continuously, but every once in a while. They almost always have things they want to take care of. Often, however a patient will say, "My wife doesn't want to hear about it." It is something like going to a dinner party where a white horse is standing on the table. The hostess never mentions it, neither does anyone else. The guests sit there for hours staring at the horse but not talking about it. In the same sense, everyone knows the person is sick, but no one wants to talk openly about it. The person may be throwing up and losing his hair from chemotherapy, but the visitor says, "You look wonderful today." Occasionally a courageous patient will point out the absurdity. A few patients do deny their conditions, but they are in the minority. The real denial is in the system around them: the nurses, the doctors, the families, and even the helping professionals who are allegedly there to deal with the issues. But everyone in fact skirts the issues.

A psychiatrist was called in to speak with a man who did not want the hospital staff to tell his wife she had leukemia. He was prepared to sue the hospital if anyone mentioned the illness to her. It was clear that he could not cope with the fact that she was dying. When the psychiatrist examined the patient and asked her why she was in the hospital, she answered, "I have leukemia." She added, "I know that and I know everyone else knows. But I also know that nobody wants to talk about it, so we don't talk about it." This is a classic situation. Patients usually know; if they don't know, it is because they do not want to know. That wish has to be respected also.

Those in the medical profession have been taught that they have an obligation to cure everybody. People constantly frustrate that goal because they die, and that is frightening for the doctors. It puts their power in question. It makes them feel helpless and guilty, and it creates a particular struggle in medical students. It is important to recognize that a patient's death does not represent a personal failure for the doctor. People do die, and it is sometimes very hard and painful for doctors to accept this fact.

It is necessary to examine where the denial and the conspiracy of silence fit in the picture.

Every member of the system must talk about the issues. The psychiatrist can communicate about the emotional problems. The social worker can help the family survive until the time of death and can help develop support systems for them. The estate planner can arrange to have business affairs attended to.

There is a fear that a patient might commit suicide if he learns the truth, but people who simply cannot cope with the knowledge of their condition and then kill themselves are rare. Most people find that the time they have left is much too precious to throw away. Most patients have no interest in suicide. What they do say is, "Please stay with me; don't run away. I need you. Please don't let me suffer."

Family members who do not want to talk about death for fear that the patient and they themselves might "fall apart" must be made to see that crying together is not a bad thing. It can be a powerful experience. Why not tell patients that they will be missed? It is a relief for patients, who most assuredly are thinking about their death, to be able to talk about it with their loved ones.

Family members are often apprehensive about discussing financial issues with the dying patient. "He will think I'm just after his money." The patient might even feel, "They're just waiting for me to die so they can get their hands on my money." Finances may not be very nice to talk about, but it is necessary to do so. The very elderly often feel others have given up on them and are only waiting to collect what they have saved in their lives. They can become so resentful that they would rather leave their money to a local animal shelter than to a son or daughter. Perhaps they are even justified. It is an issue that demands sensitivity.

There are those who feel cheated because death comes when they are young and have everything to look forward to. The young mother who feels abandoned by her husband, the young man whose life was just taking on meaning when he became fatally ill — these people have reason to rage.

When someone finally breaks the silence, often with support and encouragement from others, a tremendous release can occur. A grandfather was very sad that no one could talk to him about his death. When someone finally did, resistance was broken for all the other family members too, and this resulted in several months of a close and intense time with the grandfather. They didn't need to talk about dying all the time. They talked about many other things. The time was used constructively.

No matter how often the medical practitioner feels frustrated because solutions are not always perfect, it is important to continue to have patience with people and to give them every opportunity to communicate.

8

Psychiatry and the Challenge
of the Life-Threatened Patient

Arthur C. Carr

Quite aside from who is considered to be the subject or the object of the "challenge" mentioned in the title, the word itself offers some latitude in the manner of expressing my thoughts on this subject. In *The American Heritage Dictionary,* which orders its definitions in terms of the word's central meaning ("a method of synchronic semantic analysis," mind you), the first definition of challenge is "a call to engage in a contest or fight." In succeeding order, there are alternative meanings: "a demand for an explanation"; "a sentry's call for identification"; and "the quality of requiring full use of one's abilities, energy or resources."

The last definition seems most relevant to the task facing (challenging) professionals who deal with seriously ill patients. The "abilities, energy or resources" called for are varied: competence, dedication, and patience are essential traits in health care professionals, and are fully used. But there is more to the challenge. Professionals must be able to work alternately toward short–and long–term goals, sometimes without knowing which is which; to continue working when the rewards seem minimal; at times, to work for the impossible with the conviction that it is possible and, at times, to work for the possible with the conviction that it is impossible, always aiming at the goal of restoring to patients the greatest possible control over their own lives. And although one sign of true professionals may be that they can and do perform their best work even when they don't particularly feel like it, ideally they are also expected to convey the impression that they enjoy what they are doing, however onerous the task at hand may be. Yes, full use of our abilities, energy, or resources is indeed required.

What may be a greater challenge, however, and the one I wish to explicate, is the challenge to life–threatened patients themselves. I am not referring to the need for them to engage "in a contest or fight," although ideally they must convey the impression that they are doing so — "giving up" and "giving in" are not looked on favorably by the psychologically-minded professionals of today, who may view these behaviors as likely causes of the illness rather than as results of it. This view helps give meaning and brings order to events that otherwise would be more difficult for us to tolerate: negative outcomes are caused (so the assumption goes) at least partly by negative attitudes, thus supporting the belief that in the long run there is some justice in the world. That can be a comforting thought, although it is less so for seriously ill patients than for the professionals who are responsible for their care.

To be acceptable, the desired fighting spirit must, of course, be aimed only toward the illness or toward death itself. Certainly our tolerance for patients who would accept "a call to engage in a contest or fight" with the hospital routine or with hospital personnel is extremely limited. Experienced professionals have refined their own techniques for engaging with (or more usually, disengaging from) the "difficult" patient. One way of doing so may be to render the opinion that the patient really needs a psychiatrist!

I presume that the basic threat facing life–threatened patients, at least in their relations with the professionals who are responsible for their care, is the threat of abandonment. People who previously may have meant little to them and with whom they may have had little in common are now thrust upon them, and in positions of extreme importance. Psychological dependency, if not physical dependency as well, may be created quite suddenly. As patients are forced to redefine their life goals and to seek short-term satisfactions, abandonment becomes one of the worst possibilities that patients can face.

The challenge facing patients, therefore, is how to interest, enchant, cajole, please, or reward the numerous professionals who are in attendance as they proceed down the inevitable path toward their demise. Ironically, the more complete or comprehensive the care, the more complicated may be the task confronting the patients. They must deal with increasing numbers of professionals, all of whom may have their own ideas about what is most important. Unless close coordination is maintained, these professionals may place contradictory demands on the patients.

Surrounded by a myriad of professionals who have their own techniques for meeting the challenges they themselves face, sophisticated patients must find some specialized techniques that will help them forestall abandonment by those on whom they are dependent. In general, the adequacy of their own defenses seems to rest largely in demonstrating that they are "good" patients, while also maintaining maximum autonomy so that they can enjoy what satisfactions are still possible.

Although they are all somewhat related, there are slightly different facets to being a "good" patient. Among these factors are the following:

1. To assure oneself maximum help from all of the professionals, and to forestall abandonment, it is perhaps most important that one continue to be a "nice" person throughout a life-threatening illness. This seems to be a generalized quality: at least in a psychiatric hospital, I have noted general agreement among varied professionals, in spite of the diversity of their patient contacts, about who the "nice" patients are. Being nice includes expressing gratitude for services for which one may feel grossly overcharged; it may mean never questioning the wisdom of orders, descriptions, or prescriptions, however meaningless they appear; never challenging contradictions among the varied professionals; willingly providing the same information over and over again because professionals obviously do not share their records; being willing to testify, on call, to all one's fears, fantasies, and desires, because some professional is now ready to listen and may even be intent on doing so. Some professionals are reported to judge their own success according to whether or not the patient is giving evidence of passing through the various stages of dying hypothesized in the textbooks. Being predictable is often an important component of being nice. Patients' deviation from the assumed sequence of the expected may be considered sufficiently idiosyncratic to result in a psychiatric referral.

2. If life–threatened patients cannot succeed in being liked, they can aspire to being admired. This effort may take the form of showing how brave they are by "keeping a stiff upper lip" — no one admires a weakling. The general characteristic called for is endurance of whatever frustrations there may be, whether they emanate directly from the illness itself or from hospital rituals, doctors' schedules, or research protocols. It may mean projecting a sense of courage even when one is frightened almost to death. To be lighthearted in the face of adversity is, indeed, an admirable trait, and may help maintain the interest and dedication of health professionals. One must "keep one's sunny side up," regardless of which side is being pierced. In this effort, patients may show a euphoria that some professionals may consider inappropriate to the circumstances, and thus may constitute grounds for a psychiatric consult.

3. Abandonment can also be forestalled by being an interesting patient. One may not be likeable or even admirable, but still be of interest. Being young and attractive are obviously major assets in this regard, particularly if these attributes are marked enough to generate pleasurable fantasies in the caregiver. Interest can also be achieved by the exotic

nature of one's complaints or symptoms. Sometimes this is the only way to get the attention one feels is warranted, and sometimes it is the route by which a psychiatrist comes to be added to the health-care team. Being interesting may mean having an illness in which the hospital has a particular research investment, particularly if that research is being funded by outside money. Interest may be achieved by having a relatively rare disease or by defying the predictions that go with one's disease. What professional is not interested in the unusual? The good professional is curious. Sophisticated patients sense this and may be able to use it to forestall abandonment.

4. Patients can also respond to the threat of abandonment with an effort to be rewarding. I refer not only to paying one's bills on time — that is taken for granted — but in some way consistently showing that what is being done really is having an effect and making a difference. Good patients do well. An old professional axiom says that if what you are doing is working, keep on doing it; if what you are doing is not working, stop doing it; if you don't know what you are doing, do nothing. The patient who fears abandonment therefore has a special investment in convincing others that what is being done is working, at least to some extent. This may lead to an illusion that is readily accepted; we all grasp for evidence that what we do is meaningful. Should professionals have sufficient conviction about the positive effects of their interventions, they may view the absence of such evidence as an indication for a psychiatric consult.

5. Another technique is that of being respected. Commanding respect may be related to the position and status patients had achieved before becoming ill. Thus, by the time they are within sight of death's door, patients cannot readily assign respect in this sense to themselves; they either have it or they do not. This kind of respect, however, is not necessarily an advantage. In mental hospitals, at least, it has been noted that VIP status — particularly if that status derives from the fact that the patient is a physician — may actually work against assuring the best care, apparently because it reminds the professionals of their own vulnerability. VIP status can also elicit resentment from others and may generate envy or competition among those who share responsibility for the patient's care. Unnecessary consults, sometimes including a pychiatrist, may result from professionals' efforts to leave no stone unturned or to dilute an awesome responsibility. It is sometimes better for patients to be among the lowly. In any case, with increasing debilitation patients may lose the respect that was granted on the basis of their previous status in life — such status is often quite ephemeral.

It is to be hoped, however, that patients will find themselves in settings where they will elicit profound respect whether or not they are nice, admirable, interesting, rewarding, or socially prestigious. Mother Teresa was recently quoted as saying she hoped that the prisoners with AIDS put in her charge could "live and die in peace" because "each one of them is Jesus in a distressing disguise." Although some may find her metaphor unacceptable, her statement nevertheless conveys the sense of infinite worth she holds for all human beings, regardless of their external circumstances.

It can be hard to continue to act according to a system of beliefs that says that everyone is worth the same care and respect, whether they are aged and dying of loneliness, drunk and living on the street, or nice, admirable, interesting, rewarding, and prestigious executives. It can be hard to conform one's behavior consistently to the principle that all human beings are equally precious simply because they are human. Is this not the challenge facing all health professionals who deal with life-threatened patients? Is not the challenge facing health professionals that goal of striving to be responsible — that is, able to respond — to all patients, regardless of the guises in which they appear? To fulfill this ideal, full use of one's "abilities, energy, or resources" is indeed required.

9

Control Versus Passivity
in the Face of Terminal Illness

Samuel C. Klagsbrun

It is interesting to speculate about whether one personality type responds better than another to disability. Are there groups or categories of emotional responses to disease that would be helpful to recognize in developing a more sensitive and thoughtful approach to the care of patients? Do clusters of certain characteristics have something to do with the personalities of the patients, their backgrounds, or their life experiences? These questions suggest an intriguing exploratory approach to the relationship between emotions and disease.

Etiology is not the issue. Rather, there may be a propensity among some people for susceptibility to certain kinds of diseases or for exacerbation of some diseases if other factors are present at the same time. Some anecdotal clinical examples may shed some light on these issues.

A publisher, a mature man, well-known within his field, was admitted to a psychiatric hospital because of a suicide attempt. He suffered from multiple sclerosis. The disease had been managed well during the long history of his affliction. His family felt the suicide attempt was not warranted at that time, since he had not deteriorated significantly.

The family was not one that felt that life was worthwhile at any cost. On the contrary, they could understand that quality of life could reach such a low level that continued life would be less than worthwhile. This was an articulate, intelligent, highly educated family with a sophisticated approach to these questions. They communicated easily. Because they felt that the patient's desire to end his life was premature, however, they almost literally forced him to go into treatment at a hospital where a psychiatrist who was well-known in the field of death and dying — which they considered to be related to suicide — could attend to him.

The publisher, who shall be known as Bill, came to the hospital with a motorized tricycle, which he used because of his ambulatory difficulties. The tricycle became a marvelous tool for him to use because so many other patients constantly wanted to try it out and negotiated with him to borrow it. After a while, Bill began to enjoy watching everyone use his tricycle. It proved to be an unexpected means of entry into a communal setting and also provided other benefits to him. At the time he came into the hospital, Bill was furious that control of his life had been taken away from him by his family. Watching the other patients use his tricycle, however, gave him a renewed sense of power, a sense of contributing something to other people, of being able to add something to the environment. He could use it to negotiate certain "deals" with those who wanted to use it. How long did they want to ride the tricycle? How much of the battery would they use up? And so on.

The ability to negotiate served a therapeutic purpose. It gave Bill a sense of control. In exchange for lending the tricycle, he could extract certain services, such as having another patient bring him a cup of coffee. The bargaining was funny and done in good humor, but it also had a serious element by giving Bill a more positive sense of himself. The key factor was control. Because of his illness, Bill had lost control over his body. The reason he reacted so violently to what were, in fact, minor, periodic exacerbations of his condition was that he gradually was becoming less and less able to do things for himself. The issue of control is actually a recurring theme in patients with specific kinds of neuro-muscular disease. Another case history will serve to illustrate the pattern.

A women called Laura was referred to the same psychiatrist because of a suicide attempt made in response to her progressing disease, amyotrophic lateral sclerosis. Laura's family understood her desire to die and wished to help her. Like Bill, she had been well treated, but she had decided, in consultation with her family, that her life was no longer worth living. Actually, the quality of her life had been changing only gradually. No dramatic change had occurred, but she felt that she no longer had sufficient control over her life, largely because her energy level was so diminished. She wanted to die.

Again, the underlying issue was control. Bill, who had some energy left, could be helped to regain sufficient control of his life permitting him to emerge from his depression with tremendous vitality. He had recharged his batteries, just as his tricycle batteries were recharged. He went back to his family, his work, and a pattern of success. In Laura's case, the issue of control could not be negotiated. She refused to come out of her depression, insisted on dying, and did.

Another patient, Sandra, was a graduate student suffering from multiple sclerosis. Even before she developed the disease, she had had a long history of major difficulties in interpersonal relationships. She was a young lady who had to have her own way. Everyone knew that, but everyone respected her for her intelligence and her commitment to her studies. The therapist had to deal not only with her suicide attempt, but also with her deficiencies as a social being, specifically her inability to develop personal relationships. It was not an easy task. Sandra had to have total control, control over the therapist, control over the faculty at school, control over her grades and honors projects, and control over her roommates. The issue of control outweighed that of her disease.

John was a man in his late 40s, stricken by amyotrophic lateral sclerosis, whose overwhelming depression caused him to seek out a psychiatrist. The doctor went to see him in his home, where his bedroom was a feat of engineering. Every object was ingeniously designed to compensate for the disabilities caused by the wasting of his body. John pushed various buttons to transfer his body from the bed to his wheelchair. He grabbed pulleys hanging from the ceiling to hoist himself up and down. But even the buttons and pulleys had their limits. All his engineering skill could not compensate totally for his progressive disability. His sense of lost self-sufficiency, the loss of control, made John want to die. The psychiatrist was eventually successful in delaying the threshold of John's sense of being overwhelmed, indeed, of being paralyzed by his disease. He was able to help John accept a little bit of human assistance to replace the mechanical devices he had constructed. The depression was delayed.

What do these people have in common? The recurrent theme is loss of control. Control is a major issue in terms of personality type before disease sets in, and it certainly is a major theme after disease has worked to diminish it. Every caretaker, regardless of medical specialty, must be aware of this issue and must find a way to help the patient relinquish some control without feeling that this represents total helplessness.

The patients whose characteristics have been examined here have all been intelligent people. They were articulate about the importance of maintaining control over their lives. I do not suggest that this is a randomly selected scientific sample of a personality type, but the traits these patients shared do provide food for thought. They were an unemotional group of people. Their difficulty in expressing emotion was a serious element in their personality structure. So, too, was their tendency to perfectionism. Their threshold for frustration was also interesting. They could handle terrible difficulties, ones that anyone would find frustrating, up to a certain point, but which, once that point was reached, caused them to react dramatically. Of course, their intimate relationships depended on who the other people in their lives were. How much are such people willing to tolerate, to give, and to nurture?

On the other hand, there are people who seem very well adjusted to their diseases. The degree of passivity in accepting their condition is remarkable. These are people who cheerfully accept their lot in life in a philosophical way and just do the best they can. They are not so easy to understand, but they do seem to represent a personality type that is the opposite of those people for whom control looms large. Those who assume a philosophical passivity probably have excellent powers of rationalization. What purpose do these speculations serve? They have important implications for those concerned with the care of dying patients.

St. Christopher's Hospice in London, a facility devoted to the care of the dying, contains a section called Draper's Wing, which is populated by patients who have amyotrophic lateral sclerosis. Draper's Wing is a bustling place, almost cheerful. It's a busy, active place where the visitor has to take care to avoid the motorized wheelchairs scooting around everywhere. People seem to live a long time in Draper's Wing. It is a heartening thing for the staff of the hospice to see. The patients here seem to have that stiff upper lip quality that is so often a part of the English character. The patients are well taken care of and the need to maintain control of their own lives seems to be mitigated by the cheerful, helpful staff who devote themselves to serving the patients' needs. The patients can somehow allow the willing staff to do the incredible number of things that have to be done for them without feeling that they themselves have to maintain control of their environment. The people in Draper's Wing live much longer than people at comparable stages of disease elsewhere in the world.

Can life be prolonged by relinquishing control over it in the face of the inevitable progression of disease? Does cheerful acceptance of one's fate provide an extension of life? These are intriguing thoughts.

10

Differences in Perception Of Life-Threatening Illness

Richard Blacher and Jonathan Schindelheim

In our work with medical and surgical patients in a general hospital, we have been struck by the fact that patients' perception of the danger they are in quite often bears no connection with their physicians' degree of concern on their behalf. Some patients with truly life-endangering illnesses may be quite at ease, whereas patients with minor illnesses may react as if they were in mortal danger. For example, a 63-year-old woman who was to undergo a mitral valve replacement discussed her condition with a group of medical students. She calmly described what she understood the doctors would do and, when asked whether the operation seemed risky to her, replied casually, "I know I have a 15% chance of living." Obviously, the patient had reversed the figures that her surgeon had presented. The interviewer gasped and said, "That sounds terrible!" to which the patient replied, "Not at all. Last year, before I had another operation, I was told I had only a 5% chance of survival. My chances this time are three times better. Don't worry, I'll make it."

In this case, not only was the risk much less than the patient anticipated, but her cheery, optimistic reaction was not appropriate to her perception of the risk. Her positive outlook on life had helped her surmount many real difficulties in the past and now obviously was working toward this end.

How patients deal with illness or surgery seems to be determined by an intermingling of several factors: the illness itself; the patients' personalities, cultural backgrounds, and personal and family histories; and how the patients attempt to ward off anxieties created by both the illness and their fantasies. Let me discuss these factors briefly.

DIAGNOSIS

To many patients the diagnosis of cancer denotes terminal illness regardless of whether the cancer is of a truly life-threatening type or is a relatively benign lesion such as skin cancer. Operations on certain organs may also carry with them expectations that have nothing to do with the actual life-and-death balance the patient faces. For instance, although the actual risk of death as a result of uncomplicated coronary by-pass surgery may be only 0.5%, most people undergoing heart surgery anticipate a survival rate of just 50%. This disparity reflects not only the importance to the average person of the psychic representation of the heart, but also the fact that the heart is generally seen as functioning in a binary fashion. According to that perception, the heart beats and one lives or it stops and one dies; thus the expectation of a 50:50 chance of surviving heart surgery.

PERSONAL FACTORS

Two patients are diagnosed as having diabetes mellitus. The first patient's father also had this disease and lived to the age of ninety, controlling his diabetes by slight modifications in his diet. To outward appearances, his father had not been ill. The other patient's father had also had diabetes, but in his case the disease had been difficult to control. Consequently, he had suffered numerous diabetic comas and episodes of insulin shock, and had undergone several amputations as a result of diabetic vascular difficulties; he had experienced neuropathies and retinopathies that resulted in blindness. The two newly diagnosed patients both have the same disease, but their reactions to it will clearly be quite different. The first patient will see himself as having a minor inconvenience; the second patient will see himself as having a life-threatening illness.

Patients' underlying personalities can also play a major role in their perception of their illness. The woman who thought she had only a 15% chance of survival had lived a cheerful life despite a series of tribulations that would make most people resentful. Her positive attitude not only made her own life more tolerable, but cheered and encouraged her medical attendants as well.

Patients who take things quite literally because of their personality makeup may run into certain problems that might not occur otherwise. For example, a man in our intensive care unit asked his surgeon what the program for his care would be. The surgeon replied that if the patient continued to improve at his current rate, in a few days he would be back on the floor. At this, the patient's pupils dilated and he gasped questioningly, "On the *floor*?" He did not realize that the surgeon had meant a general medical floor. (One often forgets how the language of physicians affects their patients.)

A more serious misunderstanding came to light when we were asked to evaluate a man who had told a physician that he had recently retired from his job in order to spend his last months with his family. The physician was concerned about this, since the patient's health seemed quite good. The patient's history revealed that years before this visit he had been admitted to the hospital for a coronary bypass procedure. He was 53 years old at the time and, aside from angina, was in reasonably good health. In urging the patient to have the bypass procedure, the cardiologist had mentioned that if he did not have the surgery he might die within the year, but that the surgery could add ten years to his life. The patient elected to undergo the operation. Postoperatively, he did well and went back to a deeply gratifying professional career. The words of the cardiologist stayed in his mind, however, and after nine years he decided to quit his job, since he now had only one year to live. He wanted to give more time to his wife and children. The patient's literal acceptance of his physician's words led him to make a choice between his satisfying career and his love for his family. His was an artificial choice, and one that was much to his disadvantage.

DEFENSES

Patients often attempt to ward off the anxieties created by illness, and their fantasies about it, by means of denial. Medical caretakers who ignore this do so at the risk of not helping their patient optimally. Patients try as best they can to juggle awareness of their medical condition with denial of its dangers. Physicians' silence, their underplaying of the seriousness of the illness, or their over-emphasis of the danger can all influence patients in either a positive or negative way. Denial may make life tolerable for patients when they cannot do anything to improve their own medical status. Indeed, there is some suggestive evidence that patients with acute myocardial infarction who are able to deny the danger do better medically in the short run than those who face the dangers squarely.

Sometimes it behooves us to shore up our patients' defenses. For example, a physician with a background in research on coronary disease was admitted to an intensive care unit with a myocardial infarction. He suffered a great deal of anxiety while he ruminated over the various dangers and the statistics concerning his illness. The consulting psychiatrist suggested to him that the two of them could produce a small study on the patient's reactions to his attack, but pointed out that this would require that the patient keep notes about his condition. Soon the patient was seen calmly filling reams of notebooks with minute observations concerning his hospitalization. The bolstering of the defense of intellectualization had effectively calmed his anxiety.

Another example occurred when a young woman in her twenties underwent biopsy of a breast lesion. It was fully expected that the result would be negative.

When it was reported that the frozen section had revealed the lesion was cancerous, the entire surgical staff reacted with great distress. No one was able to discuss this finding with the patient, who was noted to become more and more anxious as several days went by. Finally, the psychiatrist went into her room with the surgical team and announced to her that indeed cancer had been found, but that the surgeons felt they had done a good job and had removed all of the tumor. Her response to this statement of bad news was to smile, throw her arms around the psychiatrist, and exclaim, "Thank God! I thought everyone's silence meant that I was dying."

The opposite problem is often presented to us in hospitals. In these instances, patients' denial prevents them from accepting procedures that can save them from life-threatening conditions. The patient who has an acute surgical abdomen but insists that there is nothing really wrong with him prevents us from saving his life. In situations like this, many physicians make the error of threatening patients with reality: "If you don't have this operation, you will die." This approach causes patients to defend themselves even more strongly by increasing their denial, and for this reason an attempt should be made instead to lower the level of anxiety and make the defense unnecessary. We suggest that it is more useful to make statements such as, "If we do this operation, then we can save you and make you well." The reassurance diminishes the anxiety and therefore diminishes the need for denial against an overpowering threat.

CONCLUSION

These examples illustrate the fact that life-threatening illness can have quite different meanings to patients and physicians. In our management of patients, difficulties most often arise when there is discord between a patient's view and our own. It is important for physicians to be attuned to those who are ill rather than to expect them to understand us.

11

The Chronically Ill Adolescent

Margaret Grey

The object of this chapter is to review the impact of chronic disability and life-threatening illness in adolescence. This task is not a simple one, since empirical data are sparse and most of the literature on the psychosocial impact of chronic illness is clinical and anecdotal. Although it is somewhat controversial to do so, I have chosen to consider all chronically ill adolescents as a single group, rather than to classify them by disease, because the stresses and burdens that chronic illnesses impose are common to virtually all diseases. Of course, this does not imply that we ignore individual differences in providing care.

Although we tend to think of adolescents as being generally healthy, the prevalence of chronic disorders in this age group is increasing. Aggregate data from the United States suggest that between 10 and 20% of individuals below the age of 17 have a chronic condition that engenders some residual disability. In the last 20 years, the percent of children with some limitation in activity has nearly tripled (Newachek, Budetti, and McManus 1984). This increase is a result of the fact that many of the previously fatal disorders of childhood — cystic fibrosis, hemophilia, and leukemia, for example — are now treated well enough to permit these children to survive into and beyond adolescence. Furthermore, some diseases, such as collagen vascular disease and inflammatory bowel disease have a high incidence during the teen years. Thirteen percent of patient visits to pediatric practices and nearly one-third of visits to subspecialists are related to chronic health problems in childhood (Gortmaker and Sappenfield 1984). Thus, the problem is a major one.

The impact of a chronic disorder on an adolescent may vary according to the individual's developmental stage, the state of the disease process, and the type of treatment available. It is useful for this discussion to consider three developmental stages of adolescence, early, middle, and late, in which the impact of an illness may be quite different. Early adolescents are primarily concerned with adapting to the physical changes of puberty and the impact of a chronic disorder focuses on physical development. Middle adolescents are engaged in developing independence from their families and forming relationships with their peer group. A chronic health problem at this state poses a threat to this process. Late adolescents are future oriented. A chronic disorder at this stage provokes concerns about vocational and academic plans, parenting, and the potential for self-sufficiency.

The transitional period of adolescence is difficult at best. During this time, children take on many new adult social, emotional, and bodily functions, and develop identities of their own that are separate from those of parents and peers. Erikson (1968) stated that the central developmental task of the teenage years is the successful attainment of personal identity, as opposed to identity diffusion. As adolescents struggle to determine their own selfhood and to gain increasing independence, they continue to rely on their parents. This conflict causes continual tension in the equilibrium between their childhood behavior patterns and their emerging adult patterns of behavior.

Cognitively, adolescence coincides with the intellectual stage of formal operational thought. Thinking at this stage becomes less concrete. Adolescents can begin to understand complex relationships. They try to master the understanding of transformations and causality in order to achieve a sense of permanence, and they search for comformity and predictable rules and regulations to order their lives (Piaget and Inhelder 1958).

The physical changes of adolescence also bring about new bodily feelings, responses, and urges that challenge adolescents daily, creating feelings of anxiety and self-criticism. These internal cognitive and physiologic changes and readjustments occur at the same time that adolescents are dealing with the external pressures of school, work, peer relationships, and dating. They need to come to terms with lifetime values, goals, and expectations, and to delineate paths for their futures. To accomplish these objectives, healthy adolescents may become introspective, evaluative, confused, and judgmental.

Physical illness adds another crisis to the already tremendous confusion experienced by adolescents, and the presence of a chronic illness may intesify the struggle for independence. Nevertheless, most chronically ill adolescents emerge from these years with relatively normal development. However, nearly all will have important concerns about their body image, sexuality, and independence. A large proportion of them will demonstrate difficulties in psychosocial adjustment. Although there are nearly as many definitions of psychosocial adjustment problems as there have been studies in the area, for the purposes of this presentation maladjustment is defined as abnormalities in behavior, emotions, or relationships that are sufficiently prolonged as to cause concern to the child or to the family and that have continued until the time of assessment (Wright 1960).

How many adolescents will have these problems is difficult to predict because there have been few large-scale population studies. In one such study, Walker, Gortmaker, and Weitzman (1981) reported that behavioral and social problems were 2.5 times more prevalent among children who had physical problems than among those who were physically healthy. According to parents' reports to a trained interviewer, 8.3% of the children who had chronic disorders had serious behavioral problems and 4.8% had social problems. Pless (1984) concluded in a recent review that those with chronic physical disorders have an increased risk of experiencing significant psychological or social problems as compared to their healthy peers. Depending on the specifics of the study, the risk has been variously estimated at 1.5 to 3 times as great.

The factors that influence the risk of maladjustment are the clinical characteristics of the disorder, the child's personal assets, and the family's background. The most important clinical characteristics are the nature of the disability created by the disorder — its severity, prognosis, and pattern of occurrence. In the past, it was assumed that the more servere the disorder in medical terms, the greater the likelihood that maladjustment would occur. However, it has been shown that those with mild disabilities may have just as many problems with adjustment as those whose conditions are more severe. The degree of visibility of the problem and the potential for the adolescent to recognize the self as disabled may influence this process. For example, teens who have diabetes or mild rheumatoid arthritis may be able to pass as normal. In that case, their peers expect their behavior to be normal. However, when medical reasons make them unable to act as expected, they are faced with a conflict that can only be resolved by sacrificing the medical requirements or by admitting to their peers that they are indeed different. Social psychologists call this ambiguous status "marginality." Recent data suggest that children experiencing marginality are as much at risk of maladjustment as those who are severely disabled.

In addition to the degree of disability, another risk factor is the pattern of symptom presentation. It is possible that the remissions and exacerbations of some illnesses, such as asthma, epilepsy, and hemophilia, may be more stressful than other illnesses that are relatively stable over time.

Studies have shown that the age at onset and the age at assessment are also important. Children whose disabilities have been present from birth seem to adjust more readily than those whose disorders begin at a developmentally critical juncture like adolescence. In addition, simply because adolescence is such a turbulent time, the more likely it is that adjustment problems will arise.

The population-based studies of Pless, Roghmann, and Haggerty (1972) in Monroe County, New York, have provided a model for explaining the development of psychosocial problems in chronically ill children. This model suggests that the presence of chronic physical disorder can cumulatively affect children's self-esteem, behavior, and ultimately, their mental health. Further, it suggests that this sequence is influenced by other factors in a child's social environment, especially the family. There is ample evidence that the way the family functions and adapts to the adolescent's illness may be the most important factor. Thus, it is important to assess not only the teenager and the illness, but also the family. In addition, all adolescents have some assets — intelligence or personality, for example — that may diminish the likelihood that they will develop psychosocial problems.

With the many physical changes that early adolescents experience, it is not surprising that they become preoccupied with their bodies. Normal adolescents are exquisitely sensitive to their own appearance and to that of others, and are particularly concerned about changes in height, weight, facial appearance, and sexual development. Cosmetic problems such as acne, obesity, and crooked teeth can be extremely upsetting. Thus, it should not be surprising that the presence of an illness that implies "differentness" and imperfection, complicates the development of a secure physical and sexual identity and a healthy self-concept. A serious illness demands acceptance of an altered body image and prolonged dependence on others. The support and approval of peers is critical to this process, so that adolescence is a particularly difficult time to be seen as different.

The conflicts resulting from their differentness may lead some teenagers to withdraw from social participation. This can hinder the development of meaningful relationships with peers of the same and the opposite sex, which may in turn delay or distort healthy psychosexual development. Those teens whose illness interferes with physical growth and sexual development are at particular risk. There also appear to be sex differences in the types of physical abnormalities that are poorly tolerated by teenagers. Boys may be more concerned about diseases or therapies that interfere with their ability to attain functional independence, whereas girls have more problems with diseases or therapies that are perceived as interfering with their ability to be attractive.

By mid–adolescence, when most of the physical changes of puberty are completed, the teenager begins to focus on the struggles of establishing an independent identity. The presence of a serious illness forces the adolescent to relinquish control and decision making responsibility to others. The developmental process of achieving independence involves learning how to make decisions and how to deal with success and failure. Experimentation and errors are the hallmarks of this struggle for independence, and these are, of course, at variance with the management of serious illness: errors in judgment may be life threatening. As they are struggling to establish their independence from their parents, adolescents find it especially difficult to tolerate the enforced dependency, lack of autonomy, and passivity resulting from illness and its regimen of care. The limitations imposed by a disorder may leave those in mid-adolescence feeling that they have nothing to decide. This is particularly true if the family or the health care providers are over-protective and do not involve the adolescent in decision making. Under these conditions, the teenager will make decisions anyway but, as often as not, these decisions will be quite different from those recommended by the health care team. For example, the mid-adolescent with diabetes may alter his insulin and diet regimen to be similar to his peers, thus increasing the potential for disaster.

Mid-adolescence is also the stage when most teens attempt to gain some degree of comfort and confidence with their sexuality, usually through experimentation. Serious illness may impose another obstacle in the adolescent's quest for mastery. Many chronically ill teenagers are at a higher physiologic risk from the consequences of sexual activity than are healthy teens. In particular, those teenagers with deformities such as paraplegias, ostomies, and amputations, which could interfere with the expression of sexuality, need counseling to correct misconceptions, avoid unrealistic expectations, and avoid later disappointments.

By late adolescence, most teens are involved with testing their chosen identity through further education, vocational choices, serious emotional relationships, and focused interests and efforts. Those with a chronic disability may experience difficulty in pursuing a chosen identity. The disorder may disrupt the quality and quantity of education. Adolescents are particularly prone to two dangers in assessing their life plans and goals in light of their illness: they may overstress the limitations and potential interferences of illness and succumb to a sense of futility and despair, or they may deny their realistic limitations, setting themselves up for disappointments when their unrealistic goals cannot be realized.

The presence of chronic disorders in adolescence may be viewed as inflicting on patients, to a greater or lesser degree, a series of losses. These losses include the loss of normal physical health and the sense of well-being that accompanies it, loss of some physical abilities and functions, loss of self-esteem and the ability to cope with everyday stresses, and the possible or implied loss of sexual development and functioning.

Despite this potential for disaster, the majority of adolescents do adjust and adapt relatively well to their illness, through the use of several defensive and coping mechanisms. Denial is often seen at the time of diagnosis, but it may also be seen in adolescents with longstanding disease to which they have adjusted well. The defensive maneuver of acting out often occurs in combination with denial. Acting out provides a method of attempting to prove to oneself that the disorder does not exist. We see this acting out relatively frequently in early and mid-adolescents with diabetes. They decide that they can "do just fine" without their insulin injections, blood glucose monitoring, dietary restrictions, or all three. Similarly, boys with hemophilia may suddenly decide that previously restricted sports are now acceptable.

As adolescents develop an increased capacity for abstract and logical thinking, they frequently use these skills in a protective manner against the painful reality of their chronic disorder. This mechanism of intellectualization allows them to substitute facts for feelings and to present themselves as good patients who are intensely interested in the details of the disorder and its treatment. This defense mechanism is helpful in obtaining compliance and educational goals, but it fails to provide an opportunity for the expression of feelings generated by the illness.

Some adolescents project their own feelings onto family members, friends, health care providers or others. Although projection can be a useful means of indirect communication, it inevitably involves some degree of denial. Feelings of anger, disappointment, and concern are commonly expressed in this manner.

Another defense mechanism commonly used by adolescents is displacement, in which they focus attention on less threatening matters. This helps to alleviate anxiety over intolerable feelings. In hospitalized adolescents a common expression of displacement of helpless and angry feelings is the abhorrence of hospital food.

Many adolescents establish behavioral rituals designed to control their internal sense of discomfort. Diabetic adolescents, for example, often adopt a strict sequence of tasks in performing their injections and cannot be talked into altering it. It is important for health professionals to recognize these mechanisms as healthy means of coping in adolescents, and plan care accordingly.

As providers of health care, we must offer not only effective therapy for the illness, but also attempt to foster normal developmental processes by involving adolescents in planning their care and by understanding their need to test rules and regulations. In addition, adolescents with chronic illnesses should be provided with help to maximize their strengths and develop positive self-images.

REFERENCES

ERIKSON, E. H. 1968. *Identity, Youth and Crisis.* New York: W. W. Norton and Co.

GORTMAKER, S. L. and W. SAPPENFIELD. 1984. "Chronic Childhood Disorders: Prevalence and Impact." *Pediatric Clinics of North America* 31:3-18.

NEWACHEK, P. W., P. B. BUDETTI, and P. MCMANUS. 1984. "Trends in Childhood Disability." *American Journal of Public Health* 74:232-236

PIAGET, J. and B. INHELDER. 1958. *The Growth of Logical Thinking from Childhood to Adolescence.* New York: Basic Books.

PLESS, I. B. 1984. "Clinical Assessment: Physical and Psychological Functioning." *Pediatric Clinics of North America* 31:33-45.

PLESS, I. B., K. ROGHMANN, and R. J. HAGGERTY. 1972. "Chronic Illness, Family Functioning, and Psychological Adjustment: A Model for the Allocation of Preventive Mental Health Services." *International Journal of Epidemiology* 1:271-277.

WALKER, D. K., S. L. GORTMAKER, and M. WEITZMAN. 1981. *Chronic Illness and Psychosocial Problems Among Children in Genesee County, Mass.* Cambridge, MA: Community Child Health Studies, Harvard School of Public Health.

WRIGHT, B. A. 1960. *Physical Disability: A Psychological Approach.* New York: Harper and Row.

12

Death Anxiety and Exposure to One's Mortality

David F. Cella, Lynna M. Lesko,
Susan Evans, and Cathy Raduns

The post-World War II era includes among its legacies an increased interest in the study of human reactions to death and dying. This interest has taken the form of numerous inquiries, both clinical and empirical, into individual concerns with death-related issues. One commonly studied death-related issue has been death anxiety, or what some might prefer to call a conscious concern with death and dying.

In some ways, it has been studied rather extensively. As far back as 1967, Lester compiled a comprehensive review of correlates to the fear of death. In this review, Lester pointed out: (1) that studies examining the relationship between death anxiety and age, sex, religion, and other demographic variables had yielded inconsistent findings; and (2) that most studies had neglected to assess the importance of apparently more salient variables, such as the impact of physical illness and nearness to death, upon death anxiety.

Pollack (1979-80), in a literature review, concluded that women and men probably show equal fear of death, that death anxiety does not increase with age, and that death anxiety will usually be higher in people who are in greater general distress. Although death anxiety and general anxiety are related, numerous past studies have demonstrated that death anxiety is a construct that is separate enough from general anxiety to justify its measurement. Two questions now arise: (1) What could be the clinical utility of measuring death anxiety? and (2) Is nearness to death or exposure to one's mortality in itself an important factor in the level of death anxiety? We focused on the second question and indirectly have arrived at some suggestions about the clinical usefulness of measuring death anxiety.

Definition And Measurement Of Death Anxiety

For the purposes of this study, death anxiety was defined as conscious concern about death and dying. Based on past research, death anxiety was conceptualized as a multidimensional construct that is a subtype of anxiety, but having unique components (Conte, Bakur-Weiner, and Plutchik 1982). Death anxiety was measured by the 15-item Death Anxiety Questionnaire (DAQ), which was chosen for its specific item content and its psychometric superiority over other popular scales (Conte, Bakur-Weiner, and Plutchik 1982).

External Exposure To One's Mortality: Cancer Diagnosis

Cancer patients were studied because they are a unique group of people in that they have to confront their mortality after a life-threatening diagnosis — they have experienced an external threat to their lives. All patients were studied after their treatment phase had been completed. These patients ranged in age from 18 to 60 years.

Surprisingly there has been little systematic study evaluating death, anxiety and fear in cancer patients. Using the DAQ, Koocher and O'Malley (1981) found survivors of childhood cancer to be no more anxious about death than control subjects with chronic illness. Similarly, Feifel and Jones (1968) found that terminally ill patients with active disease were no more fearful, and often less fearful of death than healthy comparison groups. The prevalence of suicide may be slightly increased in cancer patients, but this could be because major psychiatric disorders are slightly more prevalent among these patients (Brown et al, 1986).

Internal Exposure To One's Mortality: Suicidal Intent

Given the difficulty of predicting suicide risk, it is surprising that there has been so little effort to correlate death anxiety to suicidal behaviors. Clinical wisdom states that people who fear death will be less likely than others to commit suicide, and that it is the individual with positive attitudes toward death who must be carefully watched. This notion has been supported by a few studies: Goldney 1982; Neuringer 1979; Orbach and Glaubman 1979. However, there is some confusion among attitudes toward committing suicide, attitudes toward death and afterlife, and actual death anxiety. For example, people who are more accepting of the idea of their own suicide actually have higher death anxiety than those who are unaccepting of their own suicide (Minear and Brush 1980-81). This raises the possibility that death anxiety might actually be higher in suicidal individuals.

STUDY GROUPS

The data to be reported here were collected by a group of collaborators who shared a common interest in death-related matters in a variety of patient and non-patient groups. All patients were given the DAQ and were independently evaluated for level of depression and general anxiety. There were four groups of participants: Group I consisted of 60 disease-free survivors of Hodgkin's disease; Group II, 70 disease-free young adults who had completed treatment for leukemia; Group III, 35 suicidal adults who were patients in a psychiatric hospital; Group IV, 20 physically and psychiatrically healthy adults.

The subjects who comprised Groups I and II were people who had been forced to confront their mortality and were living with the ever-present risk of relapse or second malignancy. The subjects in Group III required hospitalization for a recent suicide attempt or for significant suicidal ideation. Group IV was a comparison group consisting of people who had not confronted personal mortality either through serious illness or suicide attempts.

RESULTS

Comparisons of mean scores on the DAQ across the four groups clearly showed that suicidal inpatients (Group III) had more death anxiety ($M = 11.5$) than any of the other groups. Scores from the three other groups were very similar, with scores within the normal range, $F(3,175) = 3.61$, $p < 0.05$.

The pattern of association between general distress and death anxiety has also been documented in two standardization samples, and indeed is assumed to be true in all individuals. However, it was not true for the suicidal inpatients, among whom death anxiety showed no significant correlation to general anxiety or depression. In all groups, however, general anxiety and depression were highly related, pointing even more sharply to the conclusion that death anxiety is more than merely a subtype of general distress, especially in a group of people with whom it has direct clinical relevance.

These data provide evidence for the specificity of death anxiety. In cancer patients leaving treatment and in cancer survivors, significant but moderately weak correlations between DAQ scores and measures of anxiety and depression ($0.26 < 0.39$) suggest a clear association among the constructs, but some unique component of death anxiety as well. The absence, if not reversal, of a correlation between DAQ scores and anxiety ($r = -0.10$) and depression ($r = 0.00$) in psychiatric inpatients reveals the breakdown of any clear association in suicidal individuals. This has potential clinical relevance in the prediction and prevention of suicide. It may be that the disparity between death anxiety and general anxiety, not the absolute amount of death anxiety per se, is the salient consideration in assessing suicidal tendencies.

Post Hoc Analysis

Given the absence, in the suicidal sample only, of any correlation between death anxiety and general anxiety, or between death anxiety and depression, one might ask whether death anxiety is *more* distinct from general anxiety and depression in suicidal individuals than in the general population and, if so, whether the separate measurement of death anxiety could be valuable in the assessment of suicidal intent.

To begin to address these questions, we divided the 35 suicidal inpatients into those who had been hospitalized after an actual suicide attempt ($N = 25$) and those who had been hospitalized for suicidal ideation only ($N = 10$). All of those hospitalized because of suicidal ideation only had never made a suicide attempt. The mean difference between these two sub-groups on depression, anxiety, and death anxiety scales were analyzed. On the Beck Depression Inventory, those who had attempted suicide ($M = 25.2$) were no different from those who had not attempted suicide ($M = 22.8$). On the Hamilton Anxiety Rating Scale, suicide attempters ($M = 25.2$) were significantly less anxious than non-attempters ($M = 29.4, t(33) = 3.89, p<0.001$. On the DAQ, however, attempters ($M = 12.5$) were significantly more anxious than non-attempters ($M = 9.8$), $t(33) = 2.83, p<0.01$.

This rather interesting contrast between general anxiety and death anxiety in suicide attempters versus non-attempters sheds some light on the confusing nature of suicidal tendencies. It is possible that those who attempt suicide are generally less anxious and more fearful of death than non-attempters before as well as after the attempt. Perhaps it is the very knowledge of one's threat to oneself that makes the truly suicidal patient more anxious about death.

It is important to keep in mind the retrospective nature of this study. These comparisons were made between past suicide attempters and non-attempters, using measures that are no doubt as sensitive to temporary states of being as to permanent characteristics. Therefore, to the extent that these patients' anxiety and depression changed after hospitalization, the results reported would not apply. Nevertheless, the data opened up an area of inquiry that has clearly been insufficiently studied, given the riddle posed to the mental health field by the phenomenology of suicide.

Clinicians often neglect the formal measurement of death anxiety, and this oversight may result in losses of unique, potentially predictive data on the tendency toward suicidal behavior. Among those whose lives had previously been threatened by medical illness — in this instance, cancer — death anxiety was not clinically elevated. However, there was a reduction in death anxiety over time. That is, patients who were temporally closer to diagnosis and treatment were more concerned about death than those who had undergone therapy in the past. This was not true of measures of general anxiety or depression, again confirming the salience and specificity of death anxiety in this population.

REFERENCES

BROWN, J. H., P. HENTELEFF, S. BARAKAT, and C. J. ROWE. 1986. "Is It Normal for Terminally Ill Patients to Desire Death?" *American Journal of Psychiatry* 143:208-211.

CONTE, H. R., M. BAKUR-WEINER, and R. PLUTCHIK. 1982. "Measuring Death Anxiety: Conceptual, Psychometric, and Factor-Analytic Aspects." *Journal of Personality and Social Psychology* 43:775-785.

FEIFEL, H. and R. JONES. 1968. "Perception of Death as Related to Nearness to Death." Proceeding of the 76th Annual Convention of the American Psychological Association.

GOLDNEY, R. D. 1982. "Attempted Suicide and Death Anxiety." *Journal of Clinical Psychiatry* 43(4):159.

KOOCHER, G. P. and J. E. O'MALLEY. 1981. *The Damocles Syndrome: Psychosocial Consequences of Surviving Childhood Cancer.* New York: McGraw-Hill.

LESTER, D. 1967. "Experimental and Correlational Studies of Fear of Death." *Psychological Bulletin* 67(1):27-36.

MINEAR, J. and L. BRUSH. 1980-81. "The Correlations of Attitudes Towards Suicide with Death Anxiety, Religiosity, and Personal Closeness to Death." *Omega* 11(4):317-324.

NEURINGER, C. 1979. "Relationship Between Life and Death Among Individuals of Varying Levels of Suicidality." *Journal of Consulting and Clinical Psychology* 42:407-48.

ORBACH, I. and H. GLAUBMAN. 1979. "The Concept of Death and Suicidal Behavior in Young Children. Three Case Studies." *Journal of the American Academy of Child Psychiatry* 18:668-678.

POLLACK, J. M. 1979-80. "Correlates of Death Anxiety: A Review of Empirical Studies." *Omega* 10(2):97-121.

13

Psychological Factors
that Affect Life-Threatened Cancer Patients

Leonard M. Liegner

The difficulties in investigating the psychology of cancer patients is related, in part, to the reluctance with which attending physicians and families respond to the idea of informing patients that they have cancer. Often, it appears impossible to get approval from department heads and physicians in general to explore, on a prospective basis, patients' reactions to cancer. Setting up a study that would deal with questions designed to elicit responses about the likelihood of having cancer is quite different from eliciting responses from patients who know the diagnosis. We can all readily discuss the possibility of developing cancer and theorize about what our reactions to this threat might be. However, this is not the same as confronting the real and immediate threat to survival.

A Personal Experience

I had a personal experience that reveals one possible sequence of reactions to the threat of cancer. A number of years ago, when I was about 45 years-old, an enlarged lymph node appeared under my chin. As an oncologist, I immediately attempted a differential diagnosis that included possibilities ranging from an abscessed tooth to either primary or metastatic lymphoma. My initial reaction to the possibility of a malignancy was one of fright, accompanied by a sinking feeling, and the thought, "Well, I've had it." The next step in my thinking was how I would handle this problem in regard to my family: would I let them know, should I impose on them the worry I was undergoing? I came to the decision that I would not inform my family, but would keep the secret and do what I had to.

The next phase was my concern about the future of my family. I anticipated taking out further life insurance in hopes of surviving the two years of incontestability. (AIDS patients now live with this horror, making my own vignette a mild event in comparison.) I contemplated other factors: were my papers in order, was my will finalized, what would the future economic status of my family be, how would my children be educated, and what would the loss mean to my wife and children? I became tearful about the prospect of losing them and about my finite existence.

The next stage in my thinking centered on the fact that I am a physician, and did I honestly believe in effectiveness of cancer therapy or was I simply an oncologist for the livelihood it provided? At bottom, I questioned whether I was going to ignore this possible cancer, or whether I should proceed as a patient, seek a diagnosis and undergo appropriate treatment. Deliberating on these issues, I finally concluded that, yes, I did believe that the treatment of cancer could be successful and that I would go to a colleague for an examination and evaluation of this node. After struggling to this conclusion and adjustment, my entire attitude shifted at the moment I made my decision. I had a feeling of buoyancy; I looked at my patients with greater empathy and interest and an unusual feeling of friendliness. I had an enhanced sense of the value of each day's experience and of each interpersonal relationship.

With all of this positive feeling, I finally did see a physician. He examined me and found nothing else significant besides the node. He noted that I had fine scratch marks on my skin, which he felt were most likely the result of a mild skin irritation and secondary infection related to shaving. This seemed reasonable, since I do have very sensitive skin.

A number of days after this examination, the lymph node, whether by natural timing, the response to local skin care, or psychological influences, seemed to regress dramatically and rapidly disappeared. This experience has remained fixed in my psyche as a positive event that enchanced my work with cancer patients (I confess that my ability, or lack thereof, has not yet extended to AIDS patients, but recently I have noted movement on my part toward these patients, whom we see more and more in our department.)

CASE HISTORY

The following case history concerns a patient who requested that I perform euthanasia upon her. Mrs. R. was a 43-year-old woman of Italian descent. She had cancer of the ovary that was generalized throughout the abdominal and pelvic cavities and was unresectable. The pathology was reported as adenocarcinoma.

Mrs. R. was married, with two children, ages 16 and 19. Mrs. R.'s mother was a widow and had inherited enough money from her deceased husband to afford her own home. Although the mother had suffered a stroke, she still visited her daughter, Mrs. R., in the hospital.

Mrs. R.'s mother indicated to me that there was great tension between Mrs. R. and her son-in-law. In order to improve her daughter's family situation, the mother sold her own home and gave the proceeds to her daughter so that she could buy her own house. Mrs. R. held a responsible supervisory position with a major insurance company and, as she stated, had always had people working under her direct supervision. Futhermore, it was she who had managed the affairs of the entire family. Her husband always gave his entire paycheck to her and said, "Don't bother me, you'll manage and you'll worry about it." She had managed so well that money was left after they purchased the house, a fact that amazed her husband. Mrs. R. proudly accepted her financial responsibility. She did not acknowledge to me that she had received any assistance from her mother, although the mother had made it quite clear to me that she had given the down payment for the daughter's home.

Prior to her hospitalization, Mrs. R.'s medical situation was tragic, although not uncommon. The diagnosis had been missed. For two years she had been under the care of two excellent gynecologists, neither of whom had detected any pelvic abnormalities. The patient had experienced upper gastric distress, and consequently had undergone a complete workup that included upper gastro-intestinal and barium studies, all to no avail (ultrasound studies were not available at the time). Because of the missed diagnosis, the patient lost complete faith in any kind of medical work-up and stated that she would refuse any future tests.

My first contact with Mrs. R. occurred after her cancer had finally been diagnosed. One of her gynecologists asked me to review the findings in preparation for subsequent care. The physician was quite upset by the initially missed diagnosis and felt completely disillusioned about preventive check-ups. He said, in effect, that if this is the way medicine goes and the way this disease goes, he might as well quit. I reassured him that missed diagnoses of rapidly growing tumors are not infrequent: I told him that I knew his capabilities and knew that it was unlikely that he would have missed a palpable mass. Whether my reassurance helped or not was not immediately evident.

Mrs. R.'s Reactions

I met the patient on her first postoperative day. She was lying in bed, in no unusual distress, and responded pleasantly to my visit. She knew I was there to discuss the radiation program. Her mother was also present, an aged woman who had obvious glaucoma and minimal residua of a past cerebral vascular accident. The patient expressed annoyance that her mother was present and asked her to leave. She stated that her mother had no right to be involved or to know what was going on. Knowing that the mother already knew, I tried to reassure the patient that her mother would not be upset by remaining. Mrs. R. persisted, however, and dismissed her mother.

The reason for dismissing her mother became apparent after Mrs. R. immediately said, "If I have cancer, Dr. Liegner, I want you to inject me with something and make sure I don't survive." I responded by saying, "I will let you know when that time comes and I'll tell you when you can do away with yourself." She did not react with shock to my statement, but simply stated, "I depend on you to do it."

I realized that although she had not been informed of the diagnosis, she assumed correctly that she had cancer because she had been told that I would speak with her about radiation treatments. She wanted to know if she had cancer, and I responded by stating she had cells that were premalignant. Although the tumor had been removed at surgery, no one could say for sure that there were not remaining tumor cells. Radiation was to be given as a preventive measure. The patient's further questioning required me to go into detail about what I meant by premalignant. I explained that these are cells that could change their characteristics and could attach themselves or invade structures of the pelvis.

Following this initial interview, I met with Mrs. R.'s mother. The mother knew of her daughter's cancer. Her only desire was that, "God willing," her daughter would die and avoid all the suffering that would occur. She wanted me to be kind to her daughter and do everything I could to make her existence easy. She did not want me to allow her daughter to come home because she herself could not manage it and didn't want the family to suffer either.

The patient came to the radiation therapy department for initial planning. She laid down on the treatment couch, but then suddenly sat up and cried and said, "Dr. Liegner, I don't want to have cancer. I have too many responsibilities — I have to take care of my home, and my family needs me." She then said, "I cannot afford to have cancer." We continued with the planning and she went through the first few days of treatment.

On the fourth day, when I visited her in her room, she was up and about, smiling and active. She said she had decided that she had to make it. She had on a nice robe, was wearing lipstick, and had her hair done attractively by the hairdresser. She appeared quite adjusted. We sat face to face and spoke very frankly, yet she still said, "Dr. Liegner, if I have cancer, you know what you have to do." I then said, "Well, suppose you did have cancer. Since we cannot guarantee that your cancer has been completely removed, and since it will take one, two, or three years of your survival to prove that there is no cancer, why don't you work on the thesis that you do have cancer at this time."

What came out of this conversation was her ability to tolerate the concept of early cancer and live with it. However, if advanced cancer meant being a complete invalid, this possibility was intolerable to her; she would rather be dead. In her mind, it would be different to die of an accident or an acute illness such as heart attack because it would be over quickly. Although her family would mourn, they would go through no undue, prolonged suffering. If she knew she had cancer, she would take her husband and children, go around the world, even go deeply into debt so that her husband would not have the economic freedom to marry another woman. Here we see the abrupt transition from a patient who asks for euthanasia to one who is going to live until she dies. An open, somewhat optimistic discussion of her disease, in which she was able to express her conceptions and misconceptions about it, turned her about.

Mrs. R. pointedly asked me, "Dr. Liegner, if you knew that you had advanced cancer, would you want to live?" I said, "No, I don't think so. But I don't know what I would do. I don't know whether or not I would actually do away with myself." At no time in the discussion did she say that she would commit suicide, but rather than she wanted me to perform a mercy killing. Although she was a Catholic, she said that she did not believe mercy killing was a sin and she would even argue with the Pope about this and some other matters. However, she still wore a Catholic medallion.

An interesting feature in Mrs. R.'s psychology was her ability to tolerate severe gas pains when she believed they were caused by the surgery and radiation therapy, not by advanced cancer. If she had known that her pains were the result of advanced cancer, she stated that they would have been intolerable and she would have wanted heavy sedation.

We wanted Mrs. R. to go home for Christmas. She thought this meant it would be her last Christmas. Although she was glad to learn it is the general policy of the hospital to encourage patients to go home, if possible, during the holiday, she did not want to go because she thought it would be a tremendous burden to her family. I said, "Why can't you be a dependent when you are ill and enjoy the care that your family gives you?" Her 16-year-old daughter then said, "Please come home. We love you and we want to do everything for you." Later, when the patient asked about going back to work, I responded by saying, "Look, enjoy your illness." The nature of this final intervention was simply to permit this person, who had always needed to control her environment, to become comfortable with her imposed state of dependency.

CONCLUSION

My experience with Mrs. R. and other patients indicates that patients who are encouraged to talk and who are given the opportunity to be heard by an interested, empathetic, and competent physician or therapist are in a position to choose options beyond their initial feelings of despair and the wish to die quickly.

14

Dilemma of the Dying —
"Why Won't People Listen to Me?"

Rae Ellen S. Stager

*When it came to my feelings, an invisible curtain seemed to drop.
The behavioral cues from my colleagues varied from lack of eye
contact to hovering over my bedside in an authoritarian posture.
They talked superficial banter about non-health topics and then made
hasty exits from my room. ... How clear it was: the message sent is
not always the message received.*

Out of context, the foregoing thoughts conflict with the reality of the situation,
but I propose to give a personal account of how I, as a health care professional
as well as a patient with metastatic carcinoma, have reacted to the impact of
cancer on my life. My purpose in sharing my observations is not to give an
intricate two-year medical history of a cancer patient, but rather to express a
personal and professional point of view about the myriad of thoughts, feelings
and interactions that one experiences as a person who is terminally ill or who
perceives himself as dying. Specifically, I would hope to impress upon readers
the importance of communicating with the patient throughout a medical crisis
which may ultimately terminate in death and the signficance of recognizing the
psychological aspects of dying and reactions to death in patients facing a life-
threatening illness.

To give some perspective to the impact of a life-threatening disease on my
own life, it is perhaps best to give a brief overview as to what has happened
during the past two years. In October 1976, at age 29, I had experienced a rather
rapid series of significant changes in my life that produced a stressful period of

time, albeit positive. A year before I had remarried and found myself enveloped in the growing pains of establishing a new marital relationship. Two years earlier I had accepted a newly created position as an assistant director of nursing at Sheboygan Memorial Hospital, a 250-bed acute care facility, and was intent upon bringing about significant changes in the psychiatric services. Added to these positive stressors was a most critical responsibility affecting my life: raising my six-year-old son. Life was both challenging and fulfilling. The goals that I had set for myself in earlier years, from a professional and personal point of view, were beginning to become a reality. I viewed myself as starting to approach the prime of my life.

In retrospect, I realize that I took my good health status for granted. Inwardly, it amused me that after 11 years of working in a hospital, the closest I had ever come to being a patient was being admitted for the birth of my son. I had never actively pondered the possibility that as a young woman, I might fall victim to a disease. Even more difficult to comprehend was the possibility of facing a life-threatening disease.

In my role as a health professional, I was accustomed to telling others to practice preventive types of health care (which included breast self-exam). However, it is fair to say that I never anticipated finding any potential abnormality in myself. Even though I consistently practiced the preventive measures that I taught, the shock and disbelief I felt upon the discovery of the nodule in my left breast will never be forgotten. Looking back over the first few days after my discovery of the nodule, I realize that one of the immediate reactions was to deny consciously that the mass could be anything out of the ordinary. Perhaps I was painfully aware of what the worst possible consequences could be: I did not want to bring myself to believe that at age 29 I might fall into the category of "cancer patient." Despite the logical concerns about the mass proving to be malignant and, therefore, challenging my life expectancy, I found myself selfishly rationalizing that I could not have that disease at this point in my life. There just didn't seem to be time "to work it into my schedule" or to tolerate and contend with a disease entity that would interrupt my life so drastically just when things were going so well.

In spite of all the reasons I could conjure up for the nodule not being anything to worry about, I went to see a surgeon who recommended that a biopsy be performed at Christmastime in 1977. Since the procedure was performed under local anesthetic, I was fully conscious when the surgeon told my husband and me that the preliminary results of the frozen section indicated a tentative diagnosis of carcinoma. I will never forget that moment: the three of us sitting so close together that our knees touched; my surgeon hunched over, leaning toward us, and talking in hushed tones. I remember looking at the clock and seeing the hands showing 10:06 in the morning. I also remember crying and disbelieving the statement about a positive pathology report. My last thought was that I had just been handed a death warrant and would not live to see the next Christmas.

A period of 12 days elapsed between the biopsy and the modified radical mastectomy which was performed in January 1978. During that time I found myself painfully going through the familiar stages of grief defined by Kubler-Ross (1969). While I did not actively perceive myself as working through the grieving process, in retrospect I feel that the period of time between the two surgical procedures enabled me to be better prepared for the amputation of the breast. It gave me the much needed time to prepare my young son with the thought that I would be in the hospital and would "not be feeling well" for several weeks to come. In addition, at that point I needed time to sort out my own thoughts and to be in better control of my emotions. It was a time for sharing, for crying, and for talking with my husband. It was a time for garnering support from each other, from other family members, and for trying to put some perspective into the nightmare that we were experiencing as a couple.

Subsequent to that surgical procedure, the physical and emotional recuperative phase was relatively uneventful and by summertime I felt physically strong and confident that the immediate crisis of adjusting to cancer had passed. It came as quite a shock to those involved in my medical care, as well as to my husband and myself, when I found a metastasis to the supraclavicular nodes in my neck in September 1978. Considering that I had received excellent follow-up care on a quarterly basis following the mastectomy, it seemed almost incomprehensible that, with negative nodal status following the mastectomy, the nodules had not been found earlier. As a result, I became a patient in the oncology service at University of Wisconsin hospitals and have been followed there since October 1978. Chemotherapy was initiated in November 1978 and continues to be the ongoing treatment plan at this time.

One cannot imagine the depth of growth experienced by a patient and his family when undergoing a medical crisis. The past two years have yielded many insights into myself as an individual and as a nurse. It is because of some of the frustrations experienced by my family and me in dealing with a life-threatening disease that it seems appropriate to speak to the issues of communication with terminal patients or those patients who have concerns about dying.

One of my first observations is that most health care professionals seem to be very uneasy in approaching patients who are concerned about their mortality or, indeed, are dying. It seems that we are raised with the concept that only old people die and that young people do not have to consider the possibility of their mortality until they have lived a long life and have succeeded in achieving the goals and milestones of a lifetime. Likewise, rarely have we as parents spent time with our children relating to issues concerning death and dying (Kubler-Ross, 1969); subsequently, a child perceives that there is some mystique surrounding death and dying which fosters the notion that death is to be feared. Therefore, it is not difficult to understand why a young woman would find it extremely difficult to accept the notion of a life-threatening illness and possible death. The health care professional is not exempt from the difficulty of relating to someone who is dying or perceives herself as about to die. Each of us as human beings carries a complex collection of thoughts, ideas, and preconceived notions about death and dying. We have carried these thoughts from our early years. Perhaps it is because we struggle to find the right words, or perhaps it is because we do not accept the idea of death at a young age, that it is difficult for us to comunicate with patients.

And what do patients see in the health care professional throughout their involvement with the health care system? I have experienced a wide range of reactions from individuals that have left me feeling empty, angry, frustrated and, occasionally, pleased about the support I have received from them. Most frustrating are the many assumptions made by health care professionals in dealing with terminal patients or those facing a life-threatening illness. Because of my expertise in psychiatric nursing, it was not unusual for me to receive cues from colleagues indicating that I should be able to cope with my situation. This rationale for this erroneous assumption was based on the fact that I had been engaged in psychotherapy with patients for 10 years and had assisted patients with problem-solving during the crises in their lives. The fact that I was a nurse apparently exempted me from having feelings. I can say with certainty that after being admitted as a patient, one takes off one's "nursing cap" and lives a different role.

I was angry when people assumed that I would be able to cope with this crisis in my life and not have the need to talk about it. Rather, I interpreted some covert expectations of others that I should internalize my feelings and somehow work out a solution which would keep me from "falling to pieces." Not until I literally shouted at one of my colleagues, "Why aren't you people talking to me? Why don't you sit down and listen to me?" was I confronted with the response, "But we thought you could handle this, especially since you are a psychiatric nurse. We just didn't know what to say."

Another assumption frequently made was that I would have other people to talk to about my feelings. This may be true in many cases. There are those patients who do not care to share their feelings with health care professionals during a hospitalization, and those wishes must be respected. But not to provide the opportunity to the patient to share how he feels is tantamount to not ensuring quality care. He must know that resources exist for sharing and acceptance of his feelings. Although a patient may not be terminal, he may still be concerned about dying and be going through the same grieving process as a patient who in fact is terminal.

Another pitfall into which health care professionals fall is assuming that patients are going to react in a predictable fashion regarding the loss of a body part.

Since my mastectomy I have had the privilege of being asked by physicians to see a variety of cancer patients within the hospital where I work. A 49-year-old woman was referred to me by the attending surgeon who had performed a bilateral mastectomy on her. The nursing staff on the unit and I conferred about this woman's ability to cope with her situation during her inpatient stay, and it was suggested to me that the patient was having a difficult time adjusting to the fact that she had had both breasts amputated. However, in face-to-face dialogue and communicating with this patient on a daily basis over a period of two weeks, it was apparent to me she was not as concerned about the loss of her breasts as she was about the fact that she did not know what was going to happen in the future and was afraid that she was going to die. How clear it is, then, that the message sent is not always the message received.

A similar erroneous assumption was made during a panel presentation in which I was involved. The panel's cancer specialists indicated to the audience that women with mastectomies should be encouraged to ask their physicians about the possibility of breast implants following surgery. Those panelists assumed that women with mastectomies would be so devastated by the disfiguring operation that "naturally" they would want to have the breast implant. In speaking with many women who have had mastectomies, I have not generally found that their greatest need was to have a breast implant. Again, health care professionals need to be wary of transferring their personal opinions and concerns to the patient with respect to after-care plans. In fact, the majority of mastectomy patients have made a successful transition from the preoperative to the postoperative state and do not feel a need to go through additional surgery which would, presumably, give them a more normal appearance. Only the patient knows what is important to him or her. Until we take the time to inquire what he or she is thinking and feeling, we cannot make assumptions in terms of what is important.

What makes it so difficult to communicate with the patient who perceives himself as dying? During my initial inpatient stay, I noticed that nurses and physicians feel very comfortable talking about non-health related issues or about giving me the results of my pathology report and laboratory tests. When it came to emotions, however, an invisible curtain seemed to drop. The behavioral cues that I picked up from my colleagues varied from lack of eye contact to standing or hovering over my bedside in an authoritarian posture. They talked superficial banter about non-health related topics, and then made hasty exits from my room. Most bothersome, however, were the statements made in an effort to reassure me, but which certainly fell short of making me feel any better. Well-worn cliches as "Things will be better tomorrow" or "You're doing just fine" or "You don't need to worry about that now" serve as sources of irritation to a patient with concerns about her life expectancy. I did *not* know I "would be better tomorrow" and while finding myself in the midst of a medical/emotional crisis, I did not perceive myself as "doing well." If patients feel their time is limited, they do not want to hear that they "don't have to worry about that now." The present and the future are important to them.

Perhaps the most contagious and pervasive fear for patients is fear of the unknown. How often do we as health care professionals promote the growth of this kind of fear? Some professionals tend to think that information about the patient and about his life-threatening illness should be shared only in certain circumstances. It is noted that the assumption is made that the patient cannot cope and, therefore, information is shared with family members or only very sparingly with the patient. We underestimate the capabilities of individuals to handle "bad news." All those facing a life-threatening illness whom I have met in the past two years have said loudly and clearly that the worst thing that has happened to them is not being told the information they need to know in order to make responsible decisions about their life. Fortunately, the majority of health care professionals realize the negative impact of withholding information from the patient and recognize the patient's right to be informed of his health status (Erickson and Hyerstay, 1979).

Another negative stressor imposed on the patient by health care professionals is the loss of control the patient experiences during the medical crisis. The loss of control, readily evidenced by the minimal involvement we traditionally allow the patient in decision-making regarding his care, yields feelings ranging from anxiety to helplessness to anger. The opportunity for the patient to function as independently as possible in his care is taken away. The patient feels that he has no control over his life and, therefore, feels very hopeless and helpless about his future. Even the smallest decisions that are left up to the patient can be meaningful. Letting him know that he has the right and the responsibility to participate in his care can be of tremendous therapeutic benefit and can ultimately assist the health care professionals in providing the necessary treatment. Those decisions may be as trivial as when the patient wants to have his bed bath to as important as to whether or not he wants to have additional surgery as a result of a biopsy.

Another way to improve our communications with patients, in addition to providing an open atmosphere in staff-patient relationships, is to look at our non-verbal communication. How many times have we been guilty of looking down at a patient who is lying prone in a hospital bed and saying, "And how are we today?" Have you caught yourself *standing* at the side of a bed with your arms folded across your chest and telling a patient what is going to happen? The covert message is one of defensiveness and lack of openness in inviting a sharing of thoughts. I submit that the humanistic way of approaching a patient (which, incidentally, does not take any more time) is to be at eye level with that patient and to communicate through eye contact, as well as through body language (Fast, 1970, pp. 117-123), that you are concerned about him. Without uttering a word the patient "reads" your body language cues and knows that the time being spent with him is the time that you are devoting *solely* to him.

Years ago, student nurses were taught never to sit on a patient's bed. It is unfortunate that such an old philosophy has carried over into the 70's, because it enhances the patient's feeling of loneliness and makes him hesitant to reach out and say, "I'm hurting, I'm scared, I'm frightened, I do not know what is happening." Not only does our body language deliver very distinct messages to the patient, but similarly we need to sharpen our skills and tune in to the patient's non-verbal behavior. When we approach a patient and find him curled up in his bed with his back to those in the room or staring out a window, do we do merely do the task that we went in to complete or do we also take a few minutes to respond to the patient's feelings? Too often we are satisfied to take the path of least resistance; we fall into that old habit described by the cliche, "Let sleeping dogs lie." Is it because we are afraid that the patient is going to ask questions, such as "Am I going to die?" or "How much time do I have left?" and because we are unsure of how we should respond to such questions that we ignore the opportunity to reach out?

Those of us who work with dying patients or those patients facing life-threatening illnesses need to consider how our verbal responses can affect the patient's attitude. Several incidents experienced over the past two years illustrate examples of insensitivity toward the crisis situation. Throughout the course of the chemotherapy regime there have been predictable days when the side effects of the medication prevent me from being at work. Because I can anticipate the illness following the chemotherapy injections and therefore "schedule" my sick time, I have several times heard colleagues tell me, "Well, enjoy your days off; it must be nice to have a vacation." Another statement made to me is what I call that of the eternal optimist, which is "Well, cheer up, things could be worse." *What could be worse?* Saying this to a cancer patient who is concerned about a potentially short life expectancy and the fact that he cannot predict the future in terms of his disease is a rude and insensitive attitude. Most cancer patients would gladly relinquish their diagnosis to anyone willing to take it. A statement that "Things could be worse" evokes very strong feelings. Perhaps the remark is made in the spirit of being supportive and genuine, although unconsciously it is used to deal with personal inadequacies and ambiguity related to coping with feelings about death and dying.

The most genuine type of response, one which patients seem to appreciate and which yields the best climate for interaction between the patient and staff, is that of providing a listening ear and being accepting and nonjudgmental of the patient's feelings and attitudes. Those feelings may include anger, frustration, denial and bargaining. It is not all right to reassure the patient that he is going to be better, but it is our responsibility to respond to the patient's concerns and questions and reassure him that these concerns are normal and important. Some of the most meaningful statements have been made by friends who have indicated their concern for my well-being by being honest enough to say, "I don't know what to say but I care and I am concerned about you." There need not be answers to questions, but there does need to be a willingness to be open, to share and to accept.

Health care professionals often underestimate the power of touch as a form of communication (Fast, 1970, pp. 78-93). It cannot be emphasized enough that a momentary holding of a patient's hand, a touch on the shoulder, or a supportive arm for a patient who is walking can communicate genuine caring and concern. The patient feels the openness and will probably venture the sharing of feelings with this individual rather than with someone who rushes in and out of his room to do only routine or technical tasks.

One final thought about communicating with the dying patient is that we, as health care professionals, need to let the patient know that we accept his feelings at any given moment. It is normal for a dying patient, or one who perceives himself as facing death, to feel "down" at times. We cannot and should not expect a patient to "put on a happy face and smile" when he does not feel that way. Perhaps it is because of our own inherent need that we find it necessary to have a pateint respond in a positive fashion and conclude that he is not making the adjustment if he, at times, seems to feel hopeless and helpless.

Lack of control, fear of the unknown, and erroneous assumptions made by health care professionals are only a few factors which contribute to the anxiety and frustration experienced by a dying patient or one who perceives himself as dying in response to a life-threatening illness. We, as health care professionals, need to realize that we can greatly eliminate these components by improving communications through verbal and nonverbal means. When we realize that we need to give of ourselves and communicate at a more feeling level with dying patients, we will indeed improve the quality of life for those whom we serve.

REFERENCES

ERICKSON, R. C. and B. J. HYERSTAY. 1979. "The Dying Patient and the Double-Point Hypothesis." In Garfield, C. A. et al. (eds.), *Stress and Survival*, St. Louis: C. V. Mosby Company, pp. 298-306.

FAST, J. 1970. *Body Language*. New York: J. B. Lippincott Company.

KUBLER-ROSS, E. 1969. *On Death and Dying*. New York: Macmillan Publishing Company, Inc.

15

The Grieving Process

Raymond Vickers

The influence of preliterate and primitive societies on the patterns of our grieving process is so great that we need to pay some attention to it. We know about many of the superstitious beliefs of primitive people through history, first recorded by the Egyptians and Sumerians. After them, the ancient Hebrews, the Greeks, and the Romans recorded beliefs that have had enormous influences on our own cultural attitude to death. In essence, we find that in early times death was seen in much the same way it is seen today by a child between the ages of two and eight years — that is, anthropomorphically. Death was seen not as "something" but as a "Someone" who comes uninvited into the mortal world to carry people off into immortality. The person of Death was often represented in the art of the Middle Ages as a cloaked skeleton or corpse-like man (death was invariable portrayed as male) resembling Father Time, but carrying a scythe to cut us down (Choron 1963).

The mythology also included the belief that Death, like other supernatural beings, might be negotiated with. One might ward off death by doing the right thing or by being lucky or protected by beneficient gods or influences. We see this same belief today in children who are approaching adolescence. As they overcome the fears of an anthropomorphic Death, they challenge it by taking "death-defying" risks — balancing atop high walls despite parental protest, for example, or trying drugs. When death does not follow, they feel exhilarated by the thrill, and can approach increasing maturity with more confidence that they will survive (Nagy 1948). Some individuals cannot make this transition and, as adults, continue to be preoccupied by thrillseeking through sky-diving, joining the army, and so on. Such people deal with grief differently than more mature persons do.

94

Most mature and rational people are not burdened by the constant fear of death, although many of us retain various superstitions and practices corresponding to the mythological lore of death. Some of these are also incorporated into religious beliefs and the rites of the funeral. In our hyperliterate society, we can view death impersonally, isolated from it by the buffer of the mass media. We do not have to smell the carcasses on the news bulletins, and we can actually be reassured by the unreality of death on violent dramas. When we leave the theater or switch off the television, we can return to a safe existence.

Scientific literature on death and dying, specifically that written from a psychosocial point of view, is a relatively recent phenomenon. Of course, the nineteenth century novel shows the preoccupation our grandparents had with the family and death as a subject of gothic literature. Beginning in 1914, the era of total war was accompanied by radical changes in the literature of death (Hoffman 1959), and this continues today in science fiction. However, until the mid-twentieth century, the subject of death was as taboo a topic for scientific discussion as sex once was. Since then it has become so popular that it is difficult to keep up with the burgeoning literature concerning death and grief (Halporn 1986). In 1959, Feifel's *The Meaning of Death* was published, summarizing much of the work up to that time. Each year thereafter, more and more publications on the subject have appeared.

It has been shown that a close contact with death often produces major changes in a person's life and personality and makes it difficult for the person to resume close ties with others. In primitive society, those who ministered to the dying in their transition to the afterlife were known as shamans; they were regarded as untouchables, and could not marry, as some priests today may not. Some patients regard surgeons with the same awe, perhaps for similar reason. Those who suffer bereavement find that in addition to their grief, they must bear the burden of becoming untouchable for a period.

The primary paradox of seeing death as evil and antithetical to life, rather than as part of life, has been challenged by some religious thinkers. Some rites are conducted by a new generation of priests who celebrate death as the culmination of life. They try to make the funeral a happier occasion, but encounter great resistance and bewilderment. There is difficulty in overcoming people's natural fear of death.

The fear of death hangs over us all. It is present as a generalized subliminal fear, contrasting with the occasional sudden panic known as anger anomie, which strikes all of us occasionally in the midst of life when something reminds us that one day, we know not when, we too will die. That acute realization is so disturbing that it causes strong defense reactions to suppress it into the preconscious, a process known as the denial of death. On the other hand, those who are dying welcome the opportunity to discuss their fears, which often surround the severing of treasured relationships rather than the process of dying.

Bowers and colleagues (1964) issued an eloquent plea for more effective communication between those who work with the dying and their patients. This was taken up and successfully popularized by Kubler-Ross (1969). Kubler-Ross described a series of stages of defense reactions used by those who are dying to deal with anticipatory anxiety and fear. They are the maneuvers that many people use to accept a loss: (1) denial (Not me!), (2) anger (Why me?), (3) bargaining (If me, then perhaps), (4) depression (I'm afraid), and (5) acceptance (Yes, me).

The word "denial," as used by psychiatrists, is a much misunderstood concept. It is important not to think about it as an objective reality or as a behavior, but as a mental process used in establishing priorities. It may be used during the time when a new concept cannot be logically accepted because it is incompatible with self-image. This is called first-order denial and is seen, for example, when a patient cannot feel a hard lump in her breast that is easily palpable. Second-order denial is seen in a person who says he accepts his death, but appears to do so in a detached way. He may neglect estate planning, or have no appreciation of the effects of his death on his family. Third-order denial applies to us all: we are cognitively unable to contemplate our own death in a real sense. Freud (1925) said that when we picture our death, we retain the eye that contemplates the scene. We cannot comprehend our nonexistence.

THE DEATH OF A LOVED ONE

Just as adapting humans can cope with the concept of their own death in a series of stages, so do we "work through" the death of a loved one in stages. Westberg (1961) described ten such stages. In normal, mentally healthy individuals, these stages of grief last from four months to a year, during which they will experience a variety of moods and encounter different aspects of their personalities.

The first stage of grief is shock, and shock is partly denial. The person is really suffering but cannot react in a way that shows it at all. The second stage of grief, often helped to emerge by sympathetic others, involves emotional release, usually expressed by crying, rage, anger, and sometimes, paradoxically, happiness. Occurrence of the latter may disturb those around the grieving person, but it provides an effective emotional release, nevertheless.

In the third stage, extremely severe depression and loneliness supervene, accompanied by isolation from others. There may be some mutual shamanistic rejection by former friends. A person may become reclusive during this stage. The wife of a minister complained that after his death no one ever invited her out to dinner. When asked, "Do you ever invite anyone else in?" she responded, "How can I, when I do not get any invitations to repay?" This lack of logic in rationalizing the isolation is clear.

The fourth stage may bring about physical symptoms of distress, causing people to see their doctors. It is to be hoped that Valium is not prescribed at these times, because the ailments are not psychological but real. People at this stage need good medical care. They develop new illnesses and have a heightened risk of mortality because of reduced resistance. Parkes (1970) and others have shown that there is an increased death rate among survivors for two years following a bereavement. Heart diseases and cancer are increasingly prevalent at this stage.

The onset of the fifth stage may be heralded by panic: "If my husband can die, then so can I!" At this stage, the therapist may expect urgent telephone calls, often in the middle of the night.

The psychological activity increases in the sixth stage, which is characterized by developing guilt. One commonly hears that the bereaved person now feels responsible for the death in some way. One widow told her psychiatrist that she had recalled that she had failed to fill the car with gasoline, causing her husband to cancel a medical checkup. A year later he was found to have inoperable lung cancer, and she felt that she had killed him. In the psychodrama of death and dying, a recurrent issue is to dwell on the unexplored potentials of a severed relationship. We have found that after living through this guilt even vicariously, student participants in psychodrama often return to their rooms and make long-distance calls to their parents. The stage of guilt is most prolonged in those who had impaired relationships with the deceased. Wives from good marriages pass quickly through this stage with no more than gentle regrets.

In the seventh stage, hostility emerges in place of guilt. This stage is one that professionals do not handle well: they become defensive. It is important to understand that the hostility is a sign of the generation of increased psychic energy, a sign of the beginning of recovery. A bereaved individual may begin to blame everyone in the family for not having done enough to help. A person in this stage occasionally consults a lawyer, seeking a suit against the doctor who failed to keep the loved one alive. It is usually a mistake to refuse to see such relatives, for they may need to review the medical care that was given before they can move beyond this stage. As they express their hostility at the physician or hospital, a professional response is essential. Outraged self-vindication may be very costly.

At the eighth stage, the person will have returned to normal activity, but will be troubled by frequent flashbacks that involve the loved one. For a time, the person may fear that the mourning has regressed, but these episodes become progressively shorter and less frequent. Grieving actually lasts a lifetime. A person in his eighties, remembering his grandmother, may shed a tear and experience the full well of deep grief, but in a moment it will pass.

Finally, a stage is reached in which hope is rekindled. Grieving people now know that they are going to make it. Ultimate acceptance of a world in which the loved one is not present soon follows, and the possibility of developing new relationships with significant others returns.

All stages respond to intervention. Some stages require only acceptance; others require interaction. It is wrong to enourage people to abandon their grief, which is not a pathological condition, but rather, a form of healing. Like healing, it can be halted, and it can regress. For the helper, knowing the stage helps to maintain hope and progress. If grief does not pass through to acceptance, clinical depression, which is a pathological condition, is likely to follow.

REFERENCES

BOWERS, M., E. JACKSON, J. KNIGHT, and L. LeSHAN. 1964. *Counseling the Dying.* New York: Thomas Nelson.

CHORON, J. 1963. *Death and Western Thought.* New York: Collier.

FEIFEL, H., ed. 1959. *The Meaning of Death.* New York: McGraw-Hill.

FREUD, S. 1925. "Thoughts for the Times on War and Death." *Collected Papers,* vol. IV. London: Hogarth Press, pp. 18-317.

HALPORN, R. 1986. *Bibliography on Death, Bereavement, Loss, and Grief.* Brooklyn, NY: Center for Thanatological Research.

HOFFMAN, F. J. 1959. "Mortality and Modern Literature." In H. Feifel, ed. *The Meaning of Death.* New York: McGraw-Hill, pp. 133-156.

KUBLER-ROSS, E. *On Death and Dying.* New York: The Macmillan Co.

NAGY, M. 1948. "The Child's Fears Concerning Death." *Journal of Genetic Psychology* 73:3-27.

PARKES, C. M. 1970. "The First Year of Bereavement." *Psychiatry* 33:444-467.

WESTBERG, G. E. 1961. *Good Grief. A Constructive Approach to the Problem of Loss.* Philadelphia: Fortress Press.

Part III

Psychiatry and
The Dying Patient

16

Psychiatric Assessment and Management of the Dying Patient

Hyman L. Muslin

The technical aspects of work with dying patients involve learning the principles of observation, both the cognitive and empathic aspects. Also required is an understanding of the principles of supportive psychotherapy, as well as an appreciation of how the operational diagnosis determines the way one approaches each patient.

The caretakers of dying people need to know the principles of observing behavior so that they can attend to the details of observing verbal and nonverbal behaviors in a sequential way. The important principle is that segments of behavior must be analyzed so that the verbal and the nonverbal behavior is appreciated (including affects).

The next learning task is to appreciate the empathic observations that need to be made. The observer must train himself to put himself in the place of the person he is interviewing so that he can experience the valence of the emotional reaction. Otherwise, he is witnessing from afar.

The next phase of knowledge must be an emphasis on rounding up the data so that the observer can make a meaningful set of diagnostic statements. We need to know: (1) Is the patient in psychological equilibrium? (2) Is the patient adapting to his state of dying? (3) What are the drives being used to assist in adaptation?

The notion of psychological equilibrium means that the patient is not experiencing nor exhibiting either massive anxiety or major depression. Anxiety is ordinarily manifest by signs and symptoms of nervousness — from tremors to panic. Depression means that the patient is exhibiting the three cardinal features of depression: the affect of grief, the loss of esteem (self-punishment or self-abuse), and changes in the psychomotor state — either retardation or agitation.

Adaptation refers to all the measures taken to master the environment, i.e., a successful interaction with the environment. At times, adaptation will require regression or relaxation of one's conscience; at other times, adaptation requires exhibiting aggression. Still another means of adaptation will involve denial, the isolation of a percept or bit of knowledge (as in the case of flying) that ordinarily requires the individual to deny the obvious knowledge of the potential danger. (Or else flying would always be an anxiety-ridden experience.)

The next aspect of collating behavior deals with translating observations into the various functions and structures of the psychic apparatus so that the observer can appreciate: (1) the nature and integrity of repressing devices — the ego defenses; (2) the nature and quality of the conscience and ideals of the person being observed; (3) the patient's reality-testing, judgment, and intelligence; (4) the nature and quality of the self system; (5) the amount and quality of drives being expressed.

Of all the defenses that are ordinarily utilized to maintain repression of drives, the most important ones to be understood in the context of the care of the dying are denial, regression, projection, reaction formation, and avoidance. *Denial* refers to the isolation of a percept so that the percept that is made is maintained in a state of unawareness. The patient has observed the lump but that percept is actually not usable information. *Regression* refers to the adoption of previous feelings, defenses from early eras in the patient's development. *Repression* refers to the removal of drives and conflicts into the unconscious zones of the personality as in an amnesia, in forgetting, etc. *Projection* means the investment of one's attitudes, drives, or conscience onto environmental objects, human or otherwise. *Reaction Formation* is the defense that entails the experience of feeling attitudes contrary to the drive that has been simulated so that conscious and articulated feelings of sympathy may harbor intense feelings of rage. *Avoidance* refers to unconscious flight from unpalatable impulses or scenes.

The self system is the collection of impressions and images that the person has of himself and includes the quality and quantity of esteem the person has. Thus, a person experiencing a depressive reaction feels himself to be of little value and a burden as a measure of his self-system and loss of self-esteem.

The superego is that area of personality that encompasses the person's conscience — his unconscious morality plus his ego ideals to live up to. Another important set of functions to be understood are the patient's capacity to test reality, to use intellectual capacity, and to make judgments. And also of concern are the amount and nature of drives that are capable of emerging. In some people there are channels for discharge of drives, adequately neutralized while in others the drives may be very restricted and the person is inhibited or rigid. In still others, the drives that emerge are not tamed (neutralized) and are too primitive for orderly social living.

We end our diagnostic considerations with a set of observations that can be collected into meaningful expressions of psychic equilibrium, with the notion of adaptation, and with a measure of the various functions of the ego apparatus. Note that we are deliberately not speaking to ordinary diagnostic appraisals but rather to a listing of the functioning of different aspects of the psychic apparatus and to the integrity of the apparatus.

An example of this approach to interview data is given below:

Segment I

Dr. M: Now, I don't know anything about your condition so, perhaps, you could just start from the beginning and tell me about yourself and your problems.

Mr. S: Well, my problem right today is that I feel useless, an unnecessary person and, uh, I just don't want to go on living anymore. That's the way I feel. This is my whole problem.

The patient is a tall, mesomorphic man, appearing to be in his early fifties. He is neatly dressed but without a tie; the collars of his shirt are over his coat lapels. His demeanor is pleasant. He walks and stands well without slouching or slowness. The muscle tonicity of the face is good. In this segment there is no affect of sadness, and there is no consternation or agitation in his affect or posture.

The verbal behavior reveals an immediate exposition of the major experience of the patient. He is suffering a major loss of esteem in his self-concept. Further, the behavior reveals a suicidal interest.

Collating this brief piece of material, the data allude to the patient's version of himself at this moment: he is experiencing a profound loss of esteem; he is expressing suicidal ideation. There seems to be an intact function of reality-testing. The interviewer's reaction was that of apprehension and inquisitiveness. There was no complete empathic recognition of the state of sadness since the affect was not that of mourning nor was a posture of dejection apparent. Perhaps this appearance did not elicit the inner feeling of an empathic recognition of depression.

Segment II

The patient, Mr. S., continues:

I had a heart attack in March of '84 that kept me in the hospital for six weeks. Before that, I was having anginas for two or three years that I kept secret from the family. And after I was in the hospital for four weeks and home for two weeks, I went back to work — I'm in business — and was working for three months and then the man sold the business and I was unable to get a job after that. I didn't feel like working and I worked part-time for about a year in a place. I couldn't make any money and I quit that job and tried to get other jobs and was turned down. I felt absolutely inadequate to do anything anymore so I've just given up the desire or will, or whatever you want to call it, to go on living. I feel inept, useless.

The *affect* was as described above. There was no sadness and tragedy in this segment. The *posture* revealed appropriate movements in conjunction with the verbal data. The *verbal behavior* reveals first an understandable sequence of behavior, i.e., the associations were not loose and could be followed. Once again the patient repeats that he has changed since his myocardial infarction and that he is without value. There were comments (almost asides) that he had angina pectoris for years before he became more ill, and that he did not tell his family about the illness. These remarks reveal a major aspect of his personality to be elaborated on later. The *essence* of this segment perhaps lies in his statement that pertains to his esteem.

Collating the behavior, we would say that data thus far reveal some material bearing on the patient's *self-esteem*. He manifestly declares his value to be nil and he expresses frank suicidal thoughts to be taken as all suicidal thoughts, quite seriously, and to be evaluated throughout the entire interview. He alluded to an aspect of his ego ideal when he commented on hiding his angina. This remark may also contain an allusion to a defense mechanism of denial — denying the seriousness of the cardiac difficulty. The data also allow us to appreciate the nature of the superego system. The intensity of the self-criticism ("I feel useless, an unnecessary person") is clear in this segment and gives us a picture of the forces of the superego in an unleashed self-destructive mode of operation. A facet of the psychic apparatus demonstrated in this segment is the patient's display of little to no drives except for the implicit meaning of the wish to see a physician for help, i.e., a neutralized and defended expression of a wish for drive gratification. There is enough data to demonstrate that there is a capacity to test reality. It can be seen when the patient says "I *feel* useless." He makes it clear that this is a perception. He is aware that he is experiencing his environment in a special way.

The interviewer's responses in this segment were the same as those in the previous segment — a feeling of waiting for more data and more affect to help in the appreciation of this material.

MANAGEMENT APPROACHES

The first approach to the management of the dying person is the diagnostic one: Is there equilibrium present? (If so, a special approach is indicated.) Are the adaptations sound? (If not, a special line of approaches is indicated based on the kinds of ego mechanism being used.) The basic principle deals with the approach of specificity — the caretaker must be (1) a competent, cognitive, and empathetic observer; must be (2) able to collate the behavioral data; and finally be (3) able to plug in a specific management approach to what he has observed to be needed.

The specific management approaches to the case of the dying are several, ranging from the notion of sympathy, pity, and friendship for a person dying in more or less a state of equilibrium to the approaches of supportive psychotherapy for a person who needs specific intervention to assist in the establishing and maintenance of equilibrium. In these discussions we are emphasizing the roles of the primary care physician and primary care staff in the emotional management of these dying people. However, it should be clear that at times a family member sufficiently attuned and empathetic to the needs of the dying person (not over-iden-tification and not affective) may function as a supervisor, an overseer of the management.

The first management approach of major importance applies to those whose terminal course is marked by a state of equilibrium, i.e., no apparent or manifest distress when the behavior may range from attitudes of sobriety and calmness to resignation. The specific approach on the part of the primary care personnel must be influenced by the knowledge that these people of course have special management needs — they need company and they need the reassurance of continued contact to the point of the final separation. This approach is based on the knowledge that death is the ultimate separation. Death always evokes in each dying person the set of feelings of abandonment and aloneness that affects every mourner and in this case the mourning for oneself.

With this set of understandings not defended against on the part of the caretaker, he or she can chart the exact reaction that is required. One must keep company, share the grief and be sympathetic, and be a companion to the mourner. What is the required action? The caretaker or the designee of the caretaker must regularly set aside a certain period of time to enter into a dialogue. The dialogue refers to the notion that even though the patient is the one to be attended to, the caretaker expresses his interest and concern and makes explicit his sympathy, i.e., he reveals his personal feelings or thoughts and thus there is an actual relationship in reaction to the patient's physiologic and emotional state. The explicit format is that the primary care person meets with the patient daily, has conversations with the patient, and keeps company as a regular visitor should, with the proviso that when the patient expresses grief or exhibits mourning, this behavior is attended to and shared so that the patient feels companionship and the respect and compassion that is deserved and given to anyone in a state of mourning.

Supportive Therapies

The primary care physicians or other caretakers must be knowledgeable about various approaches to supporting, maintaining, or reinstituting psychic equilibrium in those cases in which equilibrium is faltering and when the patient is experiencing major anxiety, depression, or other manifestations of regression of the psychic apparatus such as massive maladaptive denial or projection. These approaches to the maintenance of psychic equilibrium are labeled Supportive Psychotherapy Measures and include: Environmental Manipulation, Supporting of Defenses, Ventilation and Catharis, Transference Postures, and Intellectual Insight.

Environmental Manipulation refers to the caretaker's attempts at organizing the patient's environments in the least traumatic manner so that the patient will be less stimulated or traumatized. Operationally, it refers to special attitudes being shown to a patient; restriction or facilitation of visitors; organizing ward jobs for a patient; arranging special musical, religious, literary experiences; giving antidepressants or tranquilizers; arranging for a patient to live at a nursing home rather than with relatives, etc. It speaks to a knowledge of what causes discomfort and comfort in particular patients and is a clear reflection of the caretaker's knowledge of the patient's sources of intrapsychic and interpersonal tension. In ordinary psychotherapy, the therapist may attempt to manipulate the patient's environment in terms of job, living arrangements, habits, etc. Here the environment in a hospital or home may likewise have to be organized to promote comfort and lessened tensions.

Supporting of Defenses is a valuable technique and requires a serious understanding of the patient's psychic apparatus. It refers to the caretaker's attempts to enhance a defense or another aspect of the patient's psyche through suggestion, permission, and principally through condoning so that the particular defense, drive, or aspect of the self is accorded a greater value. Such is the case of those patients in whom denial, for example, has been a valuable defense against awareness of a disorganizing, frightening percept such as death. The patient's behavior reveals that there is a major thrust to denying the existence of the cancer and the impending death. This should define the attitude and behavior of the therapist — he too must enter into and support the denial mechanism. It is January and the patient will probably be dead in a short while, but he speaks with gusto of the opera season in the following fall. Thus the therapist enters into and speaks also of the performers and the productions to be staged. The patient, who knows clearly of the bronchogenic carcinoma of the lung that has been operated on, wishes to speak of the theater and occasionally of the "foolish doctors who won't admit she has psychosomatic asthma." This too must be appreciated and not dismantled.

One must be cautious in these supports since the existence of denial of psychotic proportions is always a lurking danger, and if the patient denies to this degree one must be careful. Thus care becomes watching behavior so that appointments are not missed and signing out against advice is not done.

If a good alliance is established, this is the best guarantee against the patient's moving away from the protection of medical care. If denial or other defenses become clearly irrational and part of a psychotic process, i.e., if reality testing becomes massively inundated, then a referral to the psychiatry service is indicated. What is referred to here as supporting of a defense only refers to those cases in which a defense such as a reaction formation (major interest in other patients' welfare), denial, or displacement, anger at medication, procedures, doctors can be accepted or enhanced while the reality testing mechanisms are generally intact. Thus, the patient can talk of asthma rather than cancer but does *not* stop taking medications or visiting her physician.

Other more subtle aspects of support relate to a special aspect of the patient's self-esteem including defenses of reaction formation, isolation, and support of the ego ideal. Thus a patient with strong pride mechanisms, needs for control of his environment, and needs to maintain repression over dependencies requires a special partnership from the staff — a discussion in general of treatment and procedures. Thus attention is paid to the narcissistic needs.

Ventilation and Catharsis refer to the capacity of the caretakers to assist in the unfolding or egress of deep feelings so that the patient can have the gratification of unburdening in a benevolent atmosphere that assists in the relief of tension and guilt. For dying people, the relief afforded when they can cry or rage with their attendants represents a vital and needed channel for discharge since so often they are unfortunately too filled with shame and guilt to express themselves with relatives.

One must be ever mindful that dying people often feel like lepers. Their relatives are insulating themselves from contaminating propensities — no one wishes to identify with death. Thus many times the dying do not have an environment where they can rage at their lesion or express wishes for love and company or feelings of mourning.

The caretaker must at times become the major *Transference* figure in the patient's life and be the authority on whom the patient rests a great deal of need. This, of course, is the essence of any doctor-patient or nurse-patient relationship in which the patient invests the caretaker with aspirations and expectations that speak of early relationships with significant objects who ordered and commanded his or her previous life.

In the dying, these relationships have great importance and the caretaker must accept this idealization knowing that it represents a vitally needed task with links to the security systems of the past — the feeling of an omnipresent parent whose reactions are always benevolent. Support of vitally needed narcissistic supplies to the dying patient is not to be taken lightly. When the patient says, "Tell me what to do about this or that ..." this question should be entered into with the feeling of a parent called on to make a pronouncement and to give advice (with proper precautions, etc.), rather than to answer: "You figure it out." Or when the patient says "I'm delighted you came; I couldn't wait to see you" he or she should be responded to with acceptance rather than humorous rebuttal.

Intellectual Insight is a supportive technique if it affords the patient a view of his or her inner workings and thus gives a measure of control and aids in adaptation to the environment or in maintenance of repression. If the patient can with the caretaker's clarification or interpretation understand some aspect of her anxiety or chagrin, the patient feels a heightening of esteem.

In therapeutic conversations with dying people from which a good deal of anxiety or guilt emerges in relationship to being ill, dependent, or dying, the interviewer's clarification or interpretation focusing on the reaction to dependency wishes that may include anxiety or guilt can help the patient see, perhaps for the first time, his or her conflict over dependency and may even enhance further explorations of past sensitization of this conflict. The patient's grasp of the problem may go a long way to acceptance of herself and may desensitize her enough to relieve a great deal of tension. The insights, although mainly intellectual, will offer a great deal of respect to her because she now sees her shame as an understandable and yet neurotic conflict and she can even begin to tolerate more and more of her normal wishes to get rest without shame.

Most of these therapeutic approaches are thought of as taking place between two individuals, but it is very helpful at times to have groups of patients engaged in meetings to discuss their reactions to the hospital, to the procedure, to being ill, to dying. It is difficult to gather together a consistent group on any particular ward setting, but it is also very rewarding if a reasonable number of sessions can take place over a period of months to see the amount of desensitization and support a group can offer. Not only do patients need support, but people actively engaged in the therapy of dying people also need support, encouragement, and supervision of their therapeutic endeavors. One approach is to have an ongoing workshop where weekly meetings are held and where people report in a somewhat casual fashion their therapeutic experiences with dying patients. At times one person may present weekly for a month in greater detail the therapy work he or she has been engaged in. Another model, especially in those caretakers who are seeing people in weekly supportive psychotherapy, is to participate in weekly supervision with a more senior colleague and to go over the details of the sessions microscopically as in the ordinary supervision of psychotherapy.

17

Psychiatric Care of Dying Patients with Head and Neck Cancer

Peter A. Shapiro

Some special psychological problems are associated with head and neck cancers. First, patients with head and neck cancer have a high prevalence of premorbid psychopathological problems. Alcohol abuse and heavy cigarette smoking, risk factors etiologically linked to the development of these cancers, are common. The persistence of some of these habits despite the efforts of friends, family, doctors to induce change, raises questions about denial, depression, self-destructive feelings, anxiety, and character styles in which actions are substituted for thinking and feeling. This has a marked effect on psychotherapeutic measures.

Second, the medical prognosis creates psychological problems. Uncertainty about the outcome for these patients is heightened by the process known as field cancerization, in which the entire upper airway and oropharyngeal mucosal surface has been exposed to the same carcinogens; this occasionally leads to the occurrence of multiple primary cancers, so that the apparently curative treatment of one tumor may no sooner be completed than a new tumor emerges.

The impact of cancer of the head and neck is further accentuated by the significance of the head and neck in terms of self-concept and body image. In daily life, it is evident that so much of what we do socially — speaking, eating, communicating, and expressing emotion, as well as much of our sexual behavior — has to do with our appearance from the neck up. Indeed, how others think of us is based, to great extent, on this same aspect of our appearance. Disfigurement in the region of the head and neck caused by disease or its treatment can have a major impact on these aspects of social living, and this can be expected to be a major source of emotional stress.

REACTIONS OF PATIENTS

There is a fairly stereotyped pattern of reactions in patients admitted to the hospital for surgery of head and neck tumors. This pattern has been noted in several studies, and, in a way, loosely parallels the stages of mourning or preparing for death described by Kubler-Ross (1969). At preoperative evaluation, many patients cannot say what is happening to them emotionally or psychologically. They experience a kind of shock and denial of the meaning of the experience. When they emerge from surgery with tubes, tracheostomies, and bandages, patients almost universally feel depressed and overwhelmed. Sometimes frank delirium ensues, although this is not common, and generally occurs only in the presence of an organic precipitant. As David and Barritt (1982) documented in a large prospective study, most patients improve psychologically once the process of healing begins and they begin to feel better physically. Fewer than 10% of patients in this study need psychiatric intervention to treat their depression and demoralization. They got better by themselves. Then real problems arise once again: how to live with what will happen now, how to adjust, or how to prepare for death. Depression, anger, and denial commonly recur and intermingle in patients' thoughts during this time.

REACTIONS OF FAMILIES

Patients' families experience a similar pattern of initial grief and mourning, followed by a time of rallying to provide the patient with support. This, of course, applies to those patients who are fortunate enough to have caring families. Sometimes the response of families involves suppressing feelings of anger or repugnance at the disfigurement, for these negative reactions are experienced guiltily. Families need to be the target of early intervention by the psychiatrist; they need to be told in a tactful way that these are understandable and normal reactions. Sometimes the psychiatrist must speak the feelings out loud in order for the family to be able to give the help the patient needs. The family also needs to be helped to deal with their fear of hurting the patient. This may mean demonstrating how to do a dressing change or give tracheostomy care. A lot of us are squeamish, especially some of us who have chosen psychiatry rather than some other branch of medicine, and we can learn from our own feelings of squeamishness that this is something we have to deal with if we are to expect patients' families to do so. Acknowledging feelings of uneasiness can help us master them.

There is another aspect of working with dying patients in general, and with patients with facial deformity or who are unable to speak in particular. It is that we feel guilty because we are glad that they have the deformity or the disability and that we do not. This feeling is the converse of the patient's outraged "Why me?" Our awareness of our feeling sensitizes us to this aspect of the patient's rage, leading us to withdraw. Family members have the same problem. Much of the depression that caretakers feel in caring for dying patients has to do with the mixture of hopelessness and guilt. We can counteract this guilt if we vigorously treat that which is treatable. We can treat symptoms of depression, pain, organic brain syndromes, and delirium. These are important aspects of care.

PALLIATIVE CARE

There are particular problems faced by those who have a disease that is incurable, that at best can be palliated and at worst, "nothing can be done." These patients experience anger, chronic pain, denial, and the fear of being abandoned. To know that you are going to die, not like everyone else in a distant, unreal future, but predictably, of an affliction that is already present, leads to feelings of isolation and abandonment. In such instances, psychiatrists can sometimes, by working with the staff and directly with the patients, help the patients to feel that they are not alone, that we are with them and care about them, and that death is not in the present but in the future.

"Removing death from the psychological present" (Eissler 1955) is a valuable treatment goal. We do this, in part, by helping patients find unfinished business that is still within the realm of possibility of completion, setting limited goals and then working toward those goals actively, rather than acknowledging only the inability to achieve other goals. For example, a debilitated elderly man spoke incessantly of his wish to kill himself rather than face his inexorable decline, and yet he made no attempt to plan or implement suicide. The psychiatrist responded to the patient's scornful rhetorical questioning of what value there could be in living in his weakened state by asking him to consider the question seriously: indeed, what did he have to live for, what did he want to do with the time left to him? The patient then used his fading energiies to express appreciation to his long-suffering and faithful wife, to make plans for a final meeting with his son and grandchildren, and to develop a relationship with the psychiatrist that became, in itself, a source of pleasure for him.

Pain can be treated very actively and suffering relieved not just by administering adequate analgesics, but by recognizing the distinct contributions of depression and anxiety to perceived pain and by providing appropriate treatment for these dysphoric affect states. Pain control can represent another aspect of unfinished business in which brief psychotherapeutic intervention can make a tremendous difference, as is illustrated by the following case.

CASE HISTORY 1

The patient was a 60-year-old woman referred for the evaluation of pain and depression a few days after she had undergone an orbital exenteration for recurrent malignant melanoma. Her surgeon, a renowned specialist, had encouraged her, after her initial operation, in the belief that she had been cured by surgery, but this hope had been shattered when the malignancy recurred a few months later, requiring further surgery and radiotherapy. She began to experience chronic pain, and a year later, as a result of another recurrence, she had now come to orbital exenteration.

At psychiatric evaluation, the patient's complaint was primarily anger at her husband. Their marriage had been strained for a long time, and her husband had had extramarital affairs. When she became ill, she felt this was unfair, since it was not she but her husband who "deserved" to suffer. After the first surgery, her surgeon's encouragement that "we got it all," had allowed her to identify with the surgeon and his strength, which sustained her, but when the tumor recurred this defense faltered. It was then that complaints of pain and depression began. Although there was an organic basis for her pain, it also represented for her the injustice of the fact that she, rather than her husband, was afflicted, the shattering of her idealization of her surgeon, and a deeply guilt provoking wish (for this rather self-righteous woman) that her husband, and perhaps her surgeon too, should be the ones to be punished. Her pain complaints certainly did serve this wish, while the pain itself served to punish her for it.

The work with her was done in three sessions on successive days. In these sessions I encouraged her to ventilate her grievances and her rage, and gave her a chance to reality-test her idea that somehow her virtue should have been a shield against the development of cancer. I also encouraged her to talk about the conflict between her angry wishes toward her husband and her concept of herself as a "good" person. During these three days her mood improved strikingly, her pain complaints decreased, she used less narcotic medication, and she was able to formulate plans to start psychotherapy in her hometown after her discharge from the hospital.

CASE HISTORY 2

A second kind of problem with this group of patients has to do with feelings of abandonment and loneliness. In working with another patient, the issue was what had happened to his face and how he felt people had rejected him on account of it. This 47-year-old man had a leiomyosarcoma of the face and, within the past four years had undergone several resections of portions of the face, first of the maxillary bone and portions of his nose, and then an orbital exenteration. He repeatedly refused radiotherapy and chemotherapy on the grounds that his own review of the literature showed that these treatment modalities did not have great efficacy. Instead, he used megavitamins, special diets, exercises, and attempts to fortify himself psychologically. He spent time visiting and encouraging other cancer patients and doing volunteer work, but a great source of distress was the rejection of his help by volunteer agencies. He felt that this rejection was based on repugnance at his disfigurement. Most of his face was covered by bandages.

I met him when he was readmitted for a total rhinectomy. Postoperatively, the patient attempted to maintain a positive outlook and cheerful demeanor, although he knew the poor prognosis, and that the loss of his nose had ravaged his face. He said, "The eyes are the windows to the soul; as long as I have one good eye, people will be able to see the real me." He maintained himself with careful bandaging and, eventually, a prosthesis in an attempt to maintain the image of his face. At times this attempt broke down, and he was depressed.

In terms of psychotherapy, there seemed to be little to say to this patient, with his horrible disfigurement, but one day I began to talk to him about how he helped others and encouraged them, and we agreed on a plan that he would make a videotape to discuss coping with cancer, and that the tape would be used in teaching medical students and others about this subject. He was very eager. Making this recording was very therapeutic for the patient, because it implied that he was still presentable, that he still had something to offer, that he was still worthwhile. This was amply confirmed in my many follow-up visits with him in the last year when he had expressed a desire to make more tapes, always in order "to help other people."

The making of the tapes meant that he was not dying yet, and that despite his disease he was still a person whom others could see for what he was. Indeed, this has been a situation in which a dying patient has received a feeling of immortality. The existence of the tapes means that he will live on. Eissler (1955) referred to the "gift situation" in the care of the dying patient, in which "the doctor finds something of himself to give to the patient." Since gifts from doctor to patient are not a usual part of the doctor-patient relationship, such a gift takes on special meaning for the patient. In fact, this patient and I have developed much greater emotional closeness as a result of this videotaping.

CASE HISTORY 3

Sometimes psychiatric intervention is less successful. Some patients exhibit very gross denial of the whole problem confronting them. They are very difficult to engage. When a psychiatrist appears and tries to speak with the patient, no emotional contact is made. The very idea of there being a psychiatrist involved implies that there is a problem, and this seems too threatening. The care of such patients is unsatisfying for all concerned, especially in those instances in which denial is paradoxically combined with demanding dependency.

One example of this situation occurred with a 38-year-old alcoholic man whose father had been an alcoholic and whose mother had died when he was still a child. This patient underwent composite resection and radiotherapy for cancer of the floor of the mouth. His tearfulness, depression, and withdrawal did not respond to antidepressants. He refused to give staff the name or phone number of his girlfriend, whom he had not informed of his hospitalization. This patient never made an emotional connection with the staff or with me. After discharge, his appearances in the head and neck clinic were erratic. He missed appointments scheduled to create a facial prosthesis, then bitterly complained about the ensuing delay. The staff responded with a mixture of pity, scorn, and contemptuous rage. The patient had declined offers of follow-up psychiatric care.

In this case, intervention was aimed at helping the involved staff understand that the patient's current behavior was formulated within the context of his life trajectory (Viederman and Perry 1980), his life's pattern of unstable, unreliable object relationships. The staff responded with a tempering of the rage response and a lowering of their expectations (Groves 1978) of the patient. They tolerated him better and eventually he did obtain his prosthesis.

SUMMARY

In summary, head and neck cancer patients pose special psychiatric problems because of their increased pre-morbid risk of psychiatric problems, the extreme effects of their illness and its treatment on their social functioning and body image, and other people's emotional reactions to them. Such patients, when they are dying, bring all of these aspects of their illness with them as they deal with problems of pain, anger, feelings of abandonment, and depression. Psychiatric work with them, and especially psychotherapeutic work, is demanding, but can be deeply gratifying.

REFERENCES

DAVID, D. J. and J. A. Q. BARRITT. 1982. "Psychosocial Implications of Surgery for Head and Neck Cancer." *Clinics in Plastic Surgery* 9:327-336.

EISSLER, K. 1955. *The Psychiatrist and the Dying Patient*. New York: International Universities Press.

GROVES, J. 1978. "Taking Care of the Hateful Patient." *New England Journal of Medicine* 298:883-887.

KUBLER-ROSS, E. 1969. *On Death and Dying*. New York: Macmillan.

SHAPIRO, P. A. and D. S. KORNFELD. "Psychiatric Aspects of Head and Neck Cancer." *Psychiatric Clinics of North America*. In press.

VIEDERMAN, M. and S. W. PERRY. 1980. "Use of a Psychodynamic Life Narrative in the Treatment of Depression in the Physically Ill." *General Hospital Psychiatry* 3:177-185.

18

The Life-Threatened Patient
in the Long-Term Care Facility

D. Peter Birkett

Many life-threatened patients are cared for in long-term facilities. In fact, statistics indicate that nursing homes are now, for white Americans, the second most common place in which to die. Some deaths in nursing homes are the end stage of inexorably progressive illnesses such as cancer, but this is by no means universal. Heart disease, stroke, and pneumonia are the most frequently listed causes of death. In some cases, such deaths represent passive euthanasia. However, terminal illness and passive euthanasia do not represent all of the severe illnesses treated in nursing homes, as will be shown in the following pages.

I wish to suggest practical methods for dealing with this group of patients. Although I will begin by categorizing these patients, this categorization emerges from no more scientific source than the top of my head and my years of clinical experience. I do not pretend that my categorization would stand up to analysis of variance or cluster analysis. In fact, one of my intents is to show the overlapping and ambiguity of these situations. The following are my proposed groupings of those who die in nursing homes:

1. Patients who are critically ill, but whose socioeconomic circumstances make hospitalization difficult.
2. Patients who are severely demented and whose consciousness is impaired.
3. Patients who seem very will, but whose need for specific medical measures cannot be established.
4. Patients who are critically ill, but for whom hospital care would have an overall adverse effect.

5. Patients who are critically ill, but whose lives would not be prolonged by medical measures.
6. Patients whose lives could be saved by medical measures available at a higher level of care; however, this care is withheld because of concurrent illness or because of the patients' advanced age or poor quality of life.
7. Patients with behavior problems that would make them uncooperative with intensive care.
8. Patients who look ill and seem moribund, but for whom no single treatable diagnosis has been established.
9. Patients diagnosed as having multiple disorders, leading to questions about which ones to give priority in treatment.

In these situations, I think it is necessary first to be clear in one's own mind about which category the individual patient is in. Ultimately, it may become necessary to smooth things over, to blur them a bit: stark presentations in black and white are then not wanted. One will look for compromise and pragmatism. If you really are going to let Mrs. Jones die when it would probably prolong her life to inject 100 mg of lidocaine into a central venous catheter, then, at least, you yourself have to know about it. That is not to say, however, that you are going to share the information with her cousin Fred when he calls from Cincinnati. If the dextrose and saline solution dripping at a keep-vein-open rate into Mr. Smith's peripheral vein is purely a stage management measure or psychotherapy, then you know this in your own mind (which is not to say that psychotherapy is unimportant in this setting).

Precise knowledge of what is in our own minds about those matters will not harm us. If we think of treating a patient and say to ourselves, "Oh, he's demented, his family isn't interested, maybe it wouldn't do much good anyway, and utilization review might not approve, and I don't want to go in there at 3 A.M.," then we should be able to say how demented he is, what his family wants for him, whether the measures would be lifesaving, whether the committee would approve, and whether we want to deal with this kind of patient. To answer the questions of others, we must first answer our own.

Who are these "others" whose questions we have to answer, whose needs we must address? In most fields of medicine, there is no question who is first and most important. As somebody once wrote, "The patient is the center of the universe of medicine, round him our thought revolves, to him all efforts tend." The customer is always right; the client is king. Yet, for the pediatrician, the psychiatrist, and others of us, at times, this is not always so. When patients in long-term care are alert and clearly able to express their wishes, then there is rarely a problem. However, this is the exception rather than the rule. Estimates vary with respect to the proportion of patients in long-term care facilities who are demented. In the skilled nursing facilities I know, it is rare to find a patient who is not demented, as determined by tests such as the mental status questionnaire. The onset of life-endangering illness is likely to impair patients' faculties further, bringing confusion, delirium, or impairment of consciousness.

Who, then, is to be considered next? Is it the family, and, if so, what family? Here we must envy our pediatric colleagues. However much they grumble about mothers, they at least know with whom they have to deal. Sometimes we are as fortunate, and there is an alert and involved spouse who will take charge. More often, however, the situation is ambiguous. A practical point here is that it is important to have done as much work in advance as possible to determine with whom to communicate when necessary. The patient's record should contain a list of family members, friends, legal guardians, case managers, and others who may be involved, together with a clear indication of which one is to be notified in an emergency. The family should discuss this and select a spokesperson. Telephone numbers should be current, include any necessary area codes, and be identified as home or business numbers. The physician or other readily available member of the health care team should have established liaison. Even these steps may not be enough. Unexpected family members, such as cousins or nieces, have a way of turning up and announcing that *they* are the ones who have been looking after the patient and should have been consulted. Occasionally, one may even have to suspect the purity of family members' motives, as in the case of an aphasic millionaire whose recent bride objected when he was given intramuscular antibiotic injections.

Repeating explanations to different family members can become a burden. Some labor-saving ways of dealing with this have been devised, but they do not always work. One common suggestion is to designate a particular family member as the recipient of the information and to have that person relay it to the others. This plan does not always work out neatly in practice and it is helpful to find one family member who is best able to understand medical information and allow that person to pass it along to the others. It is always worthwhile, in fact, to find out if there is a health care professional in the family. Families tend to have one chosen recipient of information and another who is the decision-maker. (This is seen most obviously when there is a language barrier.)

How much responsibility can be placed on a family decision maker? Here again, in real life, the answer is much less clear than it seems to be in the definite, logical world of books on medical ethics. It may be necessary to probe tactfully and avoid posing blunt questions in deciding about choices of treatment. Nevertheless, it is probably best to place on record family objections to any specific measures, such as blood transfusion or surgery. Otherwise, there is risk of incurring anger and criticism.

In the long-term care facility, as is implied by the name "nursing home," the physician's responsibility is often shared. This means that many more people may be involved than the physician, the patient, and the family. For those of us with long clinical experience, a hardening process often sets in. We have become accustomed to seeing death, dying, and severe disability. However, even the professional staff of long-term facilities will normally include many who are new to such work. For those who are inexperienced, the emotional impact of dealing with severe illness and death can be severe.

How can we deal with this problem? In these days of a pill for every ill, behavior therapy, and active intervention, my reply may sound unfashionable. First and foremost, it is necessary to listen. We must take time to know what the other members of the health care team feel. If they are horrified, resentful, frightened, disgusted, exhausted, or overwhelmed by excessive responsibility, we may not be able to do anything active about it. However, whatever we do will be more effective if we know just what it is that the others are feeling, and preferably, if we know before a crisis occurs. Do they feel able to care for life-endangered patients at all?

To a large extent, long-term facilities these days operate subject to government regulations and inspectors. We must be aware of the machinery and machinations of utilization review committees and others who monitor these facilities. The decisions of health care are not ours alone.

I have used the first person plural freely, and I should say in conclusion who I mean by "we." "We" can be any member of the health care team. There is no one standing outside the organization with such power of intellectual detachment that he or she becomes exempt from its influence.

19

The Girl Without a Face. Part I

Kenneth B. Liegner

At 2:30 on the morning of January 25, 1986, while I was on duty in the emergency department of Northern Westchester Hospital Center, we received an anxious radio call from one of our ambulance corps. It was a request for permission to bypass our hospital to transport the victim of a motor vehicle accident directly to the burn unit of Westchester County Medical Center. Details of the accident and the extent of the patient's injuries were unclear, but mention was made of burns about the face. Because of uncertainty as to the patient's status and concern about imminent airway obstruction, I ordered them to proceed to our emergency room.

As the paramedics hurriedly wheeled their stretcher into the receiving bay, we were all shocked to witness a young woman with horribly disfiguring third- and fourth-degree burns of the face, arms, and hands, who was, nonetheless, conversing intelligently with us. "I can't feel my hands," she said, clinging with a macabre blackened claw to the hand of a comforting nurse.

She had apparently fallen asleep at the wheel of her pick-up truck and crashed into a tree. The engine compartment burst into flames, and the fire was sustained by the continuous feed of gasoline from the fuel line. The gas tank did not catch fire or explode.

The young woman's ability to talk belied a severe inhalation injury with impending glottic closure. Though it was heartbreaking and pitiable to do so, she needed to be endotracheally intubated if she were to survive. Her charred and narrowed nares precluded use of the nasotracheal route, which otherwise would have been preferable. She resisted intubation, saying "Just let me sleep." She finally had to be sedated and given a muscle relaxant. With stabilization of her head and neck, the orotracheal intubation was then done with ease.

119

A subclavian line was started, volume replacement with lactated Ringer's solution was achieved, and the patient was promptly transferred to the burn unit at Westchester County Medical Center. There the extent of her burn was calculated at 30%, an amount that is not usually lethal in an otherwise healthy young person. However, her carboxyhemoglobin level several hours after the fire was close to 40%—reflecting serious pulmonary injury. If this did not kill her, she was likely to survive. It was my sad duty to call her mother long distance at 4:30 that morning to inform her of the accident. The woman was deeply concerned but calm, conveying an abiding love of her daughter. She expressed gratitude that her daughter was at least still alive. She arrived in Westchester the next day on the first available flight.

The patient followed a fairly typical course in the burn unit. Her inhalation injury, although severe, responded to appropriate therapy, while management of the burn wound presented no insurmountable obstacle to survival. The patient had to have a tracheostomy and be mechanically ventilated for a prolonged period. The extremity burns ultimately required amputation of the right forearm at the elbow and of the left hand at the mid-palm.

The reaction of health care personnel involved with this patient was anything but usual. Her grotesque, mask-like face, the loss of her hands, and the temporary absence of speech, all seemingly so central to one's identity, one's personhood, one's humanness, combined to induce horror, fear, revulsion, and intense ambivalence in virtually everyone who had anything to do with her.

Much soul-searching took place among all of those involved with her care. The paramedics, for example, who were volunteers, were aghast at what the efficient performance of their duties had wrought: the survival of a horribly deformed monster, handless and doomed to wear a lizard face. Maybe it would have been better not to respond so quickly. Maybe death would have been preferable to any kind of existence they could imagine for the victim they had "saved." They made repeated visits to the burn unit, driven by a mixture of genuine concern, morbid curiosity, and wrenching, self-doubting guilt at having had a role in saving her life.

One of the emergency room nurses the night of the accident unabashedly exclaimed, "If that ever happened to me I'd rather die! She'd be better off dead!" Fantasies of passive, or even active euthanasia were commonplace among the burn unit staff. My own attitude was that each of us acted as we had to, as we were professionally trained to, as we were morally, ethically, and legally obligated to, despite powerfully unpleasant feelings induced by the patient's horrible injuries.

Is it our role to decide whether to allow still viable individuals to die when it is readily within our power to try to save them? Should we presume to deprive any persons of their lives because we imagine that if we were placed in their situation we could not bear to live? Is that not supererogation? These questions lead to other basic questions about the value of human life. What makes it meaningful? What makes it worthwhile to continue living instead of dying?

My view is that one can only answer these existential questions by oneself, for oneself. We all know of cases in which individuals, out of the strength of their character, indomitable spirit, or plasticity and adaptability, overcome what seem to be absolutely insurmountable handicaps to live rich, meaningful, fulfilled lives. If, in due time, this patient comes to feel that life is indeed intolerable, she can always decide to end her life. That will be her choice to make. We should not make it for her.

When I visited the patient in the burn unit, she was oscillating on a rotating bed with clear cellophane shields protecting her miraculously undamaged eye globes within their partly exposed sockets. Hers was a ghastly visage. Despite the philosophical position I have articulated, I left the room emotionally shaken. I, too, now honestly felt that we should have let her die. But one week later, I visited her again, and this time engaged her in conversation. She was cheerful and highly personable. We had a pleasant and wide-ranging conversation. There was a person in there!

20

The Girl Without a Face. Part II: Team Intervention

Patricia M. Reddish

To be burned involves thirty seconds of terror and, for those who sustain the most severely disfiguring and disabling injuries, a lifetime of emotional pain, isolation, and dysfunction (Bernstein 1976). In fact, individuals who have survived injuries or illnesses that arouse our most primitive fears, such as thermal injuries or cancer, are frequently described as "victims" rather than as "survivors."

Efforts to study the life trajectory and adjustment of the facially disfigured have not been successful (Bernstein 1976). Massachusetts General Hospital attempted a follow-up study of discharged patients who had been treated there for facial burns. The study was intended to establish the course and status of these patients' psychosocial adjustment. Despite the hospital's large census of such patients, investigators were unable to obtain a sufficient sample for study because many of these patients had dropped out of follow-up treatment and could not be located. The investigators conjectured that the patients and families, frustrated by the meager results of reconstructive surgery and overwhelmed by the grief of this tragic life circumstance, had suffered the "social death" described by MacGregor et al. (1953).

Advances in critical care medicine and burn care in the last twenty years have led to unprecedented survivals (Artz, Moncreif, and Pruitt 1979). Unfortunately, esthetically pleasing reconstructive surgery and psychosocial rehabilitation have not experienced the same strides that might provide optimal biopsychosocial recovery (Lonacre 1973). Modern society, devoted to the shrine of beauty, views unappealing physical differences as repugnant and deviant (Wright 1960). Individuals with obvious deformities and handicaps experience automatic social ostracism because of others' unconscious fears of suffering a similar fate (Freud, A. 1952). The psychological impact of acquired disfigurement has been described, but little has been written about interventions that might lead to increased well-being and social reintegration (Andreasen and Norris 1972; Hamburg, Hamburg, and DeGoza 1953; Henker 1979). The treatment team at our center had few, if any, precedents or available practical advice to help it cope with our most devastating case — the girl without a face.

At the time of injury, this young woman had recently graduated from a prestigious college and was beginning a career in the business world. Her family described her as "just coming into herself"; she was experiencing a new sense of self-confidence. Her younger sister was involved in her own college studies and was beginning to recover emotionally from the sudden death of their father two years ago. Their mother was enjoying the "empty nest syndrome" and was considering dating again. On that night in January, the normal developmental life course of these three women was abruptly and irrevocably changed.

This devastatingly burned woman is currently in a state of denial and repression about the full extent of her injuries and is talking about getting a job when she is discharged from the hospital. The family desperately hopes that plastic surgery can achieve a magical restoration, but there is an overriding sense of helpless resignation. Support measures vacillate between projective identification, ethical quandaries about family members' roles in her survival, and efforts to find hope for her future. There are no simple answers to these sad and dramatic dilemmas.

It is impossible to project the ongoing or ultimate response of this patient and her family. Currently, we permit the denial, which appears to allow the family to cope with the day-to-day realities of surgery and treatment. When I attempted to test the mother's unrealistic expectations about future reconstructive surgery, she clearly told me that she needed this hope to maintain her investment in her child. At times the patient has asked, "What did I lose in the accident?" Further exploration of this question revealed that she was most concerned about a gray sweater and riding chaps rather than her face and arms. Although we have provided crisis and supportive psychotherapeutic interventions to this patient and her family, we have chosen to allow treatment issues to emerge as recovery and reality progress. The treatment team, who have experienced their own dramatic emotional response to this case, is considered a primary focus of our psychiatric liaison interventions.*

A major function of a burn team is to provide hope in what appear to be hopeless situations. Professionals in this area must experience their own process of adaptation to inflicting pain and producing a damaged end product despite

*Michael Blumenfield, M.D., Associate Director of the Consultation-Liaison Psychiatry Division at Westchester County Medical Center, is the liaison psychiatrist for the Burn Center.

their heroic efforts (Quinby and Bernstein 1971). When patients are admitted, staffs devise what Mannon (1985) has described as "recovery or death trajectories," which are based on each patient's age and extent of injury, and on complicating medical factors such as inhalation injury. These trajectories provide a framework for the medical and psychological intervention with patients and families; how to direct their expectations for outcome; and what contingencies they will encounter in the process of death or recovery.

When this woman was admitted, she presented a conflict in terms of what trajectory to choose. Although the extent of her physical injury was not considered to be in the unprecedented survival category according to current mortality statistics, we were overwhelmed by her potential for "social death" (Imbus and Zawacki 1977). In essence, whether treatment should proceed was not an issue. Based on the facts of her injury, the physicians were morally obligated to provide care. This case had an emotional impact on all levels of the staff, from the experienced surgical directors to the young emergency medical technicians who had rescued her. Although only one person had been injured, a post-disaster effect occurred that was manifested in shock, emotional numbing, and intense preoccupation with this case. Surgeons, nurses, and rescue workers experienced intense ambivalence about their aggressive life-saving efforts. We all expressed strong wishes not to be resuscitated if we ourselves should ever sustain a similar injury. Discussions centered around the question, "How can we let her live?," which was countered by another question, "How can we let her die?" The day she would be able to speak was feared. However, much anxiety was lessened when this occurred: what emerged was a pleasant, humorous person who was bravely tolerating her dehumanizing but necessary treatment.

In cases such as this, the mental health member of a burn team will be assigned a major role in case management. The psychiatric professional is delegated to fulfill (and be tested in) multiple supportive roles before gaining acceptance in an environment that is not always receptive to this specialty. It is often assumed that the psychiatrist will always be objective; be immune to the stresses that the staff encounters; provide solutions to complex ethical and problematic situations; and be the caretaker of the emotional climate of the unit. However, there is no immunity when one is faced with a case such as this. Our experience in treating more than one thousand life-threatened patients and families within the last six years has led to a different perspective about what was once an alien treatment environment. The pressure of an emergency room or rescue field allows no time for ethical deliberations. If they are to function, the staff members must focus on saving lives and consider the consequences later. Ideally, the patient should have control over choosing to live. I have observed that the vast majority of patients and families will opt for survival and adapt to the most impossible circumstances to do so. Nevertheless, life-saving activities do affect the staff in many ways including the well-documented stress pattern among intensive care unit personnel (Hay and Oken 1972). With these facts in mind, I will review some staff interventions we have used in this situation.

The primary goal of staff intervention is open acknowledgement of the distressing emotions and affects that all caretakers will experience. These emotional responses may be manifested by anxiety, projective identification, strong and differing ethical beliefs, and grief over the patient's losses. Both formal and informal opportunities should be provided for the exploration of these feelings.

At our center, we meet as a team at daily rounds and at weekly psychosocial rounds to discuss ongoing patient management, discharge plans, staff reactions, and ethical concerns. Open acknowledgement of distressing emotions and ambivalence, especially by senior surgical and nursing staff, is reassuring to newer workers. Disagreements about aggressive interventions, feelings of revulsion, and a wish for the patient's death should be permitted and tolerated, since suppression of these issues may lead to guilt and subsequent avoidance of the patient and family. Formal teaching should focus on proposed reconstructive procedures and temporary cosmetic interventions, such as the use of prostheses and make-up. It should also focus on psychological responses and behaviors that may appear bizarre but are adaptive under extreme circumstances (as in the patient's and her mother's denial in the present case.)

Informally, special attention should be paid to nurses and rotating house staff who provide the patient's primary care and who thus may be most affected. The head nurse should be especially attuned to "burnout" in staff members who care for such patients for prolonged periods, and encourage breaks from the case for them without compromising continuity of care.

The emotional responses of the rescue team must also be considered. Although their contact with the patient is relatively brief, they can develop an intense investment and can also experience their own post-traumatic stress symptoms. We have provided the rescue team in this case with individual psychological support, group debriefing, and teaching about burn management in the field.

The psychological management of the physically damaged patient cannot be limited to an individual case consultative approach. The mental health professional must be aware that these special situations have a wide–ranging impact that extends beyond the involved patient and family. Interventions must be based on a systems model. Before a treatment team can educate or assist the community or the extended social support system, they must work through their own feelings of grief and loss. With advancing medical technology, we will someday be faced not just with the question of whether or not a patient with such an unusual injury should survive, but with the question of how we can provide an existence of reasonable quality when life has been so severely compromised.

REFERENCES

ANDREASEN, N. J. C. and A. S. NORRIS. 1972. "Long–term Adjustment and Adaptation Mechanisms in Severely Burned Adults." *Journal of Nervous and Mental Diseases* 154(5):352-362.

ARTZ, P., J. MONCREIF, and B. PRUITT, eds. 1979. *Burns: A Team Approach*. Philadelphia: W. B. Saunders.

BERNSTEIN, N. R. 1976. *Emotional Care of the Facially Burned and Disfigured*. Boston: Little, Brown, and Company.

FREUD, A. 1952. "The Role of Body Illness in the Mental Life of Children." In R. S. Eissler et al., eds. *Psychoanalytic Study of the Child*. New York: International University Press 7:69-81.

HAMBURG, D. A., B. HAMBURG, and S. DeGOZA. 1953. "Adaptive Problems and Mechanisms in Severely Burned Adults." *Psychiatry*. 16(1):1-20.

HAY, D. and D. OKEN. 1972. "The Psychological Stresses of Intensive Care Unit Nursing." *Psychosomatic Medicine* 34(2):109-118.

HENKER, F. 1979. "Body Image Problems Following Trauma and Surgery." *Psychosomatics* 20(12):812-820.

IMBUS, S. H. and B. E. ZAWACKI. 1977. "Autonomy for Burned Patients When Survival Is Unprecedented." *New England Journal of Medicine* 297(6):308-11.

LONACRE, J. J. 1973. *Rehabilitation of the Facially Disfigured: Prevention of Irreversible Psychic Trauma by Early Reconstruction*. Springfield, IL: Charles C. Thomas.

MacGREGOR, F. C., T. M. ABEL, E. BRYT, E. LAUER, and S. WEISSMANN. 1953. *Facial Deformities and Plastic Surgery: A Psychosocial Study*. Springfield, IL: Charles C. Thomas.

MANNON, J. 1985. *Caring for the Burned: Life and Death in a Hospital Burn Center*. Springfield, IL: Charles C. Thomas.

QUINBY, S. and N. BERNSTEIN. 1971. "Identity Problems and Adaptation of Nurses to Severely Burned Children." *American Journal of Psychiatry* 128(1):58-63.

WRIGHT, B. A. 1960. *Physical Disability: A Psychological Approach*. New York: Harper and Row.

21

Nursing Care and Terminal Illness

Jeanne Quint Benoliel

There is probably no more difficult problem in clinical practice than the provision of care to dying patients and their families. This chapter considers the special position held by nurses in the delivery of services to these patients and outlines some general principles underlying sound nursing care on their behalf. To identify clearly the actual and potential functions of nurses when patients are dying, there is need to define the term *dying* as it is used in this chapter and to clarify the basic assumptions that underlie the viewpoint presented.

BASIC ASSUMPTIONS

Although many persons are diagnosed to have life-threatening injuries, diseases, and syndromes, they become dying patients only when someone defines them as such. In Western societies, the mandate to decide when someone is dying has generally been granted to physicians, although nurses and other members of the health-care disciplines are also in a position to make judgments about this matter.

In the world of medical practice, the term "dying patient" usually refers to those who are in the terminal stages of illness and whose disease or condition is not amenable to cure. In other words, a patient can live for years with a fatal illness such as cancer or heart disease, but he becomes a "dying patient" when nothing more can be done to promote recovery and only palliative treatment remains.

In a profound sense, the dying patient is an affront to physicians because he challenges their power to heal and to cure. Cogently reminded of the limits of their capabilities as medical practitioners, many physicians quite understandably

127

feel helpless and hopeless and frustrated by a patient's forthcoming death. These feelings can trigger a range of responses — denial that they exist at one end of the continuum, a sense of giving up at the other. Denial of the feeling may result in a continuation of active recovery-oriented treatments regardless of their worth. Giving up, on the other hand, may result in withdrawal from active involvement in the case. When the latter pathway is chosen, much of the terminal care of dying patients is left to the nursing staff, sometimes with and sometimes without effective communication among members of the medical and nursing staffs. As a consequence of inadequate communication with physicians, nurses in certain settings find themselves faced with serious social and psychological dilemmas in the implementation of sound nursing care to dying patients.

The physician's relationship with the patient is a singularly important component of care and contributes to the patient's sense of well-being above and beyond any medical treatments that are given (Balint, 1972). Yet the physician alone cannot implement an effective program of services during the final stages of life. The reality must be faced that any person's dying takes place in a socio-cultural context and hence becomes a group experience. In essence, the social process of dying for any patient is heavily dependent on the choices and actions of other people, and these other people may or may not agree on what is proper for the occasion. Furthermore, the setting of care — for example, hospital or home — heavily influences the kinds of service that can be offered and the persons who will be involved in the decision-making process and the care-giving activities. Fundamentally, however, the nature of terminal care rests in a philosophy — a system of beliefs about the rights of patients — that provides a basis for identifying general principles of nursing care.

A PHILOSOPHY OF CARE

To translate the concept of care into guidelines for nursing practice, one needs to differentiate between the concepts of cure and care as fundamental components of clinical practice. To begin with, the concept of cure centers on the diagnosis and treatment of disease, whereas care is concerned with the welfare and well-being of the person. Cure deals with the objective aspects of the case. Care is concerned with the subjective meaning of the disease experience and the effects of treatment on day-by-day living. Cure has many origins in science and instrumentation and "doing to" people. Care has its roots in human compassion, respect for the needs of the vulnerable, and "doing with" people (Benoliel, 1972).

The central premise underlying this philosophy is that each human being has value and worth in his own right and thereby is entitled to dignity in death. Extending the premise further, each human being has a right to dignity in dying, including the opportunity to share in decisions affecting how he will die. Respect for the person means that each individual has the right to be informed about his illness and about what is happening around and to him. Respect for the person also includes a recognition of each individual's special needs and areas of vulnerability. That is, each individual has the right to care and comfort — both physical psychosocial — in keeping with the disabling and limiting effects of his illness or injury and in accord with his own cultural, religious, and social values and beliefs.

In a very real sense, all health-care practitioners must find a balance between the cure goal of practice and the care goal. Changes in medical technology have brought new procedures and unusual techniques of treatment, and the options available to practitioners have increased in complexity. As Van Rensselaer Potter (1973) has noted, deciding when to intervene in the life of another person and when not to do so is fundamentally an ethical problem, and the society needs guidelines for the ethics of intervention involving the use of technology so as to avoid dehumanizing people.

Making choices on the basis of morality in combination with sound clinical judgment is a necessary component of ethical practice if the human rights of patients facing death are to be protected. In addition, however, the reality that patient care is a *team effort* must be openly acknowledged, accepted, and practiced by all of the health-care occupations concerned if the goal of personalized care for these patients is to be achieved.

As used here, *personalized care* for the dying patient contains three essential components. Each patient has *continuity of contact* with at least one person who is concerned about and interested in him as a human being. Each patient has *opportunity for active involvement* in social living to the extent that he is able — including participation in decisions affecting how he will die. Each patient has confidence and trust in those who are providing his care (Benoliel, 1972, p. 153).

By virtue of the positions that they hold in the health-care system, nurses can — if they choose — provide leadership in the provision of personalized care of this nature. Stated differently, nurses are often in position to coordinate team efforts toward finding a proper balance between care and cure and to serve as a primary communication link among the many persons involved. To do so, however, they need a clear understanding of the psychosocial and cultural dimensions of dying, as well as a sound background of clinical knowledge and judgment and a belief in a patient's right to direct his own destiny. (The latter belief must of necessity be balanced against another matter of equal importance — society's right to set and implement rules and regulations for the common good.)

GUIDELINES FOR PRACTICE

Nursing contributions to the care of patients facing death are of two general types. One set consists of the many supporting, coordinating, teaching, and

caring activities provided within the context of outpatient and ambulatory services
— including those services made available directly in the patient's home. The
other set consists of similar activities provided within the context of inpatient
services and modified to meet the varied goals and purposes of different types
of institutions, i.e., hospitals, extended care facilities, nursing homes, and other
institutions. In both types of nursing, the creation of services designed to meet
the special needs of dying patients and their families requires a framework within
which to plan, organize, and implement programs of care.

Such a framework must be built on a conceptual system that takes account
of: (1) the psychosocial dimensions of dying, and (2) the physical and physiological limitations and disabilities imposed on the patient by the illness (or injury)
and the accompanying regimen of medical and other treatments. Such a framework
must also take account of the reality that *continuity* for patients as well as *care*
must be built into the system when multiple numbers of health care workers —
including physicians — are involved.

Psychosocial Dimensions of Dying

In recent years, studies of death and dying by social and behavioral scientists
have created a set of terms that provide useful language for conceptualizing dying
as a psychosocial process and for describing its salient characteristics under
different sets of conditions. Glaser and Strauss coined the phrase "dying trajectory" to refer to the course of a person's dying as it is perceived by the various
persons involved — the patient, members of the family, doctors, nurses, and
others (Glaser and Strauss, 1968). According to this conceptualization, the dying
trajectory has two outstanding properties: *duration,* meaning that dying takes
place over time; and *shape,* referring to the graphic picture of the patient's state
of wellness or illness as it is *defined* by individuals on the basis of their expectations as to how and when the dying will take place.

The concept of the dying trajectory can serve as a useful framework within
which to *locate in time* the major changes and adaptational tasks that patients
and their families face as they live through the experience of terminal illness.
For practical purposes, the dying trajectory can be defined as follows: living
with a terminal illness is a temporal process characterized by critical events,
shifts in roles and role relationships, and other major social changes affecting
not only the person who faces death but also the social groups of which he is a
part. To conceive of dying in this way provides a structure within which to view
and understand the psychosocial dynamics of personal reactions and interpersonal
relationships as they are influenced and modified by the threat of death and/or
the actuality of death.

As Glaser and Strauss perceive the situation, definitions of dying (or expectations of death) are based on a combination of two defining terms: *certainty of
death,* meaning the degree to which people believe that death is definitely forth-

coming; and *time of death,* referring to expectations as to the point in time when death will occur or when the uncertainty about death will be resolved (Glaser and Strauss, 1965). Combinations of certainty of death and time of death provide a categorizing system for distinguishing some general types of the dying trajectory based on differences in length of time required to die and in patterning of physical signs and symptoms indicative of movement toward death.

Because the indicators of change in the patient's physical condition vary a good deal depending on the type of illness or injury, the shape of dying trajectories (patterns of dying may be a term preferred by some) can show wide variations. One pattern, such as that seen in fulminating septicemia, is marked by an abrupt onset and a rapid downhill course. Another pattern, sometimes associated with serious burns or multiple injuries, is also marked by an abrupt onset but may have a slow downhill course toward death.

Chronic diseases of all kinds produce what can be termed lingering patterns of dying. Sometimes, as with certain malignancies, the lingering pattern can show periods of apparently complete remission before the disease process returns. In other chronic problems, for example, obstructive pulmonary disease or congestive heart failure, the lingering pattern of dying continues without remission — often extending over a period of several years with slow progression toward death. A quite different pattern is that associated with unexpected and sudden death — not uncommonly produced by accidental injuries, myocardial infarction, or suicide. Although death of this type is not always a "dying trajectory" for the patient, the death does serve as a critical event in the lives of his family and often for the health-care personnel involved in his care.

The concept of the dying trajectory offers a tool for analyzing patterns of dying characteristic of different work settings. It is useful for planning and implementing programs of nursing care based on the psychosocial as well as medical needs of patients, families, and staff at different times. Since nurses often work in setting providing services for specific types of clinical problems, the concept can be especially helpful as a way of identifying problems of care that are recurrent to the setting and typical for the illness being treated. The problems of nursing care delivery can be very different depending on whether the cause of the patient's dying is cancer, chronic renal disease, emphysema, diabetes mellitus, or multiple sclerosis.

A sound knowledge base in the social and behavioral sciences and a clear understanding of the critical points for patients and families living with terminal illness provide necessary background for the development of services which can provide the kind of help that is needed at the times when such help is probably most appropriate. To be maximally effective in helping patients and families live through the experiences produced by fatal diseases, nurses need to have a clear understanding of psychological reactions to forthcoming death and of the stages of grieving in response to anticipated or actual loss. They need to be cognizant of different cultural patterns of behavior in response to death and dying and to plan programs of care that take account of differences in cultural and religious beliefs. They need to be sensitive to the importance of time and timing in their interactions with patients and families and to experiment with ways of utilizing contact time as helping time. Hoffman and Futterman, for instance, describe how time spent in a hospital clinic waiting room can be effectively organized to help families of children with leukemia cope with the adaptational tasks which they face (Hoffman and Futterman, 1971).

In addition to understanding stages of personal adaptation to life-threatening illness, knowledge about the impact of terminal illness of the family as a functioning unit is also essential for planning adequate helping services. Life-threatening situations introduce many different kinds of stress and strain into the social system of family relationships. In cases of sudden death, families face immediate adjustment to an unexpected and unforeseen loss with no opportunity for preparation through anticipatory mourning. In contrast, families that must live with a life-threatening disease such as cancer over long periods of time face a variety of adjustments, some of which are specific to a given phase of illness. Clearly the stresses for these families that are living with malignancies are different at the time of initial diagnosis, during periods of exacerbation of illness, and at the point when death actually arrives. Essentially, any family that must live for years with a chronic, life-threatening disease in one of its members must learn to live with uncertainty and ambiguity and a continuous undercurrent of tension.

The introduction of life-threatening disease into a family adds to whatever stresses and strains already exist within that group. It is probably fair to say that fatal illnesses can never be completely forgotten by those involved. The experience of living with such an illness, however, can serve as a means for drawing people into a close relationship, or it can add to their already strained problems of daily living. In my judgment, knowledge about the many psychological and social adaptations required of individuals and groups in response to fatal disease is clinical information of key importance for planning and providing nursing care services — whether in doctors' offices, outpatient clinics, oncology wards, nursing homes, or other settings. Recognition of the special vulnerabilities of "high risk" groups (those with limited personal, social and economic resources required for meeting the serious problems posed by the threat of death) is also essential if the services provided are to be effective in helping those with the greatest needs for assistance (Benoliel, 1971). Examples of high risk groups are families with dying children on hospital wards in which death is a frequent occurrence.

Physical and Physiological Limitations

Just as knowledge about psychological and social responses is essential for planning, so also is knowledge about the physical and physiological limitations associated with different patterns of dying. Although coming to terms with forthcoming death is probably the central problem faced by persons with fatal illnesses, many of them must also learn how *to live with* the physical disabilities imposed by their diseases. Nurses are often in position to help patients with chronic, life-threatening illnesses, and find constructive adaptations to the physical limitations imposed by the disease and treatment. To do so, however, nurses must be knowledgeable about the signs and symptoms of disease, its expected course and clinical complications, the treatment modalities available, and the type of medical management in progress.

By way of illustration, nurses who provide services for patients with serious heart and lung conditions need to be conversant with the various causes of their breathing difficulties and the steps that they can take to find suitable relief from certain types of distress. Nurses who work in settings where terminal cancer patients are housed need to have a clear understanding of the relationship between pain and cancer (including the fact that roughly 50% of those with malignancies have relatively little pain) and to be well informed about drugs and other measures that can be used to provide relief from the many discomforts that these patients experience (Crowley and Benoliel, 1973). In a similar way, nurses who provide services to any group of patients with specialized clinical problems can be maximally effective only if the planned program of services is soundly grounded in clinical knowledge. Needless to say, such programs also depend on a mutually respectful working relationship among the nurses, physicians, and other health care workers involved.

Just as clinical knowledge provides direction for helping patients to adapt to progressive disabilities imposed by terminal illness, this same clinical knowledge is also essential for helping the same people to learn *to live with* their diseases. In certain types of chronic disease the treatment regimen can be such as to require major adaptations by a family in its ordinary style of living. In the case of juvenile-onset diabetes mellitus, for example, insulin must be taken at the proper times and food eaten at proper intervals to avoid hypoglycemia and to prevent the onset of ketoacidosis. In effect, the implementation of a workable diabetic regimen in insulin-dependent young diabetics requires a time-bound way of living and social adjustments by all members of a family. Empirical evidence obtained in a study of young diabetics and their families showed that parental styles of behavior as agents of delegated diabetic treatment was a principal factor affecting the adaptation of the young diabetic to his disease and the family's adaptation to him (Benoliel, 1970).

The delivery of effective nursing services to patients with life-threatening or terminal illness depends on nurses who can combine the fine art of physical care with the various types of psychological support needed during different stages in the living and dying process. Such services require nurses who are able to talk with patients and families about the threat of death and other critical issues at those points in time when open talk is indicated and wanted. The provision of care also depends on nurses who recognize that a patient's pattern of not talking openly about death is not the same as denial of death; open conversation about forthcoming death is not something that everyone has to do, and some do their talking through symbolic behavior rather than through words (Weisman, 1972). To offer this kind of help, nurses must be knowledgeable about the psychosocial dynamics of personal and group responses to terminal illness. They can also profit from training in the practice of crisis intervention.

FUNCTIONS OF NURSING CARE

Because nurses occupy intermediary positions in organized systems for health care, they have a good deal of influence over the quality and effectiveness of the services that are available to patients and their families. Whether in inpatient or in outpatient settings, nurses provide assistance to dying patients and their families mainly through implementation of four important functions: support, instruction, coordination, and care.

The provision of support takes place in several ways. The ability to listen with sensitivity and concern to the emotional as well as verbal messages of dying patients and their families is central to the supporting function. In addition, however, support is provided by helping them to identify the problems they face at different points in time and to locate community and other resources useful for finding solutions appropriate to their situation. A third way by which the supporting function is implemented is through competent performance of the technical tasks of nursing, including delegated medical activities and physical ministrations of many types.

The purpose of the teaching function is to provide patient and family with information about the disease and treatment and to assist them in understanding the changes which they face. An important part of instructional assistance takes the form of teaching the patient self-care activities and delegated medical treatments to be done at home. Helping patient and family to clarify their understanding means taking the time to answer their questions and to interpret the physician's orders and explanations. The latter activity can be very important when a family has had contact with many medical specialists and is confused by differences in technical language and medical recommendations. Misunderstandings and misinterpretations can often be clarified if opportunities for discussion are regularly included in the nurse's plan of care for a patient and communication between doctor and nurse is open.

Activities that are central to implementing the function of coordination include at least two: the arrangement of regular conferences with all members of the care-giving team as needed to plan the care for and with the patient and his family; and referrals to other social and health-care facilities and services as needed by the patient — with adequate followup and evaluation to make certain that the services desired were in fact given. The coordinating function is centrally concerned with the goal of *continuity of care*, but achievement of the goal of continuity depends on clear designation of one person to serve as coordinator of patient care services.

The caring function consists of nursing activities that assist the person who is dying to cope with the subjective experience of his terminal experience *on his own* terms. The purpose of care is to personalize the experiences encountered by the patient through allowing him opportunities to maintain control over his own dying and to intervene on his behalf when his wishes and desires are not being heard. The function of care looms large in importance during the terminal stages of illness, and especially in those illnesses that cause the patient to find himself completely dependent on others.

COMPONENTS OF TERMINAL CARE

During the final period of dying, the patient's need for supportive nursing care is high. Of primary importance to both the patient and his family are physical ministrations which ensure comfort and cleanliness to the extent that they are possible. The need for nurses to utilize a variety of measures to relieve undue and unnecessary pain and distress has already been mentioned. Supportive nursing care, however, does not mean cutting the patient off from the pain of his own grief or from opportunities to bring closure to his life through open contacts with those dear to him. Indeed, supportive nursing care requires the judicious and thoughtful use of medication for pain and avoids drug dosages that cut the patient off from his final human experience.

A vital component of effective terminal nursing care is the maintenance of open communication with the dying patient for three general purposes: to ascertain his wishes, to serve as a sounding board, and to intercede on his behalf if necessary. Effective planning during the terminal period also takes account of the family's wishes and desires and attempts to facilitate open communications between the patient and his family.

If the patient's dying takes place in a hospital or other institution, provision for group planning in the implementation of patient care services is essential if continuity is to be maintained effectively over the twenty-four hours a day of coverage. Equally important, the nurse who serves as primary caretaker must have regular and open communication with the medical staff concerning plans, priorities, and goals for each of the patients. Coordination of medical and nursing plans and activities must take place if the goal of care is to be realized.

Perhaps the most important component of terminal nursing care centers in the concept of advocacy. The goal of personalized care for the terminally ill person depends on his having *continuity of contact* with someone who is concerned about him as a human being and who encourages his participation in social living for as long as he is able. Implementation of the caring function means giving the patient opportunities to let his wishes be known. It carries with it responsibility to intervene on behalf of the patient with members of his family, physicians, and others when the patient's wishes and desires have not been heard. Nurses are often the persons in best position to help the patient achieve dignity in dying, but to do so, they must be willing to function as his advocate in helping him bring closure to his life in his own way.

REFERENCES

BALINT, M. 1972. *The Doctor, His Patient and the Illness* (rev. ed.). New York: International Universities Press, pp. 239-251.

BENOLIEL, J. Q. 1970. "The Developing Diabetic Identity: A Study of Family Influence." In *Communicating Nursing Research: Methodological Issues,* vol. 3, Boulder, Colorado: Western Interstate Commission for Higher Education, pp. 14-32.

— — — — . 1971. "Assessments of Loss and Grief." *Journal of Thanatology* 1:190-191 (May-June).

— — — — . 1972. "Nursing Care for the Terminal Patient: A Psychosocial Approach." In B. Schoenberg et al. (eds.), *Psychosocial Aspects of Terminal Care.* New York: Columbia University Press, pp. 145-161.

CROWLEY, D. M., and J. Q. BENOLIEL. 1973. "The Patient in Pain: New Concepts." presented at the American Cancer Society's Conference on Cancer Nursing, Chicago, September 10-11.

GLASER, B. G. and A. L. STRAUSS. 1965. *Awareness of Dying.* Chicago: Aldine Press, pp. 16-26.

— — — — . 1968. *Time for Dying.* Aldine Press, pp. 5-7.

HOFFMAN, I. and E. H. FUTTERMAN. 1971. "Coping with Waiting: Psychiatric Intervention and Study in the Waiting Room of a Pediatric Oncology Clinic." *Comprehensive Psychiatry* 12:67-81 (January).

POTTER, V. R. 1973. "The Ethics of Nature and Nuture." *Zygon* 8:40-41 (March).

WEISMAN, A. D. 1972. *On Dying and Denying.* New York: Behavioral Publications, Inc., pp. 56-78.

22

Psychiatric Hospitalization of a Suicidal Teenager Dying of Cancer: Systems Issues

Richard Friedman, Sally K. Severino, Ken Magrath, Sandra Swirskey, Judith Giorgi-Cipriano, and Lynn C. Winther

The decision for psychiatric hospitalization, always difficult, can be over-whelmingly problematic when the patient is an adolescent with advanced cancer. The patient whose case will be presented here was admitted to a psychiatric hospital at a time when it was not certain whether she had suffered recurrence of cancer and was dying or whether she was tumor-free and predominantly depressed. Irrational factors contributed to her admission to a psychiatric hospital, including some that persisted during her stay. The health care delivery system, adequate in some ways, nonetheless failed in other ways to meet this patient's needs. The ensuing critical discussion, which resulted from extensive clinical conferences, is offered with the conviction that high quality care depends on continuous and ongoing review. We focus on systems problems at the interface between cancer care and mental health care, making this case of general relevance.

CASE HISTORY

Sheila, a 16-year-old white student, was hospitalized because of suicidal depression, her chief spoken complaint being, "I need to gain weight." Two years before her psychiatric admission, Sheila had undergone subtotal resection of a malignancy, followed by external radiation therapy. She and her parents were advised that the prognosis was uncertain. Sheila's parents chose to believe that a total cure was possible, whereas she was more skeptical. One year prior to the psychiatric admission, she had developed metastatic disease. Her parents were then informed that her condition was definitely fatal. No one communicated the prognosis to Sheila, although she was told that her cancer had returned. Privately, she had concluded that she was definitely dying. When chemotherapy was administered, Sheila experienced numerous debilitating difficulties, including decreased appetite, weight loss, hair loss, loss of sexual desire, and chronic malaise and weakness. Previously a "loner" who nonetheless socialized to some degree, Sheila felt humiliated and angry. She became completely detached from her peers.

Shortly after her admission, her metastases responded to treatment. She and her parents were then advised that she was "cancer-free." Actually the oncologist privately told the parents that prognostication was impossible, but that given her history she should already have died. Nevertheless, her parents interpreted the "cancer-free" communication to mean "possible cure." Sheila herself experienced fears of dying, mistrust of the oncologists, and a conviction that her malignancy would recur. She became progressively isolated from her parents, who insisted on maintaining a "positive attitude" and refused to acknowledge her fears. Shortly thereafter, Sheila's oncologist diagnosed depression and recommended to Sheila's parents that she receive psychotherapy. They refused in order not to "upset" her. Neither her parents or her physicians ever consulted Sheila about this matter. A brief trial of tricyclic therapy was then administered, but without antidepressive effect.

Two months after her chemotherapy was discontinued, Sheila almost immediately developed increased malaise, lower extremity weakness, postprandial vomiting without anticipatory nausea, and dizziness. She felt certain that her cancer had recurred, particularly in her legs, and she was worried that they would have to be amputated. She became more depressed and hopeless. A one-day hospitalization for diagnostic evaluation by the oncologist revealed no evidence of cancer recurrence. The oncologist again advised Sheila and her parents that there was no evidence that cancer was present. Sheila, firm in her belief that her disease had recurred, became even more estranged from her parents, who interpreted the oncologist's message to mean that the disease was now absent.

Shortly thereafter, Sheila was alone with her mother, who was making preparations for her sister's upcoming birthday party. Sheila's birthday was two months away. "Maybe I won't be around for my own birthday," she said. She then explained that if she was not already dead, she might kill herself at that time by taking pills. Her mother then anxiously informed the oncologist that Sheila was "suicidal." The oncologist immediately phoned to arrange for Sheila to be admitted to a psychiatric hospital.

A social worker in the admissions office responded to the urgency of the oncologist's request and presented the case to the admitting psychiatrist. Admission was sanctioned on the basis of "suicidal depression" and "cooperation with the oncology team." When Sheila arrived at the hospital unit she was angry at her parents, since she had no wish to be psychiatrically hospitalized. She was assigned to a ward specializing in adolescent psychiatry. The unit rarely treated medically ill patients, and had never before admitted a young person with a malignancy.

Several unusual events that affected this admission procedure demonstrate the complex nature of Sheila's entry into the mental-health delivery system. Admissions are routinely screened by the assistant unit chief and then assigned to a therapy team. The assistant unit chief immediately recognized that Sheila required psychiatric care but had grave doubts about the appropriateness of psychiatric hospitalization. It would have required much time and effort to question the admission procedure at that point and, for example, to recommend outpatient crisis intervention with family therapy.

Ordinarily, the assistant unit chief dealt expeditiously with systems problems about admissions. However, her husband had recently died of cancer after a protracted course not unlike Sheila's. After her husband's death, the assistant unit chief had taken a vacation from being a physician for a few months. She had finally resumed her psychiatric duties, but specifically excluded liaison work in order to avoid dealing with situations like Sheila's. The unit chief was also usually vigilant in maintaining the boundaries of the unit. In this instance, however, his attention was otherwise engaged. A few weeks before, he had been the only person present when a college friend died of a malignancy at the same hospital where Sheila had been receiving treatment; in addition, his wife was undergoing chemotherapy for carcinoma. The unit chief had suspended his normal vigilance about admitting procedures and "assumed" that Sheila, having been appropriately evaluated by others in the system, was an "appropriate admission."

FAMILY AND DEVELOPMENT HISTORY

Sheila's father, an executive, was emotionally distant from her, although he was concerned about her illness. There was no history of major psychiatric disorder on his side of the family. The patient's mother had a history of eating disorder. Obese from early childhood, she had weighed 250 pounds at high-school graduation. During her childhood, she had been cruelly teased about her obesity by an older sibling whom she identified as being similar to Sheila in personality. In college, Sheila's mother had lost 100 pounds by dieting. Although she had maintained the weight loss, she still thought of herself as a "fat person" and became severely anxious when she gained any weight. The mother had a younger sibling who had attempted suicide by drug overdose at age 16. Sheila's mother was consistently guarded about this event and about her relationship to this sibling. There was no other history of psychiatric disorder on the mother's side of the family.

Sheila herself was the second of five children. Two of Sheila's siblings had severe chronic anxiety and depression in reaction to her illness. Neither had ever discussed their feelings with a health-care provider prior to Sheila's psychiatric hospitalization.

HOSPITAL COURSE

Sheila's initial physical examination was notable only because of the finding of gaze-directed nystagmus and an unsteady gait, with a tendency to go to the right. Extensive evaluation by oncologists and neurologists was conducted during Sheila's two-week psychiatric hospitalization. On admission, Sheila was alert and oriented. She was apathetically depressed and hopeless, and readily revealed her plan to kill herself on her birthday if she had not already died by then. She expressed the conviction that her cancer had recurred and would soon lead to her death. Unlike the oncologists and her parents, she felt that the immediate absence of demonstrable lesions was not a reason to be hopeful.

Because of her baldness, weight loss, social isolation, and chronic malaise, she had been deeply unhappy for months before she became our patient. Sometimes detached, sometimes cynical, this patient communicated to those around her that life had lost its meaning. She did this without apparent concern for the anxiety and hostility she evoked. Cachectic and bald, her cheekbones sharp, her cheeks and eyes sunken, Sheila sat quietly in the center of our unit's "living room" area for hours while the life of the ward went on about her. She tended to hold her body motionless; the sense of movement that one usually attributes to living things was provided only by the regular drip of fluid into her arm from an intravenous bottle.

Although Sheila was clearly depressed and, in fact, manifested every symptom of a major depressive episode as defined by DSM III (Williams 1980), she perceived herself as sane but hopeless and resigned to death. She viewed the suicidal teenage patients about her as "insane" for wanting to die. She agreed to remain an inpatient voluntarily for a brief diagnostic assessment largely because she was able to communicate with her therapist and some staff members, and thus felt less isolated on our unit. The unit staff felt that a brief hospitalization focusing on diagnosis and crisis intervention for Sheila and her family could be helpful.

For other patients, the overall effect of relating to Sheila could best be described as therapeutic. Ego mechanisms were enhanced as a result of having to confront the harsh realities embodied in her condition. Although most patients were compassionate towards Sheila, none became deeply involved with her. The unit staff, on the other hand, experienced profound anguish as a result of conflicts mobilized by this patient. Feelings of anxiety and anger led staff to catch themselves in countertransference errors, usually of detachment or overinvolvement, which were rare when dealing with other patients. It was clear that issues involved in coping with a medically ill, depressed teenager who wanted to live were extremely different from those involved in coping with depressed teenagers who wanted to die. The staff required additional training and supervision in order to cope effectively. Even so, some staff members became chronically depressed or anxious in response to relating to Sheila. Her primary psychotherapist, in contrast, was able to function effectively. He formed an excellent therapeutic relationship with her, and in this context Sheila became less suicidal, as well as somewhat less hopeless and detached. Sheila's father was away on business trips during most of her psychiatric hospitalization. Her mother seemed overtly jealous of Sheila's relationship with her therapist and interrogated her extensively about the content of her therapy sessions.

During her two weeks on the unit, it became apparent that Sheila had a profoundly negative self-evaluation and saw herself as nonhuman — as "creature-like." Within a week after her admission, she reported a decrease in suicidal ideation. Although she was quite anhedonic, she reported feeling positive about her participation in physical therapy and her ability to attend school. Her improved mood appeared to stem from her therapist's and the staff's acceptance of the truly agonizing nature of her predicament. She never wavered in her conviction that she was dying as a result of undetectable recurrence of the malignancy. Our staff did not challenge this conviction, but acknowledged the possibility that she was correct and accepted her conviction as a topic worthy of discussion.

Efforts were made to engage Sheila and her family in a more realistic and mutually supportive way than had previously been possible. After two weeks, however, Sheila suddenly developed headaches, slurred speech, and pupillary dilation. She was transferred to a cancer care hospital. Shortly thereafter, she became comatose and died. Postmortem examination revealed diffuse carcinomatosis with central nervous system metastases.

DISCUSSION

Seriously ill patients have diverse needs, and in order for them to cope successfully, these needs must interdigitate with the equally diverse components of a highly complex health care delivery system. Despite everyone's good intentions, it is possible for patient care to suffer because of failure to integrate parts of the health care system, with resultant failure of response to the totality of the patient's needs. In our view, this occurred in Sheila's case. Four major guidelines that are particularly important in the care of adolescent patients emerged from our critical review of this case:

1. The family system must be evaluated as soon as cancer is diagnosed. Mobilization of family support must be monitored by health care providers.
2. Clearly demarcated pathways of communication among physicians, the patient, and the patient's parents must be established and maintained throughout the course of the illness.
3. Health care providers should conceive of the patient in biopsychosocial terms, seeing the patient as a whole person whose identity transcends the illness.
4. If intervention by mental health professionals is required, liaison models for care should be used if at all possible. If such patients are to be hospitalized for predominantly psychiatric reasons, they should be placed in units devoted to the treatment of adolescents with cancer or other serious medical illnesses. Hospitalization of adolescents like Sheila in settings that focus on functional psychiatric disorders should be avoided unless no practical alternative exists.

The family's influence on Sheila's course cannot be overestimated. The family dynamics that affected the quality of her life were not clearly identified until after she had become a psychiatric inpatient. It would have been in this patient's interest for the core family dynamics to have been assessed at the onset of her illness. Active support of this family against the predictable stresses might have prevented the fragmentation that occurred.

This patient became ill during early adolescence, a time when normal developmental processes alone impose a strain on families. During her subsequent course, Sheila increasingly became emotionally detached from her parents and siblings and they became estranged from each other. Sheila's father withdrew from her and from her mother. Neither parent was able to provide support to Sheila's siblings, who floundered under the impact of her prolonged illness. Sheila's mother found herself cut off from the "healthy" husband and siblings; of necessity, she formed an intrafamilial subsystem with the chronically ill child. The ambivalent aspects of her bond with Sheila were manifested, on one hand, by anxious overcontrolling maneuvers and, on the other, by rejecting attitudes. Sheila's mother, always in power struggles with her own overeating, was fearful that Sheila would starve to death. As her eating disorder was exacerbated, she became preoccupied with her daughter's eating habits and her weight. Using mechanisms of projection and projective identification, she alternately equated Sheila with her own fear of starving, with one of her siblings who had abused her (justifying anger), and with another sibling who had attempted suicide, thereby contributing to her motivation for Sheila's emergency psychiatric hospitalization. The family members' isolation from each other occurred over a substantial interval and finally contributed to the sense of desperation that each experienced.

This family's behavior was consistent with that described in the literature on stress and coping by the families of cancer patients. The early literature on this subject emphasized parental coping with the child's impending death. More current literature has emphasized both the practical and emotional stresses parents experience because of their child's continuing need for cancer treatment. These include the stress of getting the child to outpatient cancer therapy while meeting the needs of healthy siblings, the stress of planning for the child's future while uncertain about how much time is left, and the stress of unresolved anticipatory grief if the child survives. The importance of fostering mutual support among the family members of adolescents with cancer is well understood and has been extensively described (Koocher and O'Malley 1981). The fact that such fostering of support did not occur in Sheila's case testified to the power of the tendency to regress in the face of forces beyond human control.

Lack of clarity in understanding family dynamics led to poor communication among the patient, physician, and parents. Poor communication, in turn, contributed to Sheila's and her family's distorted understanding of the status of her illness and the physicians' inadequate understanding of the state of the family's awareness of health–illness issues at any point. For example, following Sheila's treatment for metastases, when the physicians described Sheila to her parents as "cancer-free," they pointed out that they did not actually know her prognosis. This message, accurate as far as it went, was delivered in a context in which the family and patient interpreted "not knowing" according to their individual needs and avoided discussion, so that the discrepancies could not become apparent. To the parents, "not knowing" meant that there was the possibility of a cure; to Sheila it meant that the physicians were ignorant of the truth about her condition. Since these same physicians were responsible for her day-to-day survival, her isolation from them appeared to contribute to her detachment, pessimism, and, ultimately, her hopelessness.

In general, the patient's family, based on their interpretation of messages from the care providers, conceptualized her health status in the form of a simple equation in which structural evidence of active cancer meant being sick and absence of such evidence meant being well. Only the patient remained aware that these equations were inapplicable to her. This aspect of the case illustrates the necessity to formulate health–illness matters in biopsychosocial terms, as described by Engel (1977) rather than through use of a simple, closed-ended medical model.

Throughout the course of her illness, others tended to equate Sheila's *identity* with her role as a patient having a particular type of illness. This approach, in our view best described as defensive, is common in medicine (for example, physicians refer to patients as "a diabetic" or "a schizophrenic"). This view helps physicians contain their anxieties by dealing with "illnesses" instead of people, and seems to be a manifestation of regression that is analogous to countertransference regression in psychotherapists. The way in which the psychiatric diagnosis of depression was used in the management of this patient illustrates this point.

As is often the case with patients who have severe illnesses (Hirsch, et al 1979; Kashani and Hakami 1982; Levine, Silberfarb, and Lipowski 1978), Sheila met symptom criteria for major depression according to DSM III. Her health-care providers interpreted this *dynamically* despite the fact that DSM III is descriptive and theoretical. It was tacitly assumed that Sheila's pessimism and suicidal ideation were consequences of depression and were therefore treatable with the traditional modalities for treating depression. It is possible that the people with whom Sheila interacted preferred her to suffer from depression, a psychiatric disorder with an excellent prognosis, rather than from the existential realities of metastatic illness. In the scenario the providers followed, Sheila became "suicidal" as a complication of a depressive disorder and therefore was hospitalized. Actually, Sheila appeared to contemplate suicide more for existential reasons than psychiatric ones. What we mean by this is that she did not suffer *primarily* from a mental disorder that created a bleak background of despair for the events of her life. Rather, she seemed to feel that her potential for pleasure was realistically so minimal that she could find no reason to live.

Studies relating suicide to cancer have not been conclusive. Only rudimentary data have been collected, and there have been no specific studies of adolescents (Barraclough 1978; Faeberow, Schneidman, and Leonard 1963; Forman 1979; Louhivouri and Hakama 1979; Petty and Noyes 1981; Whitlock 1978). Furthermore, we are aware of no discussion in the literature of an adolescent considering suicide because chronic illness or the treatment of it had impaired quality of life. The aspect of Sheila's life that seemed to be most associated with her suicidal fantasies was social isolation. To be sure, this was in some degree a consequence of depression. To a greater extent, it appeared to result from others' inability to relate to her because of her cancer. The interpersonal relationships she established in the hospital were accompanied by the apparent cessation of her suicidal fantasies. Even when Sheila felt less isolated and was able to experience the pleasure of companionship, however, she retained the conviction that her malignancy had recurred. In her view, she was dying, even though modern technology could find no validating evidence that this was so. It would appear that her suicidal fantasies were more a response to loneliness than a need to assume control over death.

A review of the literature revealed no articles on criteria for the admission of seriously ill adolescent cancer patients with depression to psychiatric hospitals. In retrospect, we believe that Sheila should not have been hospitalized in a psychiatric facility, although she and her family certainly required extensive psychiatric intervention. Once she became a psychiatric inpatient, she experienced a radical change in social role. No longer a "cancer patient," she became labeled as a "mental patient." Within the context of her history, the message she believed that she was required to hear was clear: "This person, in whom no present evidence for cancer exists, is mentally ill because she is depressed, hopeless, suicidal, and believes, falsely, that she still has cancer." In fact, when Sheila began talking of commiting suicide, stating that she planned to do this six weeks hence, her mother panicked and called the oncologist, who arranged for Sheila to be seen in the admissions office of our hospital. At several levels, there was avoidance of formulating the major question: "Yes, this patient needs psychiatric help, but would it be best for her and her family if it were *not* offered in a psychiatric inpatient setting?" The chief and assistant chief of the unit to which Sheila was admitted transiently withdrew from her emotionally. Both were taken by surprise by the unwelcome intrusion into their ward of someone who symbolized issues about cancer that they sought to avoid.

Despite the sequence of events in Sheila's case, some constructive interventions were made. The inpatient staff did, in fact, identify and cope with salient issues. Systematic evaluation and treatment of the entire family unit was begun. It seems clear, however, that the advantages that did result from Sheila's psychiatric hospitalization — involvement of the family system and open communication with Sheila — could have been achieved in a different treatment setting, using a liaison model (Lang and Mitrowski 1981). We agree with those who have suggested that adolescents should be involved in decision-making and should have as much control as possible over their minds and bodies (Adams 1979; Nitschke, et al 1982). Psychiatric hospitalization raised both the family's and the patient's hopes. On the other hand, Sheila's self-esteem seemed to be undermined by her placement in a type of hospital where she was so very different from her peers. The mental-hospital label deeply disturbed her at the end of her life.

Throughout the course of events described above, Sheila maintained a clear sense of reality about the state of her disease and the unrealistic expectations of others. She steadily refused to allow her inner sense of herself to be determined by authority figures. As we wrote this manuscript, we wondered whether Sheila's story might have been told better by fiction writers than by clinicians, and were particularly reminded of the works of Franz Kafka. In *The Metamorphosis*, for example, Kafka depicted the astonishing transformation of a man into a beetle during an otherwise normal night's sleep. Much of the irony of this story stems from the characters' insistence on maintaining their accustomed social habits in the face of inexplicable dehumanization. Sudden intrusion of incomprehensible, uncontrollable influence is part of the human condition. One of the most common of these intrusions is, of course, illness. We suspect that, at least in our culture, more people experience dehumanization as a consequence of illness and its treatment than for any other reason. Patients, particularly those with serious chronic illnesses, are at risk of a metamorphosis remarkably similar to that described by Kafka. The dehamanization process is by no means inevitable, however, and health care providers must struggle to protect patients from it.

REFERENCES

ADAMS, D. W. 1979. *Childhood Malignancy: The Psychosocial Care of the Child and His Family.* Chicago, Il: Charles C. Thomas.

BARRACLOUGH, B. M. 1978. "Cancer and Suicide." *British Journal of Psychiatry* 133:287.

ENGEL, G. L. 1977. "The Need for a New Medical Model: A Challenge for Biomedicine." *Science* 196:129-136.

FAEBEROW, N. L., E. S. SCHNEIDMAN, and C. V. LEONARD. 1963. "Suicide Among General Medical and Surgical Hospital Patients with Malignant Neoplasms." *Veterans Association Medical Bulletin* 9:1-11.

FORMAN, B. F. 1979. "Cancer and Suicide." *General Hospital Psychiatry* 1:108.

HIRSCH, J. F., D. RENIER, P. CZERNICHOW, L. BENVENISTE, and A. PIERRE-KAHN. 1979. "Medulloblastoma in Childhood: Survival and Functional Results." *Acta Neurochirugica* 48:1-15.

KAFKA, F. 1981. *The Metamorphosis.* S. Corngold, trans. New York: Bantam Books.

KASHANI, J. and H. HAKAMI. 1982. "Depression in Children and Adolescents with Malignancy." *Canadian Journal of Psychiatry* 24:474-477.

KOOCHER, G. P. and J. E. O'MALLEY. 1981. *The Damocles Syndrome.* New York: McGraw Hill.

LANG, P. A. and C. A. MITROWSKI. 1981. "Supportive and Concrete Services for Teenage Oncology Patients." *Health and Social Work* 6:42-45.

LEVINE, P. M., P. M. SILBERFARB, and Z. J. LIPOWSKI. 1978. "Mental Disorders in Cancer Patients: A Study of 100 Psychiatric Referrals." *Cancer* 42:1385-1391.

LOUHIVOURI, K. A. and M. HAKAMA. 1979. "Risk of Suicide Among Cancer Patients." *American Journal of Epidemiology* 109:59.

NITSCHKE, R., G. B. HUMPHREY, C. L. SEXAUER, B. CATRON, R. N. WUNDER, and S. JAY. 1982. "Therapeutic Choices Made by Patients with End-Stage Cancer." *Behavioral Pediatrics* 101:471-476.

PETTY, F. and R. NOYES. 1981. "Depression Secondary to Cancer." *Biological Psychiatry* 16:1203-1220.

WHITLOCK, F. A. 1978. "Suicide, Cancer and Depression." *British Journal of Psychiatry* 132:269.

WILLIAMS, J. B. W., ed. 1980. *Diagnostic and Statistical Manual of Mental Disorders (DSM-III).* Washington, DC: American Psychiatric Association.

23

Dementia in the Cancer Patient

Mary Anne Zubler

Patients who have cancer often develop dementia as a result of changes in mental status caused by the primary disease, its treatment, or intercurrent illness. It is important to differentiate the cause of dementia in cancer patients in order to treat it effectively and to determine the prognosis. Specific causes of dementia in these patients include:

Cancer
    Meningeal metastases
    Brain metastases
    Paraneoplastic syndromes
Emotional effects
    Depression
    Change in life style
Drugs
    Therapeutic
    Symptomatic
Infection
    Sepsis
    Meningitis, abscess
Intracranial bleeding
    Trauma, commonly from falls
    Coagulopathies

Meningeal metastasis is common with many forms of cancer. When the tumor spreads to the meninges, it may produce a change in mental status. This is not a focal change such as seen with metastasis to the brain, but a subtle difference. Usually, spouses tell us that the patient has been having increasing problems with disorientation or confusion, or that they have noted a change in personality. This may in fact be one of the first signs of meningeal metastases. Such subtle changes are not as dramatic as those that occur in patients who develop hemiparesis, but certainly can indicate spread of disease. Appropriate diagnostic tests can confirm the diagnosis. Brain metastases can also produce a change in a patient's thinking and personality, but this is usually not so much a simple change in mental status as it is a reaction to loss of function (for example, of an arm or leg). This, in turn, can affect mental status by changing the patient's attitude and outlook on life.

Mental status changes may also result from the development of paraneoplastic syndromes. Most of these syndromes do not affect mental status directly; however, leukoencephalopathy or some of the necrotizing myelopathies can have secondary effects such as personality change or disorientation. In such cases it is important to keep in mind that the alteration of mental status is not a direct effect of the tumor and does not reflect spread of the tumor to the meninges or the brain, and that improvement will occur if the cancer responds to treatment.

Obviously, emotional responses secondary to cancer may affect mentation and personality. Patients often develop depression as a response to malignancy, and this in itself can severely influence mental status. Almost all patients who have cancer experience changes in lifestyle that are quite dramatic, at least temporarily, and sometimes permanently; quite naturally these changes have a bearing on mental status.

Certain drugs can cause dementia in cancer patients. Anyone receiving such drugs should be observed closely for changes in mental status. Fortunately, if the problem is indeed iatrogenic, it is readily treatable. For the most part, the offending drugs fall into two categories: those used to treat patients' symptoms and those used to treat the cancer (chemotherapy). Among the most common offenders with respect to altering mental status are pain medications, including narcotics and nonnarcotics; sedatives, including anxiolytics, hypnotics, antiseizure medications, such as Dilantin and phenobarbitol; antinausea and antiemetic drugs; and steroids, given for brain metastases or other tumor-related problems. Any of these drugs can cause behavioral changes and emotional instability, sometimes manifested as dementia.

Pain medications are at the top of the list and cause many problems. Although controlling pain is essential, most of the drugs used for this purpose can produce marked disorientation. For example, I recently saw a patient who was having considerable pain from rectal cancer. He was taking the pain medications at home, but he told me that he couldn't understand what was happening to his supply; he said that they seemed to be disappearing. When I questioned him further I realized that he was so disoriented he could not remember when he had last taken his medication, or for that matter, whether he had taken it at all. Having unwittingly increased his dosage, he had fallen victim to a drug-induced distortion of his time sense, and the problem was building upon itself. He was hospitalized so that he could be given his medications on a regular schedule under supervision, after which he recovered his normal time sense and could manage his own medications again.

Some nonsteroidal medications, such as those used to treat arthritis, can affect the central nervous system (CNS), e.g., mild disorientation syndromes. Sedatives can also be a problem; some patients experience what they describe as a "hangover" from their sleeping pills, and this leads to some morning disorientation. Antiseizure medications such as phenobarbital can cause CNS sedation.

Some of the chemotherapeutic drugs used to treat cancer can affect the CNS. Encephalopathy that can be manifested as confusion or stupor is often associated with the administration of L.-Asparaginase, which is used in the treatment of leukemia. It is important to understand that although these reactions can be a problem, patients sometimes have to endure them in order to receive effective therapy. Patients and their families can be reassured that the problems are temporary and that they are related to treatment rather than to their cancer or to some other cause that is not going to resolve. Although 5-fluorouracil does not change mental status, patients who develop cerebellar syndrome (ataxia, clumsiness, and slurred speech), which makes them appear intoxicated, can be quite disturbed by these side effects. Other drugs, like cis-platinum, do not affect the CNS, but certainly can cause neurological problems in the peripheral nerves. Procarbazine has been described as causing confusion and lethargy, and hexamethamelamine has been reported to cause encephalopathy.

Certainly, tumors themselves have the greatest effects on the CNS, but some of the less common effects related to use of drugs are infections, including meningitis and abscess. Some drugs used in treating tumors can cause impairment of the immune system, which of course increases the likelihood of infection. A change in mental status is often manifested early in the course of sepsis, so it is important to be alert to evidence of such changes in order to prevent any infection present from becoming more severe.

One should be alert to the possibility of intracranial bleeding as the cause of a change in mental status. A weakened patient may sustain a subdural hematoma as a result of a fall, which might go unreported. Intracranial bleeding can occur in patients who have coagulopathies.

The treatment goal for patients who have experienced a change in mental status is, obviously, to eliminate the cause of the problem wherever possible. If the cause cannot be identified, certain measures can still be taken. For example, making sure that these patients' rooms are lit during the day and darkened at night is helpful in avoiding the syndrome we call "sundowning," in which patients become much more disoriented at night. Having a family member present so that the patient can see someone familiar when he does have periods of orientation is often valuable. If possible, having the same nurse care for a patient, at least on each shift, is reassuring.

Drug therapy is useful for some patients. We generally use Haldol as our treatment. There are other drugs available, but Haldol has been the most useful for our patients. The important thing to remember is not to use drugs that will increase the sedation of an already sedated patient. The benzodiazepenes usually worsen the situation, as do barbiturates.

Physical restraints can be used to keep patients from falling out of bed or harming themselves during periods of disorientation. The Posey restraints that we use now are not too constrictive to patients and are acceptable in most cases. When patients who are disoriented get out of bed at night and fall and injure themselves, it is distressing to them and their families, as well as to the staff and other patients. If this situation cannot be handled in any other way, the use of restraint seems appropriate.

The final point to remember in taking care of patients with disorientation or some other form of dementia is the importance of continual monitoring. Suggestions have been made for the use of some sort of elementary psychological testing that could be done on each shift. Objective measurements of patients' mental status could then be charted and intervention taken as required.

24

The Influence of Societal Factors
on Life-Threatened Existences

Marcella Bakur Weiner and William Weiner

Whereas the threats to patients' lives are usually formulated within the confines of known illnesses perceived to be lethal in nature, little attention has been paid to societal factors that help shape patients' existences. Heinz Kohut, the father of self-psychology, defined these factors as psychotropic, suggesting that they are society's values, enforced by religious, social, political, and professional demands, and that they are capable of modifying mental activity. Using this framework of self-psychology, we hope to demonstrate how society is currently affecting our patients, threatening their self-cohesion and rendering them vulnerable to self-fragmentation that they experience as life-threatening over time.

Kohut never clearly defined "psychotropic factors," but a dictionary definition of psychotropic is "capable of modifying mental activity, as opiates, tranquilizers, etc." In considering the full implications of "modifying mental activity," it must be recognized that mental activity includes values, especially when these are enforced by religious, social, political, and professional demands. Kohut suggested that the relevant psychotropic social factors of today's world include the facts that parents work or are away from home a great deal, that families are small, and that most people have no servants or ones who come and go. He felt that these conditions "promote either the creation of an understimulating, lonely environment for the child and/or expose the child, without the opportunity for effective relief, to the pathogenic influence of a parent suffering from self-pathology, especially when the self-pathology is not gross and overt — i.e., when other members of the family do not feel compelled to take remedial action."

A major psychotropic factor in today's world is the prospect of nuclear war.

This particular psychotropic factor may explain the 300% increase in the suicide rate among young people within the last 20 years. According to the National Center for Health Statistics (*The New York Times* 1985), the suicide rate among those 15 to 24 years of age had risen to 11.7 per 100,000 in 1983, the last year for which complete figures are available. The likelihood of nuclear war is, undoubtedly, a major factor in this grim increase in teenage suicide, along with an increase in drug addiction, alcoholism, school dropouts, and unemployment in this age group.

A recent experience seems relevant in this regard. The senior author was dining with her son in a New York City restaurant. Three young women in their mid-20s were sitting at a nearby table. Since the tables were rather closely spaced, their conversation could easily be overheard. The topic was the recent bombing of Libya. The focus of their discussion was on the impact this bombing could possibly have on their lives. What could be gleaned from their talk was tremendous defensiveness and anxiety couched in terms of their political and professional lives. For example, they spoke about how they would vote in the next election and, if the present military intervention were expanded, how it would affect the availability of young men, already in short supply. Sensitively attuned, one could feel the life-threatening impact of the Libyan situation on their lives. Riding abreast the flow of conversation was a feeling of bitterness, disillusionment with authority figures and, most of all, an overriding helplessness, in that any attempts at control over the environment would fail. Politicians, they stated, would do what they needed to do for their own political advantage, while human beings such as they would be damned, if not doomed!

Translated into self-psychology terms, a de-idealization was taking place in that leaders and other influential persons were not perceived as having feet of clay, but feet of sand, with no substance and no stability to be counted on. As far as their inner experience was concerned, these young women saw the world and its situation as life–threatening in both a large political sense and, most urgently, in a very personal and meaningful inner sense. Their anxiety, no matter how sophisticated the defenses, had the nature of a tidal wave, and the self, which is so central to the concepts of self-psychology, was fragmenting. Similarly, the feelings of helplessness they expressed as, "What can we, the American public, do to turn things around — we have no real power," can be interpreted as a feeling that world leaders and possibly, early parenting figures, are unresponsive to their needs.

Thus, it is possible, from an ego psychological approach, that even persons such as these three young women, who probably had received good mothering, have little chance to use that experience fully in the de-idealization process that goes on when the protective parents fail. The possibility that regression to the grandiose self will inevitably take place under such circumstances is very real, for, if parents will not take care, then one must be totally in charge of oneself, exercising omnipotent control, unable and unwilling to accept limitation. The culmination of much of this is that individuals in this predicament become our patients. We in the mental health field offer our services to defeated, deflated selves, selves fragmented and suffering from early wounds imposed by a society that is seemingly uncaring.

Although our patients seek us out as healers and soothers to their wounded psyches and bodies, we ourselves are not impervious to societal demands and psychotropic factors. Along with our own anxieties about nuclear war, we, too, respond in highly selective ways in our professional roles, for during our formative years we either did or did not receive adequate chances for mirroring, for idealization, and for twinship relationships (White and Wiener 1986).

Our difficulties are couched, however, in professional terms, and are often subtly implied in professional journals within the confines of scientific studies. One such instance may be the way in which we treat different populations of patients who are critically ill. For example, according to Weisman (1972), cancer patients are viewed differently from cardiac patients with the same limited life expectancy. He found that although the staff considered cancer patients to be hopelessly ill, cardiac patients were viewed as seriously ill, but having good chances of recovery. Although staff tended to encourage isolation and denial in the cancer patients, cardiac patients were both better informed about their illness and better liked by staff.

One speculative interpretation is that cancer still has an unknown and to-be-feared quality from which staff shy away, but that this is not true of cardiac disease. In our society, with its strong Protestant work ethic, cardiac disease connotes hard work. Thus, cardiac patients are respected, even if the end result of the work ethic is that the heart proves to be fallible, after all. Cancer, contracted in ways that are still unknown, engenders a sense of ambiguity and discomfort, for mysteries titillate, but also raise anxiety levels. Stress, underscoring most theories of cardiac illness, is clearly understood. These patients were too conscientious, too demanding of themselves, and this is the price they pay. Their illness may sound a warning to professionals whose own investments in life may not be too different from their patients'. Hence, the professionals can identify without retreating. With cancer patients, they retreat without the identification.

Other patient populations also fill professionals with anxiety. This is true for those working with AIDS patients. These patients, shunned by society, are also shunned by health care professionals. This is not to say that these fears are founded on either truth or falseness. Our purpose is not to moralize, for sensitive professionals, in touch with their own feelings while attuned to their patients, must ultimately make their own choices. We are saying, however, that the underlying feeling is anxiety, which arises from the perception that working with such patients may be life–threatening. The underlying theme of deviancy also seems to enter into responses to AIDS patients since, for the most part, they are either homosexuals or drug addicts. Our own moralistic view of both of these factors seems to determine our manner of treating this population.

As with the treatment of all patients, our own identifications, early parenting, and current, continuous search for a caring and responsive environment — in self-psychological terms, the "good self object" — dictate our responses. It is of interest to note, too, that when queried as to which type of population they most enjoyed working with, groups of young nurses stated that they wished to work with those who had some "serious illness" and not the usual limitations associated with aging. Again, to be old involves the acceptance of limitations, a boundary to one's archaic grandiosity and, if in early experiences one needed to be grandiose as a means of surviving, why place oneself in a situation where old wounds will be re-opened? The "seriously ill" patient stirs up none of the identifications, the aged person does.

Every era, it seems, has its own special brand of "psychotropic factors." Whereas some historical eras have been marked by plagues, wars both small and large, and other major happenings, life-threatened existences continue into our modern age. Although some events, such as war, still infiltrate our everyday reality as dramatic and "real," other events are no less essential to our patients and to ourselves.

A familiar topic at every social gathering concerns places to live: Where should one live? Where can one live? And where *will* one live — if? Life and the "if" are linked by a concentration of energy on the former and a concentration of anxiety on the latter. Both authors have experienced the tremendous fear and apprehension our patients express when they feel that they will have no place to go. Some have told us that their fear of becoming "bag ladies" appears like reality in the existing housing crisis. Others who have struggled for independence for years have had to return to their parents' homes. The assurance to every child that he or she will be protected in a secure, safe, and stable environment is turned on its head as known environments seem to disappear overnight. The environment seems unresponsive, at best.

The values of a society directly affect the individual. When a person feels cared about, and in particular when this repeats childhood experiences, the self nestles securely within the nucleus of the person. When the environment appears uncaring, again repeating earlier devastations, borderline and psychotic states appear. These states may be reversed for patients by psychiatric or psychological therapy through the empathic, supportive, and responsive environment in the person of the therapist. It may be that through this union, patients can be most effectively stimulated to attain their own self-cohesion, thus enabling them to function more effectively. As this process cements over time, the patients, and perhaps we ourselves, will be able to tolerate the pressing psychotropic factors of the moment, knowing that, as in the past, they too shall pass, but that our self-experience, that inner core of our own reality, will continue over time, assuring us of stability in an ever-changing world.

REFERENCES

KOHUT, H. 1977. *The Restoration of the Self.* New York: International Universities Press.
The New York Times. November 11, 1985.
WEISMAN, A. D. 1972 *Dying and Denying: A Psychiatric Study of Terminality.* New York: Behavioral Publications, Inc.
WHITE, M. T. and M. B. WEINER. 1986. *The Theory and Practice of Self Psychology.* New York: Brunner/Mazel.

25

Towards a Cartography of Thanatology

Allen Fertiziger

"It then occurred to me that this was not the first time I had been given a map which failed to show many things I could see right in front of my eyes. All through school and university I had been given maps of life and knowledge on which there was hardly a trace of many of the things that I most cared about and that seemed to me to be of the greatest possible importance to the conduct of my life. I remembered that for many years my perplexity had been complete; and no interpreter had come along to help me. It remained complete until I ceased to suspect the sanity of my perceptions and began, instead, to suspect the soundness of the maps" (Schumacher 1977).

The task of this chapter is, in principle, a simple one. It is to make a point that I believe is essential to the future well-being of thanatology. It is a point that is made in the quotation from Schumacher. Is there reason for thanatologists to begin to suspect "the soundness of the maps" we are using to guide us over the terrain of professional practice? I will argue that we are using a map which, though more than adequate for most health professionals, is far off the mark for those who work in the domain of thanatological thought and practice.

The map currently in use by most health professionals is that defined by the biomedical scientific paradigm that views humanity as a complex machine consisting of many organic, cellular, and subcellular functioning parts. In philosophical terms, this map can be thought of as the logical extension to human existence of materialism, a school of philosophy that holds that the only reality is what we can see, touch, hear, smell, and taste (i.e., that which is accessible to our senses). Thus, in the context of the biomedical map that is so widely and effectively used, humans are things!

Although there is reason to believe that the exclusion of the human spiritual nature from many aspects of clinical thought and practice is problematical, that is not the issue I will examine. Far more specifically, I will argue that the biomedical model provides those of us in thanatology with what Schumacher calls "hardly a trace of the things" that we care most about and that seem most important to the conduct of our professional lives. Because of this, I will argue that if thanatology is to grow and prosper, it will be absolutely essential for thanatologists to begin to develop a map of their own, in which humanity will be depicted in terms that are far more relevant to our day-to-day work.

The day-to-day "stuff" of thanatology — terminal illness, human physical and psychological pain and suffering, the meaning and purpose of continuing life, physical deterioration, the many seemingly insoluble human dilemmas and tragedies that abound in most clinical settings, and death itself — are almost wholly unapproachable through the simplistic logic of biomedical scientific materialism. These aspects of experience cannot be simply reduced to the nuts and bolts of mitochondria, enzymes, or even brain activity. They demand a logic and, so to speak, a map of their own, in which they are understood diagnostically and treated therapeutically on their own terms.

It is always difficult and threatening to question a map that has provided a valid, logical framework for a long time. It is even more difficult to question a map that continues to function quite well. Such is the case with the biomedical model, which is by no means in danger of being replaced. It is just that this model has nothing to offer when the human machine passes that point-of-no-therapeutic-return that death and dying symbolize. When those who rely exclusively on the biomedical mechanical map pass this point of irreparability, they have literally no choice but to attempt one last ditch "experiment" after another until time runs out. This logic may make sense to the clinician, but it is often wholly unacceptable to patients who would rather not be treated in these mechanical terms.

Although thanatology enters when biomedical materialism leaves off, it will not fully come to terms with this profound philosophical distinction until it begins to develop its own map of humanity on which it can begin to chart the many non-material human qualities that constitute the bulk of our day-to-day work. We may aid and assist many of our clients' biological functions, but our concern and energy is far more directed to their non-material, subjective world than it is to their bodies (which, by the time they reach us, are generally deemed "hopeless.")

TOWARDS THE CREATION OF A THANATOLOGICAL MAP

The modern materialist biomedical map has become so deeply ingrained in today's health consciousness that it is often extremely difficult to see its limitations and to think in terms of a philosophical alternative. This map is so richly textured and so highly refined that without the assistance of a man like Schumacher to tell us that it is missing the mark, we would not suspect that it could be so deficient and so fundamentally unsound in meeting the needs of the thanatological community. But it is a map only of people's physical existence, and we are working in the spiritual domain. It is as though in today's would of high technology and scientific advances there is no need for health professionals to give serious consideration to the question of whether we are only physical beings or if we are also constituted of spirit. Although that question seems more appropriate to the church and the synagogue than to the clinic, this philosophical distinction is crucial for thanatology.

Insofar as it is a materialist map, modern biomedical science is in no position to enter into a discussion of human spiritual existence, let alone to consider the possibility that such a spirit exists. To a great extent, modern health professionals have been able to side-step this fundamental distinction without creating any epistemological chaos; indeed, the closest approach to this issue appears to be in modern clinicians' acceptance of the legitimacy of psychosomatic phenomena. However, thanatology will not profit from dodging this philosophical bullet. It is high time for thanatology to begin a serious effort to consider humanity in spiritual terms. Thanatology is so intimately connected with such spiritual issues as the human mind and subjective experience, the meaning of death (including the volatile issue of life after death), and the very meaning of life, that to continue to ignore them at this stage of our discipline's development would be unfortunate.

We do not ignore these issues with our clients. On the contrary, we are among the rare few in health professional circles who are freely open to the existence of these issues, rather than devoting all of our attention to physiological and physical matters. Why, then, don't we simply begin to put these issues onto the maps of our clinical practice? Are we afraid of being ridiculed by our colleagues for being "unscientific"? We should not be afraid of this criticism, because unscientific is exactly what we are. It is of the utmost importance that we in thanatology begin to understand that science, by definition, cannot engage in issues or phenomena that involve the spirit. We are being "unscientific" when we minister to the needs of our clients, but that is exactly the reason why they come to us. To deny this for fear of being called "soft" or "unscientific" by our more scientifically oriented colleagues seems to be a frank denial of the very work we all consider so important. To thanatologists, people are not simple biomechanical machines, but profoundly complex blends of spirit and matter who deserve more than can be provided by the widely held view of our clinical colleagues.

THE MEANING OF DEATH — THEY SHOOT HORSES, DON'T THEY?

Throughout its short lifetime, thanatology has done much to encourage health professionals and their clients to open to the reality of death instead of denying its inevitable presence. Although it is important to fight disease and organic disintegration, we must all reach that inevitable point of no therapeutic return where continuing to fight is often associated with exacerbated suffering, whereas surrendering can create remarkable dignity and transcendent acceptance. We have all had to work hard to negate the narrow-minded tendency — an extension of biomedical materialism — to fight death at any cost. We have all learned how destructive these last-ditch pitched battles can be to the emotional lives of the terminally ill and all who love them.

Even though we try to encourage the dying and their families to accept, as fully as they are able, the truth of their condition, I have always been puzzled by one aspect of this fundamental thanatological strategy. What is the point of laboring so hard to confront the grimness of these impossible situations when any success one may achieve will be so obviously short-lived? Certainly, by accepting their condition, many dying patients have risen to heights of awareness that verge on the miraculous. But how can we assess the cost-effectiveness of such demanding, difficult, and painful work, when the achievement of that awareness, if in fact it does occur, is so fleeting?

I pose this question more in a Socratic sense than out of personal curiosity, because I know the strong personal and spiritual commitment most thanatologists bring to their clients. Nonetheless, I wonder why we are so reluctant to articulate more fully our thoughts on this seemingly irrational approach to guiding people through the difficult course of their life's final moments. Why encourage people to work so hard when they may not even have the gratification of using what they learn? Wouldn't it be easier and far less painful for people to go out as quickly, quietly, and even as unconsciously as possible — that is, if we knew in advance that there would be no future in which they could apply all that they had so painfully learned?

As a teacher, I always try to remain aware of what my students will be gaining from the educational experience we join in. If I knew in advance that my students would never learn what I was teaching them, or if they might only be able to use what they learned for a fleeting moment, I believe I might spend our time together in different ways. In studying how other cultures justify the acceptance of death (and most cultures do this quite forcefully) I find an almost universal recognition of the fact that anything gained in these final difficult moments will be carried forward by the dead and used in their next life. Ancient Egyptian priests, Socrates, Tibetan lamas, and poets like Wordsworth all have spoken of an afterlife. What I find so puzzling about thanatology is the almost taboo-like quality that keeps us away from this seemingly threatening subject.

Although philosophers and theologians alike seem to be under no such constraint, I believe it is our continued allegiance to science and its materialist philosophy that keeps us from exploring this subject, which seems a perfectly natural one for thanatology to consider. I believe this to be a perfect example of what Schumacher had in mind when he spoke of the way that tried and true maps can begin to fail us. In tracing a broad sweep of historical time, one quickly learns that this spiritual antipathy is a recent addition to medical history. For thousands of years, physicians have treated both body and soul. In fact, the physician's role has origins that are closely tied to the performance of priestly functions. Man's psyche or soul has always been a part of the physician's responsibility.

I think there is now an unfortunate confusion between religion, on one hand, and genuine recognition of the spiritual nature of man, on the other. Because of this confusion, physicians have seemingly abandoned their client's souls in favor of a scientific approach to their bodies, which are widely held to be some sort of soul-less machines.

The name of Sigmund Freud is of special relevance to this issue, not only as the father of modern psychoanalysis, but because of his outspoken views on the connection between medicine and religion. One of Freud's students, Erich Fromm, (1950) wrote an entire book on this issue, which perhaps should be required reading for every thanatologist. I quote from Fromm:

> Freud goes beyond attempting to prove that religion is an *illusion*. He tends to sanctify bad human institutions with which it has allied itself throughout history; further, by teaching people to believe in an illusion and by prohibiting critical thinking religion is responsible for the impoverishment of intelligence (p. 12).

Although Freud rejected religion per se, it is important to recognize that he did not reject the fundamental spiritual notion that humans have souls or psyches that are distinct from their physical bodies. On this, Fromm wrote:

> The analyst is not a theologian or a philosopher and does not claim competence in those fields, but as a physician of the soul he is concerned with the very same problems as philosophy and theology: the soul of man and its cure (p. 7).

The question of life after death is a fundamental issue that involves the fate of the human soul after its separation, at death, from the physical body. Although this is often interpreted in one of a number of religious contexts, we in thanatology ought to begin to recognize that it is an issue of much broader humanistic significance and concern than is generally narrowly interpreted. Since antiquity, philosophers and sages have grappled with the fate of man's psyche (i.e., soul or mind) after death. It seems reasonable that this would also be a subject of considerable concern to the dying. Thus, it seems strange that thanatology has not yet begun to a systematic exploration of this issue.

No doubt part of the blame for this oversight has to be attributed to the widely held view that any serious talk of life after death is wholly irrational and "unscientific." As a teacher of courses on death and dying, I have discovered that although many students "believe" in some sort of life after death, there is an almost universal recognition that science has proven this belief to be little more than a vacuous, childish wish. It is always a mutually pleasant experience when I explain to my students that this is a question that science can in no way test and by no means prove. In fact, because of science's materialist framework, it is a question that science cannot even consider.

Is man a spiritual being? Does some form of life continue after death? Is it possible that the hard-earned fruit of life's final labor is actually retrievable and held in our psyches after our bodies have ceased to function? Although these are not easy questions or ones any of us have been trained to consider, I suggest that the thanatological community begin to consider the value of probing these and other aspects of humanity's spiritual nature. The answers will not readily be found in a routine Medline search or through perusal of *Biological Abstracts,* but there is a vast repository of philosophical thought that is richly informed in this area. In fact, there are even some modern clinical data that actually support the notion that our spirits are dissociable from our physical bodies and may be able to survive our physical death. The strange phenomena known as near-death experience and out-of-body-experience support the disssociability of body and mind; the former actually suggests that the subjective human mind is capable of surviving after the physical body has been declared clinically dead.

MIND–BRAIN DUALISM: A KEY TO THANATOLOGICAL THOUGHT

It is clear that the materialist map of modern medical science has led us to some of the most remarkable healing discoveries in the history of civilized man. It is hard to fault a map that has led to the discovery of DNA, transplant technology, and antibiotics. Nevertheless, it is becoming increasingly clear that these discoveries have not come without a hidden price, for unwittingly, by accepting the scientific materialist philosophy that comes with these discoveries, modern health professionals have had to strip from their maps of clinical practice any vestige of the notion that humans are spiritual beings. Foremost among the human spiritual qualities that have been eradicated from the modern materialist map is the spiritual substrate of subjective experience known as the human mind. Today, the human mind has no existence of its own, but is a functional by-product of the physical brain.

The relationship between man's mind and brain is one that can be traced back to the French philosopher René Descartes, whose work formed the basis for the modern dualism between man's matter and spirit. It was Descartes who laid the groundwork for modern materialist science by splitting the then dominant Natural Philosophy into two discrete branches. One, the forerunner of modern science, involved the study of what might be called objective reality. The other, which developed into modern psychology and modern philosophy, involved what might be called subjective reality. The former dealt with matter; the latter with spirit.

Descartes saw each of these two extremes as real and identified each as including "things." Things of the spirit (i.e., the mind) he called *res cogitans*. Things of matter were called *res extensa*. As if we have forgotten this crucial distinction between two diametrically opposite realities, modern science has trivialized the mind into a nonentity and categorized it as one of the physical brain's manifold functions. Thus, what Descartes called *res cogitans* no longer exists as such, but is now part of *res extensa* (i.e., the physical brain). And all the while, what has been done on the basis of a philosophical assumption is now misrepresented as a scientifically verifiable "fact."

If mind and brain are one and the same, then the death of the latter must preclude the continued life of the former. But if they are not one, but two, then an individual's physical brain could die and the spiritual mind live on (and with it all that the individual had learned in this life). Although this may sound like a script for the Twilight Zone, the fact is that it is wholly consistent with traditional wisdom. Even more remarkable is that there may now be some clinical evidence that this notion could be more than wishful thinking. Let us now consider this evidence more closely.

THE NEAR–DEATH EXPERIENCE

Recent advances in biotechnology have made what has come to be called the near-death experience an occurrence of some regularity in today's high-tech intensive care units. Patients who at an earlier time could not have been resuscitated have returned from unequivocal clinical death with reports that have enough consistency to suggest a pattern. What is the pattern? In all cases, survivors report a continuity of subjective experience. Although the details of that experience have been systematically studied (Moody 1977), these details are somewhat tangential to the point. If the brain is nonfunctional, how then could the individual be capable of having a continuous stream of conscious experience? How can consciousness continue unabated when the brain's EEG is so flat as to suggest that the brain is turned off?

Despite the tendency to write off this phenomenon as a curious oddity (it is extremely threatening to the materialist biomedical model, since that model can make no sense of it), there are similar types of findings that support the dissociability of the physical brain and the spiritual mind. For example, many recovered coma patients report having had a continuous stream of conscious experience during their coma. They remember visitors and other hospital experiences despite the fact that their brain function was largely suppressed. The so-called out-of-body experience in which consciousness seems to be set free of the physical body is another clinical oddity that supports the separate existence of a spiritual mind.

Although one can undoubtedly come up with explanations other than that of the mind's separate existence, my point in raising this issue is that in the end there may be no experimental means of answering this question unequivocally. The biomedical view is built on the faith that only matter is real. A more spiritual view is predicated on the assumption that a "thing" need only be directly experienced by the physical senses to be determined to be real. Both views, like all philosophical systems, are built on the faith we have in the presuppositions we make but can by no means prove. It is not surprising that most biomedically oriented scientists are puzzled and even troubled by giving any serious attention to the clinical relevance of humanity's spiritual nature. There are, however, a few notable exceptions that thanatologists would do well to study.

Wilder Penfield, a neurosurgeon and one of the experimental architects of the mind-brain monism, reversed his position during the final stages of his life and wrote a fascinating book entitled *The Mystery of the Mind* (1975), in which he explained his rationale for adopting the view that the spiritual mind has a life of its own. There are, in addition to Penfield, two other significant spokesmen for this mind-brain dualism, and each of them has the distinction of having received the Nobel Prize. Sir Charles Sherrington (1951) and Sir John Eccles (1979), both celebrated and skilled students of the brain, have each gone on record to advance the view that mind and brain are not the same and that each is real. Although, understandably, these writings are given little serious attention by biomedical science, I believe that these works have tremendous importance to thanatology. They point to a philosophical departure that our profession may have to consider if it is to create a map of professional practice that contains the "things" we and our clients care most about.

Conclusion

The demands of thanatological work have brought its practitioners into a spiritual gray zone which, at present, is almost completely neglected on the current maps of clinical practice. Lacking a representation, these crucial existential issues are generally disregarded and denied a credibility. Thus we find that materialist-dominated health-professional culture tends to regard any serious attempt to consider humanity in spiritual terms as though it were the regressive, child-like fantasy of less-than-adequate critical thinkers. I suggest that we have reached a point in our own professional development where we should sidestep this ideological tyranny and establish our own maps that will more adequately describe the professional terrain we travel each day with our clients and colleagues.

It has taken a long time to operationalize and legitimize quality care for the terminally ill. There remain many other areas of neglect and confusion that demand the attention of those who, like thanatologists, are willing to forego the tidiness of the materialist medical model and meet these human dilemmas head on, despite the chaos and the havoc they wreak on our epistemological order.

REFERENCES

ECCLES, J. C. 1979. *The Human Mystery*. New York: Springer International.
FROMM, E. 1950. *Psychoanalysis and Religion*. New Haven: Yale University Press.
MOODY, R. 1977. *Life After Life*. Atlanta: Mockingbird Books.
PENFIELD, W. 1975. *The Mystery of the Mind*. Princeton, NJ: Princeton University Press.
SCHUMACHER, E. F. 1977. *A Guide to the Perplexed*. New York: Harper and Row.
SHERRINGTON, C. S. 1951. *Man and His Nature*, 2nd ed. Cambridge: Cambridge University Press.

Part IV

Psychiatric Patients with Terminal Illness

26

Life-Threatening Illness
and The Psychiatric Patient

Marilyn Lewis Lanza

People with chronic mental illness face death in different ways: some exhibit the same reactions "normal" people do, whereas others react in ways that are unique to the mentally ill. Despite the prevalence of chronic mental illness, little has been written about the ways these individuals experience the grieving process and the implications of their experience for health care providers.

STAGES OF GRIEVING

Many theorists have suggested that there are a series of stages of grieving, and that these stages have certain points in common. The stages of grief suggested by Hofling, Kubler-Ross, Engel, Aguilers, and Fine are diagrammed in Figure 1, adapted from Freihofer and Felton (1976).

The theorists have suggested that, in general, the dying person moves through a series of steps from rejection to eventual acceptance of death. These stages overlap; one does not pass through them without many stops, starts, and returns to earlier stages.

Although clinicians are concerned with movement through the grief process, they must also consider the type of grief reaction that individuals experience. Peretz (1970) listed the following types of bereavement: normal; anticipatory grief; inhibited, delayed, and absent grief; chronic grief (perpetual mourning); depression; hypochondriasis and exacerbation of pre-existing somatic conditions; development of medical symptoms and illness; psychophysiological reactions; and acting out, or becoming involved in activity to avoid the pain of grief.

As patients consciously or unconsciously anticipate death, they think about

167

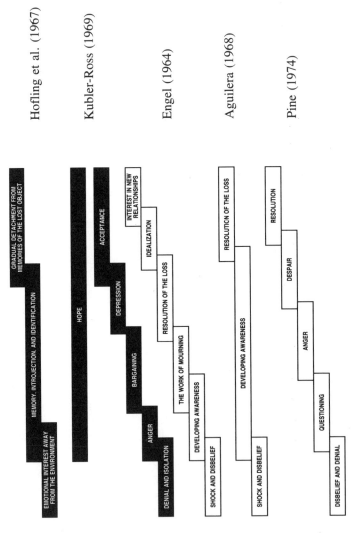

Figure 1   The Stages Of Grief.

and fear separation from valued persons and things in their world. Also, dying patients face loss of self. Rapidly or gradually, they will lose various activities and functions: cognitive skills, motor skills, and the capacity for pleasure.

NORMAL GRIEF

The psychoanalytic approach to the understanding of death is based on the assumption that the human mind is incapable of conceiving death as the absolute end of life. Freud's view was that "our unconscious does not believe in its own death; it behaves as if it were immortal." Klein (1948) believed that there is an unconscious knowledge that death means a total end. Jacques (1965) claimed that the unconscious contains experiences that may later equal conscious perception of death. Adaptation to death is related to individuals' maturation and to the various phases of crisis in their lives, and differs at various ages — childhood, adolescence, midlife, and old age (Alexander and Adelstein 1965; Easson 1968; A. Freud 1960, 1967; Hinton 1967; Jacques 1965; Stern 1968).

Normal grief involves intense mental suffering, deep sorrow, and painful regret (Peretz 1970). Initially there is shock, numbness, and denial. When faced with the reality of death, one undergoes certain changes. Protection against death is sought by use of all the ego defenses, foremost among them being the mechanism of denial (Hagglund 1978). When denial diminishes, the mourning process begins. There is bewilderment, weeping, and the despairing acknowledgement of loss. The dying person then relinquishes objects, life, and body. Simultaneously, the wish for the immortality of one's own personality leads to the formation of an "auxiliary ego" to maintain object relations after death in one's work, children, or accomplishments. Physiological reactions during the grieving process include dyspnea, deep sighing, "lumps" or tight sensations in the throat, weakness, feelings of emptiness, exhaustion, decreased appetite, and insomnia. Anxiety and tension are commonly experienced. Irritability may serve to keep others at a distance. Intimacy may be a painful reminder of loss. Depression, feelings of numbness, and helplessness are also part of normal grieving. As death approaches and regression intensifies, a splitting mechanism often develops whereby the dying person divides emotions and objects into good and bad. For example, the world they are leaving is considered bad, while fantasies of death or identification with the therapist, or anyone who has provided support, are good (Hagglund 1978).

The mourning process of a dying person involves the loss of the external world and loss of one's body. As the dying process advances, fantasies increasingly take on the quality of real objects in the person's mind (Hagglund 1981). At the end of the dying process, this is manifested in difficulty of discriminating between fantasy and real communication with the external world.

Fantasies of death fill the void that this unknown condition leaves in individuals' minds. In these fantasies, death can be represented as a continuation of life in some other form (Hinton 1967) or as punishment or reward for a morally bad or good life (Feifel 1959; Stokes 1966), or it can be personified in the shape of an animal, man (Kemppinen 1967), or a threatening figure (McClelland 1964). Fantasies of death may take a pleading form or may represent a return to the frustration-free intrauterine state. Death may be personified as a seducer (Bromberg and Schilder 1936) or offer the prospect of reunion with lost objects or others who have died (Eissler 1964; Freud, S. 1926a; Greenberger 1965; Waelder 1960).

In order to mourn the ever-weakening, dying body, one must solve the narcissistic conflict between the weak and ailing body and the wished-for, ideal state (Hagglund 1981), imagining one's own body on some other level of existence or in a condition in which the body-self attains specific libidinal value. Examples are "survival" through one's own creativity, children, or achievements, and the mental image in the minds of others.

The ego can only defend against the threat of death and unendurable anxiety in the beginning of the dying process. Denial begins to fail, and fear of death begins to overwhelm in the form of separation anxiety or fear of annihilation (Hagglund 1981). When one is at the threshold of death, there is fear of losing contact with one's fantasies and fear of losing the possibility of communicating these fantasies to another person or inner object.

ANTICIPATORY GRIEF

Dying is a process that ends in death, but a process from which there is a possibility of escape. For example, a chronic patient may look for remissions and, perhaps, a cure (Pine 1974).

Anticipatory grief, according to Peretz (1970) is a time when the person is faced with declining health and may grieve in much the same way as one would grieve for another. The reactions may range from sadness and crying to those associated with actual grief. Anticipatory grief begins before actual bereavement occurs (Arkin 1974). In fact, it is the first stage of bereavement (Weisman 1974). It is followed by serious problems of disorganization, crying and craving, perceptual aberrations, and then, by gradual coping, the return of effective behavior, and closure (Weisman 1974).

Anticipatory grief may interfere with the ability of dying patients and survivors to maintain their relationships (Peretz 1970). Patients who express anticipatory grief when the possibility of loss is low are predisposed to hopelessness and pessimism. They are often guilty and self-punitive. When loss does occur, they often show depression rather than grief.

FACING DEATH: THE CHRONICALLY ILL PSYCHIATRIC PATIENT

My search of the literature indicates that few studies have dealt specifically with the issue of how chronically ill psychiatric patients face death. Christ (1965) interviewed 1,000 patients age 60 or older who had been admitted to psychiatric units of San Francisco General Hospital in 1959. He concluded that psychiatric patients were upset about death and used denial, suppression, and repression as defenses. Prior to the study interviews, 87% of the patients had not talked to anyone about death. Only one-third of the patients had made a will.

Feifel (1965) conducted an exploratory survey at a Veterans Administration Hospital to assess the meaning of death to 85 psychiatrically ill patients. These patients resided on both closed and open units and represented a cross section of diagnostic categories. The results follow.

Asked at what age most people fear death, the most frequent answer was in their 50s, followed by in their 40s. The patients' responses indicated that fear of death was lowest in childhood, increased to a peak in the fifth decade of life, and then decreased in the sixth and seventh decades. It was suggested that the drop might be accounted for by resignation or adjustment to the ideal of death. However, when asked to rank the most-to-the-least-favorable age groups, the 70s and older were rated as the time during which most people feared death, followed by early childhood. Old age and childhood were reported as the times to have the most and the least fear of death.

Commonly, patients viewed death with a kind of philosophic rationalization, as the inevitable final process of life. The next predominating outlook, a religious theme, was that death represents only the dissolution of bodily life and, in reality, is the doorway to a new life. This was followed by the conception of death as a time of rest and peace, a supreme refuge from the turmoil of life. Less than 15% of the patients found death so anxiety-provoking that they denied having any ideas about it. A prominent theme in patients' drawings was death by a traumatic event. This may reflect inner aggression toward others and self.

When asked hypothetically what they would do if they could only do one thing before dying, patients' most common response was that they would like to do something to benefit others. This response was followed equally by the wish to engage in activity of a religious nature and to have reunions with close relatives and friends. Next in order was the wish to travel and have new experiences, then, to live better economically, and, finally, to achieve some goal. These responses are in contrast to those of normal groups, who put self-interest and self-gratification before religious or social activities. Because of strong guilt feelings and a desire for peace of mind, mentally ill people may have a greater need than others to make amends to others before dying.

In a later study, Feifel and Herman (1973) investigated the hypotheses that mentally ill persons manifest greater fear of death than normal persons, at least at unconscious levels, and that the greater the degree of emotional disturbance, the more widespread the fear of death. The subjects for this study were 90 mentally ill patients, 63% of whom had psychoneurotic and personality disorders, and 37% of whom had psychotic disorders. The control subjects were 95 healthy individuals. The patient population came from the Veterans Administration, university and community hospitals, and private practice. The normal subjects included more women and had higher levels of education and higher socioeconomic status.

This study assessed subjects' attitudes toward death on different levels: conscious, fantasy, and below the level of awareness. The investigators also inquired about the frequency of patients' thoughts about death and perception of life after death.

No significant differences between mentally ill and normal subjects were found concerning fear of death on any of the three levels examined. What was apparent was the overall similarity of response in the two groups. Two-thirds of both groups consciously disavowed fear of death, giving the reason that "it's inevitable." Those who did admit to fear of death ascribed it to "fear of the unknown" or "leaving the good things behind." On the imagery level, both groups shifted to perceiving death ambivalently. Below the level of awareness, anxiety toward death was evident, but there was no significant difference between the groups with respect to frequency of death thoughts or views of personal fate after death. The pattern in both groups linked conscious repudiation of fear of death to one of ambivalence at the imagery level, and apprehension at the level below awareness.

No differences were apparent between psychotic and neurotic groups except that psychotic persons required a longer recall time on a word association test and differed with regard to personal fate after death, focusing on a religious view. It was suggested that this is because psychotics expect a more violent death. This mirrors their struggle with aggression toward self and others. Neurotic persons had a materialistic orientation. The difference between the psychotic and neurotic groups held when using analysis of covariance to control for differences in demographic variables.

Feifel and Herman concluded that there was not a significant difference between mentally ill and normal subjects in their reactions to death and that the degree of mental illness was not a major factor relating to fear of death. They suggested that the dominance of cultural imprinting with regard to the outlook on death appears to be such that it overrides any differences in emotional health.

Feifel and Branscomb (1973) conducted a large study in which they compared 90 patients who had psychoneurotic, personality disorders, and psychotic disorders with 92 seriously and terminally ill patients, 94 chronically ill and disabled patients, and 95 healthy individuals. The purpose of the study was to scrutinize and isolate major demographic variables, including nearness to death and recent experience with death, that are associated with fear of personal death. Fear of death was measured as, in the previous study, on a conscious level, fantasy level, and below the level of awareness.

Again, the mentally ill were not significantly different from the control groups in response to the fear of death. At the conscious level, the dominant response to fear of death was repudiation. At the fantasy or imagery level, it was one of ambivalence; and at the non-conscious level, outright negativity. This apparent counterbalance of coexisting avoidance–acceptance of personal death most likely serves adaptational needs, allowing individuals to maintain communal associations and yet organize their responses to contend with oncoming death.

None of the demographic variables except age and religious self-rating appeared to influence the personal dread of death. Institutionalization as a factor was more marked for the terminally and chronically ill than for the mentally ill, but it did not appear to be a significant variable related to personal fear of death.

Dahlberg (1980) described the reactions of his patients in analysis who faced death. It should be noted that these subjects were not suffering from mental illness to the same degree as those described in the earlier studies. Dahlberg's patients experienced anger, depression, sorrow at the thought of leaving their loved ones, and sudden, almost manic joy at being alive. The intense joy of being alive was not a defense against depression. The patients also experienced sudden mood shifts. Catharsis, abreactions, and ventilation were useful and valuable releases. Rage put an enormous strain on even sound relationships. Dahlberg suggested that narcissism is a normal state, especially for the very ill, and should not be pointed out pejoratively. Patterns of leave-taking were highly individual. Some patients rushed to get in everything they wanted to do, others found surrogate parents and spouses for their families, and still others held onto their spouses or displayed jealousy, self-pity, withdrawal, and passivity.

Although there are variations in the way the mentally ill face death, this is also true among those who have not suffered from mental illness. Moreover, it appears that there are more similarities than differences in the ways that the mentally ill and those who are not mentally ill approach death.

CLINICAL OBSERVATIONS*

Psychotic symptoms seem to decrease as physical illness becomes more prominent. Patients become subdued because of their physical illness. If there is a

---

*When I undertook to write this chapter, I selected comments from those who work with dying psychiatric patients. The above discussion is based on comments from two psychiatric clinical nurse specialists and members of the nursing staff of two medical units where care is provided to terminally ill psychiatric patients.

remission in their physical illness, they often become psychotic and agitated again. This is particularly so if they have not been receiving their psychiatric medications. This behavioral pattern leads to speculation that when a psychiatric patient is transferred to a medical unit, the environmental interactions may be different from those that applied when the patient was on a psychiatric unit. The staff of the medical unit talk to the patient more about the physical illness and treat the patient as "normal," whereas the psychiatric staff focus more on the mental illness.

A particular problem for staff is that when a psychiatric patient is admitted to a medical unit, the administration of antipsychotic medications is often discontinued (because of the medical problem). As a result, the patient becomes increasingly psychotic, often exhibiting bizarre behavior. Psychiatric patients may have difficulty identifying their feelings. They may express their feelings in a distorted way, and need help to recognize that their feelings are normal and appropriate.

It is important to carefully observe nonverbal behavior. Managing pain can be difficult if a patient is not verbal. Psychiatric patients seem to complain less about physical pain than do other patients. Careful assessment of their pain is necessary: a quiet patient is not always a pain-free patient.

Patients suffering from chronic obstructive pulmonary disease often did not comply with requests to give up self-destructive behavior such as smoking. (One wonders if, in this, they are any different from nonpsychiatric patients?) Self-destructive tendencies may manifest themselves in many ways. Indeed, some nurses felt that psychiatric patients are very similar to nonpsychiatric patients. There is a great variety in how they handle death. One psychiatric patient undergoing urinary dialysis was very depressed and wanted to die. Another psychiatric patient was a real "fighter." He could not verbalize anything about his own death but was very interested in facts about other patients' deaths. In reference to himself, he always said he was feeling better.

Several nurses noted that long-term psychiatric patients with end-stage pulmonary disease become increasingly psychotic when they are on a ventilator. They become psychotic, irritable, and isolated, often ignoring friends and family and refusing to interact with others. These patients also regress, a fact that is reflected in behaviors such as refusing to wipe themselves after going to the toilet. This observation, however, again draws attention to the conclusion that mentally ill and mentally normal individuals do not face death so differently. All physically ill people regress. Although the mentally ill may express regression through less socially acceptable behavior than do the non-mentally ill, the difference is one of degree, not kind.

The nurses also noted a difference between psychiatric patients' experience on medical and psychiatric units. These patients are used to individual attention on psychiatric units, where many staff members meet with them individually or in groups. On medical units, this is not possible to the same extent. Patients and their families may not understand and the staff may feel guilty, leaving everyone feeling more isolated and abandoned.

Sometimes conflict can arise between families and staff. For example, psychiatric patients are often unconcerned with personal hygiene and may resist taking showers. The family may then be critical of the nursing care. At times, families are remote. Family members must go through their own grieving, but sometimes it can be difficult for the staff to deal with their demands. It must be remembered much of a dying person's concern centers around family. The maintenance of hope remains important, and concern about others becomes paramount (Dubrey and Terril 1975).

Often, the staff become the patient's surrogate family, particularly if the patient's hospitalization has been lengthy. Kent (1983) presented the case of a woman who was dying of cancer and who had been treated with electroconvulsive therapy for depression. This woman adopted the staff as her family, using individual members to fulfill her various needs. When the staff from the patient's original unit are the patient's only existing support system, their visits after the patient has been transferred to another unit are most helpful.

IMPLICATIONS FOR HEALTH CARE PROVIDERS

As the population in our country ages, so will the population of long-term psychiatrically ill patients. In many ways, psychiatric patients react to the prospect of their death as anyone else would. Thus, the health care team should treat these patients in the same way they would anyone else who is facing death. Yet, in some ways, there are important differences in the meaning of death to these individuals that should be taken into consideration.

It is essential to explore with patients what their own death means or symbolizes to them. For example, does death bring the prospect of relief from a tortured inner life? Is peace the anticipated outcome, or does a patient expect further trails and trauma in an after life? What does the patient feel will be the cause of death — for example, will death be the result of suicide or of natural causes? What is the meaning of either alternative? What effect does this perception have on this patient and on the patient's significant others?

Death forces people to take stock of their lives. They look back on past accomplishments and failures. For those who have been psychiatrically ill and who may have been institutionalized for much of their lives, failures may overshadow successes. These patients may have missed many opportunities that are considered to be "normal" for a fulfilled life. Close personal relationships may have been difficult and the result, often, is that these people are alone, without spouses, children, close family, or friends. They may not have been lonely; they may have preferred a solitary existence. The approach of death, however, may bring a life of emptiness into sharp focus and the pain of loneliness may then be acute. A defense for many people in this situation is to think about the next generation and about what they have passed on to them, both genetically and environmentally. Such thoughts provide little comfort for a patient who feels like a "bad seed," and who has generally been a burden rather than a support to others. Loneliness is not so much a sense of social isolation or a lessening of social contacts, but rather a rupture in one's history, a cutting away of meaningful ties (Nash 1977).

Mental illness may also have prevented patients from succeeding in school and in their careers. The more intelligent the patient, the more apparent the discrepancy between potential and actual results will be. Despite high hopes at an earlier stage in life, even the patient's intellect was not enough to deal with the disabling psychotic process. At best, the individual may have had to accept menial work that did not make great demands but that offered some protection. Inability to concentrate, overwhelming fears and anxiety, and problems in relationships may have been some of the symptoms that doomed a career.

Other areas of patients' lives need to be explored. No matter how thoroughly patients are cut off from reality, both in inner life and external surroundings, all individuals have a set of norms by which they judge their lives. Health care providers must help patients come to terms with disappointments and successes.

Consideration of the successes in the life of a long-term psychiatrically ill patient may require educating both the health care provider and the patient. Health care providers may need to evaluate life within a framework quite different from their own. The best a patient may have been able to do is to be a productive hospital citizen or to offer small amounts of help to another patient. The positive aspects of each patient's life must be emphasized without condescension or feigned admiration. Patients must be acknowledged as valuable and capable of accomplishment despite limitations that are beyond their control.

Reviewing their lives is a therapeutic process for all dying patients, giving them an opportunity to experience joy at happy events and to reconsider things they may yet be able to change. For example, there may still be a chance to resolve some painful or broken relationships. A sensitive clinician can often help a patient to do this by assisting with a phone call or letter.

Patients must not blame themselves for life's disappointments, but instead take pride in their successes. If this is not done, overwhelming guilt may intensify feelings of negative self-worth and result in increasing despair. Above all, the health care provider needs great sensitivity and compassion for the patient. The health care provider must begin to see the world through the patient's eyes. "Clear, honest and sympathetic communication with the dying patient is essential. Sham, pretense, and a 'conspiracy of secrecy' have no place in the behavior of responsible and responsive professionals" (Davidson and Lichter 1981).

GUIDELINES FOR CARE

Brody (1974) has provided some fundamental guidelines for working with those facing death:

1. Attention to social as well as medical needs must not be neglected. Though dying, the individual is still alive — a fact that should always be remembered.
2. Hope should be maintained by the staff. Dying people should not feel that those who are responsible for their care have given up.
3. The fact that a patient is dying should not mean that his wishes are not to be considered. Those who are dying should have as much autonomy and choice as possible, even in small matters. Patients' priorities may differ from those of the staff. Patients' ability to determine priorities is an illustration of their need for autonomy and choice.
4. Communication with staff, peers, and family should be encouraged. Interpersonal relationships should be preserved to the fullest extent. Loneliness, one of the most frequently voiced psychological pains of dying, increases as patients draw nearer to death. Others also withdraw, perhaps out of their own sense of helplessness.
5. That an individual is dying should not mean that his established roles — for example, as a family member or friend — are obliterated.
6. Attention should be given to patients' need for privacy and meaningful possessions. Again, remember the person is still alive and should be treated accordingly.
7. Competent behavior should be encouraged to the fullest possible extent.
8. Individualization of care is essential. It is important to listen carefully to dying patients. Clinicians must address and treat each patient with respect, making it clear to the patient that they care about them. They must also provide patients with opportunities for discussion and listen to them carefully, while helping them maintain a dignified image.
9. The physical milieu should recognize the patients' social as well as physical needs. Sometimes the staff inadvertently contribute to patients' isolation by placing them in private rooms or at the end of a corridor. Patients may, in fact, prefer to be with others and sit in the day room.
10. It should never be assumed that patients are unaware of surroundings and do not hear or understand discussions among others about their condition.
11. Staff members should be aware of their own feelings as they influence their reactions to and treatment of dying individuals. These matters should be included in in-service education programs. Staff should have an opportunity to develop understanding of the reactions and behavior of patients' families as well as those of the patients themselves.

Baker and Sorenson (1963) have described behaviors that clinicians should avoid in talking to patients about death. For example, a clinician can terminate a conversation by manipulating the patient into a position in which the patient's expression of feelings is secondary to the clinician's own comfort. Or, the clinician may give false reassurance as a way of cutting off the patient's need to talk. Sometimes, the clinician may indirectly prompt the patient to feel guilty about trying to talk about death because the clinician is not really prepared to deal with the subject. Other behaviors to avoid are (1) referring the patient to another person for answers, (2) moralizing or philosophizing, (3) stating facts or possible facts that disagree with the feelings the patient is expressing, (4) directly denying the fact that the patient may die, (5) changing the subject, (6) avoiding questions by silence or turning away from the patient, (7) kidding the patient out of expressing further feelings, and (8) filling "silent time" with irrelevant conversation. There are times when quiet must be permitted. Allowing the patient to talk without interruption may bring forth issues on which the patient wants to work, such as making a will or planning a funeral.

Patients may be inconsistent as they deal with reality. For example, they may discuss their plans for their burial and, at the same time, speak about "when I get stronger, I will ..." It is important to not confront the inconsistencies or refute what the patient is saying.

LeShan and LeShan (1961) suggested the two major reasons for clinicians' avoidance of discussing death are their own fear of death and the dying patients' inability to use counseling as a springboard to a long future of improved functioning. Kubler-Ross (1978) aimed to teach physicians to deal with their own fears of death. She found that physicians often did not reveal their own fears to themselves and did not tell their dying patients that they were dying. The physicians projected their own fears and anxieties onto the patients, preventing them from discussing their knowledge of their own impending death.

Kubler-Ross has said that patients should not be referred to thanatologists, but that the usual health care providers should learn to deal with dying patients. She hoped that staff would evaluate their own unresolved losses, pains in their own lives, and their own attitudes toward dying, thus freeing themselves to communicate with dying patients. Although Kubler-Ross's wish may be the ideal, it must be recognized that not everyone can work comfortably with the dying. It is well to know if one cannot, so that one can then try to provide the patient with someone who can.

LEARNING ABOUT ONE'S SELF

Vigor and productivity are greatly valued by society. Our energies appear to be vested in a "High Noon" vision of the human condition. Consequently, there is avoidance of people whose lives are marked strongly by suffering or death (Kastenbaum 1974). It is frequently said that it is not death itself that the dying fear, nor the pain associated with their physical condition. Rather, they fear being relegated to the periphery, the loneliness and the indignity so frequently associated with the dying process (Marcovitz 1973). Patients who are in the last stages of their lives are not just dying; they are also living. Whether or not they have the opportunity to live this final human experience to the fullest is influenced in great measure by the environment and by who takes care of them (Nash 1977).

Curran and Kobos (1980) explored the learning that takes place for clinicians when they work with dying patients. Clinicians can learn to feel deeply, to get in touch with their own humanness, and to risk sharing. They also become aware that patients are highly sensitive to verbal and nonverbal communication, and are subject to distress when their questions are dismissed, ignored, brushed aside, or treated as though they were unimportant. Clinicians learn that patients are strong and that psychotherapy is a participatory relationship rather than one of predictable and anticipatory maneuvers. Experienced clinicians can learn to relinquish control — to be present, to listen, to feel, and to share — and to increase their gentleness and sensitivity. The finality of patients' lives has a definite impact on the pace, content, and process of the therapeutic involvement.

Specific Treatment Approaches

Dahlberg (1980) maintains that psychotherapy of the dying patient includes a sympathetic ear, reassurance (especially about anger), encouragement, assuagement of the ever-present guilt, cautious interpretation of characterological problems that interfere with adjustment, and some attempt to hold the patient back from acting out the normal craziness.

Schwartz and Karasu (1977) discussed the interaction between the dying patient and clinician during therapy. They noted that clinicians and patients often share in the denial of death. As mentioned previously in dealing with dying patients, clinicians are forced to face the idea of their own death and the death of those close to them. The gratification for clinicians working with dying patients is in seeing and taking part in the resolution of intrapsychic conflict. When a patient dies, the clinician's reward is in having helped the patient to die easily and without pain.

Affective empathy is most important. It involves honest and direct communication without any semblance of value judgments. The empathizer must be able to share in reliving and living through the dying person's experiences. The dying person gains a sense of this experience and becomes aware of the fusion, which is brief, but certainly realized. The patient may reverse roles with the clinician for brief moments. The fusion permits identification and empathy with the clinician, thereby diminishing the sense of extreme loss for both. Empathy provides fusions with the patient's unconscious and transmits the feeling that part of the clinician will die with that person. Empathy requires a substantial degree of ego development, specifically with respect to memory, thinking, and good conceptualization. It is enhanced by age and experience.

Clinicians must help staff and family manage collective grief. This includes guilt and helplessness in regard to themselves and the dying patient. They must be constant, reliable, and available to their patients. Fear of abandonment is strong, and leads to panic and dread. Superficial optimism must be avoided. It fosters suspicion and mistrust. With people for whom optimism is a character trait, denial should not be challenged, but viewed as homeostatic and ego-syntonic for maintaining self-esteem. People die as they have lived, using the same coping mechanisms.

McKitrick (1981) has compared and contrasted various counseling approaches to dying patients, based on Kastenbaum and Aisenberg's delineation of four ways in which individuals respond to the prospect of their own death: overcoming, participating, fearing, and sorrowing. The following summarizes the counseling approaches appropriate to dealing with each reaction:

1. *Overcoming*. There is focus on religion and striving for ways to overcome death. Approaches consistent with this reaction are psychoanalysis, crisis approach, and methods for reducing loneliness and isolation.
2. *Participating*. One is involved in one's own death. Two approaches are patient-centered counseling, which protects and emphasizes the dying person's individuality, and self-actualization, which helps the dying patient use the dying process as a growth experience.
3. *Fearing*. The dying fear personal suffering and indignity in the dying process, punishment and rejection in the afterlife, and extinction. Two approaches with patients who have intense or prolonged fears of dying are the use of mood-altering substances along with counseling and a focus on resolving guilt conflicts through insight.
4. *Sorrowing*. This response to the thought of death is not to be confused with depressive reactions. The approach to its treatment focuses on the patient's anticipatory grief.

The final approach to be discussed here is Kubler-Ross's (1969) stage approach, which does not fit within Kastenbaum and Aisenberg's four primary reactions to death. Rather, Kubler-Ross's stages include all four categories of the major reactions to death. The stage approach offers an alternative to considering the dying patient in terms of a single major response to death. Kubler-Ross's guidelines for counseling help the patient go through five distinct stages. Listed are Kubler-Ross's stages and Kastenbaum and Aisenberg's associated reactions (McKitrick 1981):

	Kubler-Ross	Kastenbaum and Aisenberg
Stage 1:	Denial	Overcoming
Stage 2:	Anger	Overcoming
Stage 3:	Bargaining	Fearing
Stage 4:	Depression	Sorrowing and participating
Stage 5:	Acceptance	Sorrowing and participating

There are many approaches to helping the dying patient face death. Through sensitivity to the life experiences, wishes, and needs of all those who are dying, including those who have chronic mental illness, all patients can be helped to live more fully as they die.

REFERENCES

ALEXANDER, I. E. and A. M. ADELSTEIN. 1965. "Affective Responses to the Concept of Death in a Population of Children and Early Adolescents." In R. Fulton, ed. *Death and Identity*. New York: Wiley, pp. 111-123.

AQUILERA, D. C. 1968. "Crisis: Death and Dying." *ANA Clinical Sessions*. New York: Appleton-Century Crofts. pp. 269-278.

ARKIN, A. M. 1974. "Notes on Anticipatory Grief." In B. Schoenberg, ed. *Anticipatory Grief*. New York: Columbia University Press, pp. 10-13.

BAKER, J. M. and K. C. SORENSON. 1963. "A Patient's Concern with Death: Do Nurses Recognize the Needs of the Patient Who Wants to Talk About Impending Death?" *American Journal of Nursing* 63(1):90-92.

BRODY, E. M. 1974. *A Social Work Guide for Long-Term Care Facilities*. Rockville, MD: National Institutes of Mental Health.

BROMBERG, W. and P. SCHILDER. 1926. "The Attitude of Psychoneurotics Toward Death." *Psychoanalytic Review* 23:1-25.

CHRIST, A. E. 1965. "Attitudes Toward Death Among a Group of Acute Geriatric Psychiatry Patients." In R. Fulton, ed. *Death and Identity*. New York: John Wiley and Sons, pp. 146-152.

CURRAN, M. C. and J. C. KOBOS. 1988. "Therapeutic Engagement with A Dying Person: Stimulus for Therapist Training and Growth." *Psychotherapy: Theory, Research, and Practice*. 17(3, Fall):341-351.

DAHLBERG, C. C. 1977. "Perspectives on Death, Dying, and Illness." *Journal of the Academy of Psychoanalysis* 8(3):361-380.

DAVIDSON, G. P. and I. LICHTER. 1981. "Nursing the Dying Patient." *New Zealand Nursing Journal* 74(3):5-6.

DUBREY, R. J. and L. A. TERRILL. 1975. "The Loneliness of a Dying Person: An Exploratory Study." *Omega* 6(4):357-371.

EASSON, W. M. 1968. "Care of the Young Patient Who Is Dying." *American Journal of the Medical Association* 205:203-205.

EISSLER, G. L. 1964. *The Psychiatrist and the Dying Patient*. New York: International Universities Press.

ENGEL, G. L. 1964. "Grief and Grieving." *American Journal of Nursing* 64(Sept):93-98.

FEIFEL, H. 1959. "Attitudes Toward Death in Some Normal and Mentally Ill Populations." In H. Feifel, ed. *The Meaning of Death*. New York: McGraw-Hill, pp. 114-130.

FEIFEL, H. 1965. "Attitudes of Mentally Ill Patients Toward Death." In R. Fulton, ed. *Death and Identity*. New York: John Wiley and Sons, pp. 131-141.

FEIFEL, H. and A. B. BRANSCOMB. 1973. "Who's Afraid of Death?" *Journal of Abnormal Psychology* 81(3):282-288.

FEIFEL, H. and L. J. HERMAN. 1973. "Fear of Death in the Mentally Ill." *Psychological Reports* 33:931-938.

FREIHOFER, P. and G. FELTON. 1976. "Nursing Behaviors in Bereavement: An Exploratory Study." *Nursing Research* 25(5):332-337.

FREUD, A. 1960. *The Writings of Anna Freud,* vol. 4. New York: International Universities Press, pp. 302-316.

FREUD, A. 1968. *The Writings of Anna Freud,* vol. 5. New York: International Universities Press, pp. 173-186.

FREUD, S. 1915. "Thoughts for the Time of War and Death, Part II. Our Attitude Toward Death." *Standard Edition,* vol. 14. London: Hogarth Press, pp. 289-300.

FREUD, S. 1926. "Inhibitions, Symptoms, and Anxiety." *Standard Edition,* Vol. 20. London: Hogarth Press, pp. 87-172.

GREENBERGER, E. 1965. "Fantasies of Women Confronting Death." *Journal of Consulting Psychology* 29:252-260.

HAGGLUND, T. 1981. "The Final Stage of the Dying Process." *International Journal of Psychoanalysis* 62:45-49.

HINTON, J. 1967. *Dying.* England: Hunt Barnard.

HOFFLING, C. K. 1967. *Basic Psychiatric Concepts in Nursing,* 2nd ed. Philadelphia: J. B. Lippincott Co.

IMARA, M. 1975. "Dying as the Last Stage." In E. Kubler-Ross, ed. *Death: The Final Stage of Growth.* Englewood Cliffs, NJ: Prentice-Hall, p. 147.

JACQUES, E. 1965. "Death and Mid-Life Crisis" *International Journal of Psychoanalysis* 46:502-514.

KASTENBAUM, R. J. 1974. "Gone Tomorrow." *Geriatrics* (Nov):127-134.

KASTENBAUM, R. J. 1977. *Death, Society, and Human Experience.* St. Louis: C. V. Mosby.

KEMPPINEN, I. 1967. *Life Beyond Death in the Light of Ancient Carelian Beliefs and Comparative Theological Sciences*. Helsinki: Carelian Research Society.

KENT, J. 1983. "Care with a Big C." *Nursing Mirror* 157:32-34.

KLEIN, M. 1948. *Contributions to Psychoanalysis*. London: Hogarth Press.

KUBLER-ROSS, E. 1969. *On Death and Dying*. London: MacMillan Co.

KUBLER-ROSS, E. 1978. *To Live Until We Say Good-Bye*. Englewood Cliffs, NJ: Prentice-Hall.

LeSHAN, L. and E. LeSHAN. 1961. "Psychotherapy in the Patient with a Limited Life Span." *Psychiatry* 24:318.

MARCOVITS, E. 1973. "What Is the Meaning of Death to the Dying Person and His Survivors." *Omega* 4(1):14.

McCLELLAND, D. C. 1964. *The Roots of Consciousness*. Princeton, NJ: Van Nostrand.

McKITRICK, D. 1981. "Counseling Dying Patients." *Omega* 12(2):165-187.

NASH, M. L. 1977. "Dignity of Person in the Final Phase of Life: An Exploratory Study." *Omega* 8(1):71-80.

PERETZ, D. 1970. "Reactions to Loss." In B. Schoenberg, ed. *Loss and Grief: Psychological Management in Medical Practice*. New York: Columbia University Press, pp. 20-35.

PINE, V. R. 1974. "Dying, Death, and Social Behavior." In B. Schoenberg, ed. *Anticipatory Grief*. New York: Columbia University Press, pp. 31-47.

SCHWARTZ, A. M. and T. B. KARASU. 1977. "Psychotherapy with the Dying Patient." *American Journal of Psychotherapy* 32(1, Fall):19-35.

STERN, M. M. 1968. "Fear of Death and Neurosis." *Journal of American Psychoanalytic Association* 16:3-31.

STOKES, A. D. 1966. "On Being Taken out of One's Self." *International Journal of Psychoanalysis* 47:523-530.

WAELDER, R. 1960. *Basic Theory of Psychoanalysis*. New York: International Universities Press.

WEISMAN, A. D. 1974. "Is Mourning Necessary." In B. Schoenberg, ed. *Anticipatory Grief*. New York: Columbia University Press, pp. 14-18.

27

The Borderline Patient With Life-Threatening Illness

Virginia R. Crespo

Patients with pre-existing psychiatric difficulties, such as those that occur in borderline conditions, may experience further severe disorganization of the self when confronted with a life-threatening illness. Correspondingly, staff members confronted with the amalgamation of psychiatric and physical symptoms face an especially difficult task. This may greatly effect the quantity and quality of care provided to these patients.

Patients who regress in response to serious physical illness may experience exacerbation of such symptoms as impulsiveness, dependency, feelings of entitlement, rage, and depression. The staff may not respond to these situations in a clinically optimal manner. Countertransferential issues such as avoidance, fear, and anger in staff members' reactions to these patients can greatly influence the quantity and quality of care.

Psychodynamic Exploration of the Borderline Condition

A borderline personality involves a severe but stable character disorder associated with a profound developmental disturbance that occurred early in life, in the pre-Oedipal period of psychological development. In normal development, children learn to distinguish and eventually to separate psychologically, cognitively, emotionally, and physically from important objects, such as mother, and learn increasingly to tolerate such separations, along with sadness and anger. The child with a borderline condition cannot tolerate the negative affects associated with separation. This child reacts with deep despair and rage, which continues into adulthood. Pre-Oedipal yearnings for fusion between the self and important objects persist; these important objects are viewed as desperately needed parts of the self, rather than as separate entities (Modell 1963). The psychological and emotional boundaries between the self and others become so blurred that emotional closeness or intimacy plunges the borderline person into the deeply paradoxical position in which either fusion or separateness carries the threat of emotional death (Zetzel 1971).

Borderline individuals' sense of self is fragmented, and their sexuality is confused with their aggression; needs are experienced as rage. Because of their severely impaired ego functioning, they are unable to master painful or ambivalent feelings or to channel these needs and feelings into creative or productive areas in their lives. In addition, they experience a keen sense of emptiness and emotional fragility that renders painful or ambivalent feelings intolerable; their impulse control is deeply impaired. Borderline individuals see themselves, as well as others, as either "all good" or "all bad," as "all weak" or "all powerful." These perceptions may be accompanied by feelings and images of fear, shame, impotency, and grandiosity.

Also, these individuals have serious flaws and impairments in reality testing. They can easily regress into primary process thinking and perceiving when under stress. This can occur, for example, during physical illness or in situations in which there is too little structure (Friedman 1975).

Much theoretical data about borderline persons have been derived from object relations theory, which provides us with a model for "developmental shaping of these images as the child begins to separate the image of himself from that of his mother" (Shapiro 1971: 1309). Shapiro speaks of three major developmental tasks in this developmental process: (1) self–object differentiation; (2) the integration of loving and hating images and the development of object constancy; and (3) the further integration of the images into flexible psychic structures, e.g., superego and ego ideal. In the borderline personality, internal images of the other are greatly distorted, with stereotyped, rigid, and unchanging patterns of relating (Shapiro 1971).

Self–object differentiation implies that children are able to make an intrapsychic separation between their own experiential boundaries and their experience of their mothers. With attainment of the capacity to view one's self as both a loving and hating person in response to the internal image of the other who will alternately both gratify and frustrate, the child will achieve that stage of object constancy. This will allow the child to tolerate and master separation and loss by maintaining a comforting image of the mother (constant object image) despite her frustrating separation from the child (Zetzel 1971). The capacity of the child to acknowledge and accept angry feelings toward the mother will help the child develop the capacity to tolerate guilt, empathy, frustration, and depression over the lost internal image of the mother, rather than experiencing the more primitive sense of impotent rage and defeat by external forces (Shapiro 1971).

Mahler and Furer (1963) have written about the following crucial developmental periods in the child's life: the symbiotic period, from the second to the fifth month, in which mother and infant are joined with no separate boundaries, and the separation–individuation period, which occurs when the child is five months to three years of age. During the period of separation–individuation, the mother's tasks are to satisfy the child's needs and to act as an auxiliary ego, basically through her empathic responses to her child, and to create a "holding" enviornment in which the infant's "absolute need for empathy" is met (Shapiro 1971).

The mother's empathic responsiveness to her child is blocked when she cannot acknowledge her own conflict in this symbiotic interaction. If the mother perceives her own needs and conflicts as "bad" and projects this feeling onto her child, she may withdraw and become empathically unresponsive to her child's needs. This may result in the child's detachment and formation of a "false self," in which the child "passively adapts to the mother's needs and abandons his own, since they would represent a threat to the mother, whom he needs and who is relatively immune to his feedback" (Friedman 1975: 143). As a result of this severing of the symbiotic line before the internalization of empathic maternal functions, the child is left with a sense of detachment. This is accompanied by a profound sense of emptiness and undeveloped potential for the direct personal experience of living (Friedman 1975). Detachment is a distancing, protective maneuver to defend the self against the negative experience of the mother's continual and chronic empathic failure.

Mahler and Furer (1963) subdivided the separation–individuation period into four subphases: (1) differentiation (five to eight months); (2) "practicing" (eight to 16 months); (3) rapprochement (16 to 25 months) and (4) object constancy (25 months to three years). During this last period, the child's task is to emerge gradually from the relationship with the mother and to develop increasing internal and external autonomy, together with increased tolerance of frustration, mastery of separation anxiety, and maintenance of self-esteem. As Shapiro (1971) has said, "It is during these subphases of separation–individuation that the issues central to the dynamics of borderline psychopathology first appear. It is here that the conflict between the push for autonomy and the wish to unite is for the first time apparent in the behavior of the child."

In the "practicing" subphase, the intense "stranger anxiety" that Mahler observed is so fraught with anxiety for the child, owing to the frustration experienced in the symbiotic phase as a consequence of empathic emotional failure, usually on the mother's part, that any additional frustration threatens the infant's loving experiences. This results "in a prolonged defensive splitting and projection of fearsome negative experience onto the 'stranger'" (Shapiro 1971). The child is beginning to learn the primitive defense mechanism of splitting and projective identification, and cannot tolerate the mother's departure. The child finds it difficult to differentiate between positive images of self and mother, and has similar difficulty in self–object differentiation within the images of negative experiences (Kernberg 1975).

In the rapprochement subphase, the conflict between autonomy and reunion are most clearly seen in the borderline child, who cannot tolerate increased separateness, loneliness, and helplessness, and has difficulty developing a sense of clear, firm boundaries between experience of the self and experience of the mother (Shapiro 1971). According to Mahler and Furer (1963), the child alternately wishes to be reunited with the mother and also fears engulfment. Mahler and Furer observed that children who experience difficulty in this subphase show aggressive behaviors, alternately clinging to and repudiating their mothers. These children experience frustration and depression by emotional departure and abandonment, and are overwhelmed with rage that is only assuaged by loving images of mother in her absence. The children dissociate this loving image from the hateful image they have of themselves as "bad" children who are being abandoned by their mothers (Shapiro 1971). "The mother may chronically withdraw because of her inability to distinguish between her own unresolved needs [for the child's response to her] and her recognition of the needs of her child for autonomy and support" (Shapiro 1971).

There is a chronic failure of empathic sensitivity in these mothers. If, by the end of the rapprochement subphase, the mother cannot contain the child's aggression while continuing to give her child love and support, and if she cannot show her child that she is separate from him and not a creation of his projections, the child cannot develop a relationship with her as a real and autonomous person (Kernberg 1975). The child then cannot tolerate his own anger, because it might destroy his loving mother, turning her into a bad, angry, or anxious mother. The child's conviction about his own good self-image and that of his mother is weakened, increasing his fears of his own aggressive tendencies and his inability to achieve integration (Groves 1975). The child generates increased rage and makes greater demands in the presence of the mother's withdrawal, thus intensifying the conflict in their interaction. For the child, a profound and basic mistrust of self and others is the result; from the beginning, the child's sense of identity and being "good" is severely damaged. Expanding libidinal needs are affected by constricted possibilities of gaining pleasure and satisfaction. Thus, in the initial encounter between mother and infant, "mutual trustworthiness and mutual recognition" (Groves 1975) do not develop. Because of this impairment, the child's capacity for mutuality with others is severely limited.

As a result of this early empathic failure with the mother, the child's weakened and damaged ego is unable to master the phase-specific tasks of trust and separation-individuation that are needed to achieve autonomy in interaction with the physical, social, and emotional environment. The child is incapable of tolerating frustration. Intense rage and depression diminish the child's capacity to learn and to cope with transitional, developmental, interpersonal, and physical life crises. Specific modes of responding to stress become apparent in the borderline condition.

OVERVIEW OF SYMPTOMS

Most authors mention six characteristics of the borderline condition: (1) the presence of intense affect, often hostile; (2) a history of impulsive acting-out, often with self-destructive behaviors; (3) superficial social adaptiveness; (4) a history of brief psychotic experiences under stress; (5) loose thinking in environments or contexts that have too little structure; and (6) relationships that vacillate between transient superficiality and intense dependence (Groves 1975). Borderline individuals usually exibit various provocative behaviors in various combinations, along with clinging dependence, disproportionate fear, intolerable rage, profound depression, a deep inner sense of emptiness and, at times, raw aggressive sexuality.

It is important to understand the primitive defense mechanisms used by borderline individuals. These behaviors are often highly visible, and are especially noticeable when these people are within the contained environment of a medical hospital. According to Groves (1975), the following defenses may be employed:

1. Splitting, or the active process of keeping separate from each other perceptions and feelings of opposite quality. Borderline patients categorize staff members as "all-good" or "all-bad," because they cannot tolerate the anxiety-producing idea that their caretakers can be both good and bad at the same time. Included in the splitting process is the use of primitive idealization, in which these patients view some staff members as totally "good" in order to protect themselves from "bad" staff members and painful experiences. Splitting also involves projective identification, in which these patients perceive some staff members as negatively as they perceive themselves. Kernberg (1975) has noted that in the characteristic use of projective identification, borderline individuals project the unacceptable parts of themselves (impulses, rage, etc.) onto another person, identifying the other person as having the same "bad" qualities that they see in themselves and, as a result, repudiating the other person.

2. Primitic denial, in which the patients repress from consciousness any perceptions having opposite qualities. Thus, a powerful wish or need may obliterate crucial aspects of reality that are contrary to it. For

example, borderline patients may deny any serious medical illness and reject all medical treatment.

3. Omnipotence and devaluation, when manifested in the hospital environment, represent borderline patients' shift between the need to establish a relationship with the magically powerful staff and the conviction of their own omnipotence, which renders all others impotent by comparison. When omnipotent caretakers are unable to protect borderline patients from the "badness" of sickness, pain, and suffering, then these patients perceive the staff as impotent and hateful (Parrish 1981).

HOW LIFE-THREATENING ILLNESS CAN AFFECT THE BEHAVIOR OF THE BORDERLINE PATIENT

Confrontation with a life-threatening illness and the necessity to adapt to a complicated and arduous treatment regimen have powerful, profound, and varied ramifications for anyone. Even psychologically healthy patients may manifest a variety of psychological disturbances and stresses. Those with serious illness have lost or will lose one or a number of important bodily or cognitive functions. They usually experience loss of financial status, loss of a job, as well as the decrease or loss of sexual potency. Reactions to these stresses are manifested in various ways. Patients may withdraw from membership in groups, from social commitments, and from planning for the future. They may use different types of defense mechanisms that will either help or hinder their adaptation. Varying degrees of dependency are expressed, as are feelings of uselessness, helplessness, hopelessness, depression, regression, anger, hostility, anxiety, and fear of death and dying (Reichsman and Levy 1972).

For borderline patients, with their severely weakened egos and impaired perception of reality, these reactions become even more acute. The profound difference between psychologically healthy individuals and borderline individuals when they confront life-threatening illness lies in the fact that borderline patients have gone through the grief process repeatedly prior to the onset of their physical illness. When they become physically ill, borderline patients' psychological symptoms may be acutely exacerbated.

One of the biggest initial problems for borderline patients is accepting the fact that they have a serious disease. Often, intense fear and anxiety causes them to refuse to recognize their illness and the need to be treated. They may deny the diagnosis and refuse the medical treatment program or may engage in medically dangerous activities. Through their primitive denial, crucial aspects of reality are obliterated. Some patients may have unrealistic fantasies of their future lives. In time, however, borderline patients may enter into an even deeper state of denial. They become more aware of the obvious diminution of their capacities and become increasingly aware of their dependency on medical personnel, their families, their medications, or certain foods. To deal with their growing awareness of these realities, as well as the consequent stresses and disappointments, border-line patients may intensify their "struggle against dependency." Failure of this defense often leads to still deeper depression (Groves 1975).

Sometimes, because of their dependent premorbid condition, borderline patients lose all motivation to do anything for themselves, including caring for their personal hygiene. Acute clinging dependency may also be expressed in constant demands for care and attention, accompanied by feelings of entitlement. Border-line patients may openly express hostility and rage toward medical personnel. They will complain of insufficient or unprofessional care and lack of understanding or support. Because of their feelings of omnipotence, these patients will often attempt to devalue their caretakers, rendering them impotent and making them objects of hatred, much as the patients are to themselves.

These patients' ambivalent love-hate relationship with their caretakers can lead them, upon the termination of treatment, to attempt to prolong their care through self-destructive acting-out behaviors that may seriously undermine their health. Groves (1975) mentions having knowledge of a patient "secretly infecting his dressings or intravenous lines with saliva or feces to run a temperature." Patients may also just refuse to leave treatment, demanding additional care, as did one of my own patients, who refused to leave the hospital. Borderline patients may act out violently or impulsively. They may threaten or actually attempt suicide. The fear of living a restricted, deprived life seems almost as intolerable to these patients as the fear of imminent or slow death. They will alternately demand and reject treatment; split, idealize or make scapegoats of staff members; and complain of relentless anxiety and depression, thereby consuming considerable amounts of time, energy and patience of the staff.

STAFF MEMBERS' REACTIONS TO BORDERLINE PATIENT BEHAVIOR

If caretakers are unaware of the dynamics, the primitive defense mechanisms, and behavioral manifestations of the borderline condition, the behaviors of these patients can greatly disorganize them and undermine their efforts in treatment. In this circumstance caretakers may, indeed, begin to manifest some of the same behaviors as the patients. They may regress into countertransferential hatred and fear, as well as feelings of guilt, anxiety, and helplessness. They may withdraw or engage in punitive behaviors toward the patients. Groves (1975) has spoken of some of the defenses used by staff members — repression, turning against themselves, reaction formation, projection, distortion, and denial of hatred — all of which can indirectly increase the danger of patients' suicide or can force the patients to flee medical treatment (Burnham 1966).

The more unconscious caretakers are of these feelings, the more likely it is that the patients will act in self-destructive ways. As a result of covert staff splitting and disagreement, borderline patients can become victims of this conflict (Adler 1973). When this occurs, communication among the staff lessens, disagreements arise about the care of the patients, and reactive behaviors by both the patients and the staff thus increase. Anger, hostility, scapegoating, devaluation, and punitive behaviors among staff members can often occur in this collusive relationship with borderline patients. Self-esteem is lowered on both sides.

STRATEGIES FOR ADDRESSING PATIENT AND STAFF BEHAVIORS

In order to provide and maintain optimum care, several effective strategies have been suggested. Adler (1966) proposed that the acting-out behaviors of borderline patients have to be controlled through "firm, non-punitive limit setting ... because the patient has to learn that he cannot destroy the object or be destroyed by it, no matter how much he may wish this, or fear it."

Mesnikoff (1964) pointed out that the focus should be on the behavior responses to specific situations that delineate these patients' ego strengths and weaknesses, conflict areas, defense mechanisms, and compensatory mechanisms. By controlling the patients' impulses and acting-out of frustration, rage, tension, anxiety, and depression, the patients may be helped to begin slowly developing greater inner control of impulses, together with increased tolerance for anxiety, frustration, rage, depression, and so forth. In other words, a safe "holding" environment should be created for this type of patient. This may help to establish equilibrium between internal resources and the environment. In this way, the patients are helped to respond to and adhere to the various required regimens.

Although it is difficult not to react to and angrily confront patients who too often make narcissistic demands of deservedness and entitlement, Adler (1973) warns against confrontation, stating that "often the borderline has only this sense of entitlement to keep his personality together during the multiple stresses of hospitalization. Entitlement is to him what hope and faith are to some normal persons. Preserving it requires a deliberate effort by an un–split staff." Adler offers additional precautions and strategies: (1) acknowledge the real stresses in the patients' situations; (2) avoid breaking down needed defenses; (3) avoid overstimulation of patients' wish for closeness and (4) avoid overstimulation of the patients' rage (Caplan 1970). Thus, setting limits, avoiding confrontation, and averting overstimulation of the desire for closeness and rage are crucial strategies, although, at times, they are difficult to accomplish.

Obviously, the earlier the borderline patient is diagnosed and the strategies described above are implemented, the better it is for both the patient and the staff. Also, as Caplan (1970) has pointed out, mental health consultation is a helpful tool that "involves thinking of the patient and staff as a single entity and dealing as much as possible with the strong, healthy part of that entity." Caplan (1970) has recommended that when mental health consultants are called into such situations, they ally themselves with the healthy part of the entity — the staff — and suggests that doing so will help in dealing with borderline patients' pathologic defenses, especially in the area of splitting. Interpretation of the staff's pathology must be pursued with caution and support, however, because the staff is often "closely linked in an unwilling, hateful and guilty alliance with the patient, and its collective self-esteem is already damaged by encounters with the patient" (Groves 1975).

Initially, the patient may attempt to split the consultant — to see if the consultant is "all good" or "all bad." In addition, the staff may make a scapegoat of the patient, and may wish the consultant either to take over complete care of the patient or to help remove the patient from their care. Thus, the consultant's job is to focus on working with the staff rather than the patient. Groves (1975) has recommended that the mental health consultant use the following procedures:

1. Form an alliance with the staff, seeing the patient only briefly and intermittently. For the specific purpose of strengthening the alliance with the staff, no alliance should be sought with the patient. The consultant should also establish firm limit–setting with the patient. This also serves as a protective measure for the staff.

2. Implement behavior management by educating the staff about the following factors in their dealings with the patient:
   (a) Communication is essential — it is important to tell the patient simply and truthfully what the medical regimen will be. The consultant should forewarn the staff that the patient may attempt to split them by relating different stories to different staff members. To counter this, it is recommended that daily staff conferences be held to plan the patient's treatment and to reach a consensus about the information to be related to the patient.
   (b) There is need for the same personnel to deal with the patient consistently, to the extent that this is possible. Ideally, one main caretaker will make the decisions and negotiate with the patient. Since this cannot always be achieved, especially on a hospital unit, it is recommended that with each shift, a staff member be familiarized with the patient's treatment plan. That staff member should then introduce himself to the patient, letting the patient know how long he will be on duty.
   (c) The staff should be informed about the dynamics and meaning of the patient's sense of entitlement and deservedness, and should be

helped to understand that this is the patient's way of expressing anxiety about the stress of physical illness and a way of holding himself together emotionally. It is recommended that the medical personnel be alert to signs of the patient's feeling of entitlement. They should also be aware of their own anger in response to the expression of this feeling, and should cope with the anger without confronting the patient or indicating that the patient does not deserve care or attention. Instead, staff members can respond empathically to the patient, telling the patient they do understand what he is demanding, but that because they feel that he deserves the best possible care, they will continue to pursue a medical regimen which is based on their experience and judgment.

(d) The staff needs to set firm limits when the patient makes conflicting demands. They should not argue with the patient, but quietly, firmly, consistently, and repeatedly set limits on the patient's acting-out behaviors, entitlement, and rage. If the patient threatens to behave in a self-destructive way, the staff should tell the patient that physical restraint will be used for his own protection.

In addition to undertaking behavior management of the patient, the mental health consultant, as part of the effort to build an alliance with the staff, should explore, through their interactions, the staff's transference to ther consultant. This transference may be positive or negative, which, of course, will affect how the problems will be dealt with. The consultant must also attend to staff members' countertransferential feelings toward the patient. The consultant should help to legitimize expressions of hostility about the patient to himself rather than to the patient. The consultant should also help the staff to identify and interpret the patient's pathologic defenses, such as splitting. Groves (1975) recommends that brief daily conferences be held to prevent staff splitting, as well as to set firm limits when the patient's rage and sense of entitlement become apparent.

Groves (1975) also speaks about staff members' countertransferential hatred toward the patient, including malice and aversion. It is important for the staff to talk about this openly with the consultant, who can act as a role model in helping the staff to voice these forbidden feelings. Thus, the consultant must try to help the staff work through countertransferential feelings by pointing out that it is impossible to meet the patient's constant demands; that it is not the staff's job to cure the patient of psychiatric illness, but only to care for him while he is in the hospital; and that the staff may feel guilty about not being able to cure or satisfy the patient.

The consultant can also act as a role model for the staff in setting limits with the patient. After the alliance between the consultant and the staff is secure, it also may be helpful for the consultant to educate the staff about the underlying dynamics of the borderline condition and the various defense mechanisms such patients use, always pointing out, however, that the staff members should focus their energies on observing, but not curing. This educative process can help to sublimate some of the staff's anger. It can also help the staff deal with its despair and feelings of helplessness, and can foster cohesion and healthy alliances among the staff members (Groves 1975).

Thus, by understanding the psychodynamics of the borderline condition; the primitive defense mechanisms these patients use, especially when confronted with the stress of serious physical illness; and the ways they themselves may react to the patient's behaviors, medical personnel can effectively address these difficult situations for the purpose of providing and maintaining optimum health care services.

REFERENCES

ADLER, G. 1973. "Hospitals Treatment of Borderline Patients." *American Journal of Psychiatry* 130: 32-36.

BURNHAM, G. 1966. "The Special-Problem Patient: Victim or Agent of Splitting?" *Psychiatry* 29:105-122.

CAPLAN, G. 1970. *The Theory and Practice of Mental Health Consultations*. New York: Basic Books.

FRIEDMAN, L. J. 1975. "Current Psychoanalytic Object Relations Theory and Its Clincial Implications." *International Journal of Psychoanalysis* 56:137-146.

GROVES, J. E. 1975. "Management of the Borderline Patients on a Medical or Surgical Ward. The Psychiatric Consultant's Role." *International Journal of Psychiatry in Medicine* 6(3):337-348.

KERNBERG, O. 1975. *Borderline Conditions and Pathological Narcissism*. New York: Jason Aronson.

MAHLER, M. and M. FURER. 1963. "Certain Aspects of the Separation-Individuation Phase." *Psychoanalytic Quarterly* 32:1-14.

MESNIKOFF, A. 1964. "Therapeutic Milieu for the Seriously Disturbed." *International Psychiatric Clinics* 1(4, Oct):891-910.

MODELL, A. H. 1963. "Primitive Object Relationships and the Predisposition to Schizophrenia." *International Journal of Psychoanalysis* 44:282-291.

PARRISH, A. E. 1981. "End-Stage Renal Disease." In W. Stolov and M. R. Clowers, eds. *Handbook of Severe Disability*. Washington, DC: U. S. Department of Education Rehabilitation Services Administration, pp. 334-345.

REICHSMAN, F. and W. B. LEVY. 1972. "Problems in Adaptation to Maintenance Hemodialysis." *Archives of Internal Medicine* 130(Dec):845-863.

SHAPIRO, E. 1978. "The Psychodynamics and Developmental Psychology of the Borderline Patient." *American Journal of Psychiatry* 135:11.

ZETZEL, E. R. 1971. "A Developmental Approach to the Borderline Patient." *American Journal of Psychiatry* 128:867-871.

28

The Psychiatric Patient With AIDS

Robert S. Lampke

Acquired immune deficiency syndrome (AIDS) has been referred to by some as the number one health problem in the United States today. It is a major life-threatening illness that strikes relatively healthy individuals in the prime of their lives, has no known cure, and has a very high mortality rate within two to three years of diagnosis. There is a growing body of literature on the psychosocial aspects of AIDS, including reports on such areas as psychosocial reactions and neuropsychiatric sequelae. For the most part, these reports concern patients with no prior history of psychiatric illness.

The way a patient copes with AIDS depends on variables in three major areas: medical, psychological, and social. Medical aspects include the patient's symptoms, the clinical course, and complications of the disease, especially with respect to the central nervous system (CNS). Psychological factors include the patient's previous level of psychological adjustment and personality integration. Social considerations include the patient's social supports, as well as the sociocultural stigma attached to the illness and afflicted groups (Holland and Tross 1985). A patient's coping ability depends on how many areas are affected: if one area is affected, coping is potentially reduced; if two areas are affected, coping is moderately reduced; and if all three areas are affected, coping is severely impaired (Wellisch 1985).

Many AIDS patients are, of course, affected in the medical and social areas. There are frequent and debilitating infections, often of the CNS. In addition, there is considerable stigma attached not only to the disease but also to the two main groups that are most conspicuously subject to the illness: homosexual men and intravenous drug abusers.

Early signs of brain damage in AIDS include persistent headaches, difficulty in concentrating, fatigue, apathy, and withdrawal. The etiology is an HTLV-III infection of the brain. The functional psychiatric syndromes that accompany AIDS are anxiety reactions, depression, and suicidal behaviors. The organic brain syndromes that result are delirium and dementia.

NATURE OF THE STUDY

How does a psychiatric patient cope with AIDS? Does the presence of pre-existing psychiatric illness affect coping ability? What is the impact of psychopathology on patients' behavior? Does AIDS exacerbate the emotional status of patients with past psychiatric illness? This chapter reports the results of a study of 25 patients with confirmed or suspected AIDS who either had a past psychiatric history or who were hospitalized on the psychiatric service and then transferred to the medical service. All patients were seen in psychiatric consultation by the psychiatric liaison service of Kings County Hospital Center at the request of their primary (non-psychiatric) physicians. All but one of the patients were seen while on the medical service of the hospital. Data were obtained from the original psychiatric consultation reports and, when possible, from patients' present and past medical and psychiatric records.

There were 25 patients (20 males and 5 females) who ranged from 20 to 49 years of age. Seven of the patients (28%) were Haitian. Of the remaining patients, four were homosexual and 10 were intravenous drug abusers. Three patients had questionable histories and no risk factor could be identified in one patient.

RESULTS

The past psychiatric history revealed 22 (of 25) patients had known psychiatric disorders, as follows:

Psychosis	9
Depression	8
Bipolar disorder	1
Diagnosis uncertain	4
No known disorder	3

The reasons for psychiatric consultation were as follows:

Assessment of competency	6
Suicidal behavior	5
Behavioral disturbance	4
Psychiatric hospital transfer	4
Refusal of medical treatment	3
Evaluation of drug therapy	2
Disability evaluation	1

Upon evaluation, the diagnostic impressions of these patients were that seven (28%) had depression, five (20%) had atypical psychosis, three (12%) were mentally competent, three (12%) had chronic schizophrenia, two (8%) had adjustment disorder, two had functional psychosis, and one (4%) had dementia.

Four patients who were transferred from the psychiatric service had been hospitalized only briefly, but two patients who had been transferred from a local branch of the state psychiatric hospital had been hospitalized for approximately two and ten years, respectively, before transfer. In summary, 12 of the patients (48%) had a history of prior psychiatric hospitalizations and six of the patients (24%) had been transferred from the psychiatric service. This gives a combined total of 72% of the patients who had a past or present history of psychiatric hospitalization.

Of these, approximately half had been hospitalized for the first time within the past two years. It has been estimated that AIDS has a two- to five-year incubation period, giving rise to speculation that some of these first psychiatric hospitalizations were the result of undiagnosed AIDS that was first manifested psychiatrically.

Suicidal Behavior

Psychiatric consultation was requested for five patients because they had exhibited suicidal behavior. Specifically, two had threatened to kill themselves if the AIDS diagnosis was confirmed, one had been admitted because of a suicide attempt, one was assessed as being at risk of suicide, and one had attempted suicide in the past. Within the entire group of patients, three others had a history of previous suicide attempts. Another patient had begun making suicidal and homicidal threats a few months earlier, after he had been diagnosed as having AIDS.

There was one fatality by suicide. This patient had a history suggestive of chronic schizophrenia, and it was decided that he was not competent to refuse admission for treatment of presumed CNS toxoplasmosis. He would go in and out of delirium secondary to the toxoplasmosis, and thus required tranquilization and restraint. When he realized he could not return to the adult home where he had lived prior to his admission, he became increasingly depressed. The week before his death, he reported to a nurse that he was having suicidal thoughts, but this information was not acted on. The day before his death he was again delirious and had to be restrained. The next morning he managed to get out of his restraints and gave them to an intern, saying that he didn't need them anymore. Shortly thereafter, he jumped to his death.

It is apparent that staff attitudes toward this patient were ambivalent. Someone heard a warning, but did not want to hear it. Because he was ill with AIDS, the patient was unwanted by the adult home where he had lived, and he was perhaps unwanted by the medical staff, who felt frustrated because they could not cure his terminal illness.

Disposition

At the completion of their medical treatment, four of the six patients who had been transferred from the psychiatric service were returned to it. One patient was transferred to a chronic-disease hospital and one died. In addition, three patients were admitted to the psychiatric service at the completion of their medical treatment: two for suicidal ideation and one because he was felt to be a danger to himself in the community because of his drug abuse and functional psychosis with auditory hallucinations. Prior to their transfer, none of these patients' families had supported the possibility of their coming home, and this had contributed to their suicidal behavior. Shortly after two of these patients had been admitted to psychiatry, their families became supportive and agreed to take them home. This led to a resolution of their suicidal behavior. The third patient had a relapse and was returned to the medical service, where she died shortly thereafter. Needless to say, an association between depression with suicidal behavior and lack of family support is evident in these cases.

To summarize these data, although 48% of the patients had a history of previous hospitalizations, only three patients, or 12%, needed to be admitted to the psychiatric service at the completion of their medical treatment. Although not put to statistical examination, there was not a marked exacerbation in the emotional state of the patients.

To Tell or Not To Tell?

Current medical custom, in contrast to that of the past, is for patients with serious illnesses like cancer to be informed of their diagnosis. Be that as it may, whether or not to inform patients remains a broad and complex issue. Since a cure for AIDS does not yet exist, and since there is very high mortality among patients within two to three years of diagnosis, this is a profoundly serious diagnosis to have to tell someone. The situation is similar to that which prevailed when there were few effective treatments for cancer, although the survival rate for cancer patients then was better than the present survival rate for those who have AIDS.

What do you do when patients may threaten to kill themselves if they are told their diagnosis? One possible solution would be not to tell them, but such a course of action would be at best questionable where AIDS patients are concerned. AIDS is spread by intimate contact and the sharing of bodily fluids between affected persons. Because of the extreme health risks to others, both ethics and practical considerations make it imperative to tell affected persons what precautions to take. AIDS patients must be told of measure for safe sex, and intravenous drug abusers must be warned against sharing needles with others. The urgency of these issues can hardly be overstated.

It becomes virtually impossible to keep diagnoses from patients when, for example, they are housed in isolation rooms or when they see the medical and nursing staff taking such precautions as donning masks, gowns, and gloves before approaching them. Consents for patients' participation in research protocols to test new drugs require that the condition be listed on the form. Hospital practice is to refer all patients with AIDS to the AIDS clinic on discharge. Obviously, there is no easy solution to this dilemma.

In the present study, two patients said they would kill themselves if they were diagnosed as having AIDS. One 24-year-old said that he had been told a year ago that he might have AIDS, but no diagnosis had been made at that time. He told me that he did not want to kill himself if he were found to have AIDS, but that if they didn't find out what was wrong with him within "five to seven days," then he "just might decide to kill himself." He had been depressed since the age of 10, when his mother had been fatally shot by his father, but he had never received any treatment for his depression. Because he was quite anxious, I advised that he be given an anxiolytic. The next day he appeared calmer and less distressed. Following an open-lung biopsy that was diagnostic for AIDS, he was placed on a respirator. His condition deteriorated rapidly over the next two weeks, and he died. Given the rapidity of his deterioration, he probably did not know of his diagnosis.

The second patient had a history of two previous suicide attempts and intermittent suicidal ideation in the past. He said that as long as he was not told he had AIDS, he would not kill himself. The psychiatrist's initial recommendation was not to tell him his diagnosis. His sister was told, and he seemed to be aware of this, but he did not attempt to kill himself. It was as if he were saying that as long as he was not told directly that he had AIDS, then he would not kill himself. He was one of the three patients previously discussed who were admitted to the psychiatry service at the completion of their medical treatement.

Myths

In the course of this study, several misconceptions were observed regarding medically ill psychiatric patients:

1. *It Must Be Psychological.*

According to this myth, the patient has a psychiatric history and now presents symptoms that the medical staff believe are purely psychological in origin. They are quick to forget that psychiatric patients are not immune to medical illnesses that may cause alterations in their thinking, feeling, and behavior. Such alterations are especially observable in AIDS, now that it has been shown the AIDS virus has an affinity for nerve tissue.

Since symptoms can be organic or functional in origin, it will be useful to offer some guidelines to assist when the patient has a past psychiatric history. Patients with recurrent functional psychiatric illnesses who have delusions and hallucinations tend to have the same delusions and hallucinations in each recurrent psychotic episode. If new delusions and hallucinations develop, they are likely to be organic and not functional in etiology (Glickman 1980). It is also important to verify the past psychiatric history, since it is easy to give a psychiatric label to a patient where none, in fact, applies.

Psychiatric consultation was requested for a 43-year-old man who was a patient in the medical prison ward. The patient had a past psychiatric history and the physician wanted advice about medications for his uncommunicative state. The physician stated that he did not know much about the patient's psychiatric history other than that his previous doctor had told him the patient had been at Bellevue Hospital in New York City, presumably for psychiatric reasons. I reviewed the medical chart and learned that the patient had been almost entirely mute since his admission approximately three months ago. The neurological examination done at admission noted that he had an abnormal gait and clouded consciousness. Because of his altered mental status, he was seen by a psychiatrist to assess his competency to consent for medical procedures. The psychiatrist concluded that he was suffering from dementia and was not competent to give consent for procedures. A subsequent CAT scan of the patient's head was also abnormal. Elsewhere on his chart it was mentioned that he had been at Bellevue. I called the family and learned that he had never been at Bellevue for psychiatric reasons and that he had no previous psychiatric history.

When I went to examine the patient, he was in a deep stupor and had bilateral Babinski's reflexes, indicating neurological dysfunction. I felt that his uncommunicative state was organic and not psychological in nature and that the use of psychotropics was not indicated.

2. *Psychiatric Patients Are Incompetent to Consent to Diagnostic Tests.*

Two of the patients in this study were referred for consultations because of past psychiatric history. The requests for consultations were worded thus: "Patient had a past psych history. Is he competent to consent for endoscopy?" In fact, a past history of psychiatric treatment or hospitalization is not in itself sufficient evidence to say that a patient is incompetent. Patients are assumed to be competent; incompetence must be proven. It must be shown that a patient is suffering from a mental illness and that the mental illness is currently interfering with the patient's understanding of co-existing physical illness and of the proposed treatments.

The two patients referred to above were felt to be competent to consent. A third patient in the study was felt to be competent to leave the hospital against medical advice. Three other patients were felt not to be competent to refuse treatments and admission to the hospital. Two of the were drug abusers who had developed organic brain symdrome; the third patient had chronic schizophrenia. In another study of AIDS patients (Lampke 1985), I observed that patients who were found incompetent to refuse tests or treatments commonly had organic brain syndromes and were likely to have a past history of drug and or alcohol abuse.

3. *Present Behavior Reflects Past Behavior.*

Sometimes it is difficult to identify the influence of the setting on patients' symptoms, as the following two case vignettes illustrate. Both patients concerned talked about the devastating effects AIDS was having on them emotionally; both admitted to thoughts of suicide.

The first patient was being seen for disability evaluation. He had what was then called pre-AIDS, which meant that he had some symptoms of the illness but not enough to meet current diagnostic criteria. Ten years previously he had made two suicide attempts related to his homosexuality. Such difficulty in hand-ling crises strongly suggested he would have difficulty handling a suspected illness such as AIDS. During the examination, he appeared agitated and depre-ssed. He said that he was hearing voices saying that he would die of AIDS. The week before he had started taking antidepressants, but with little apparent effect. He was the only patient in the study whose psychotic symptoms — the voices he heard — were related to AIDS (in this case, pre-AIDS). He was also the only patient seen for a disability examination. It was difficult to determine — especially since he was seen only once — how much of his distress during the evaluation resulted from his illness and how much arose from a desire to present himself as disabled.

The second patient was in the hospital prison ward and had asked to see a psychiatrist because he felt depressed over his illness and wanted someone to talk to. He was in jail for attempted burglary. He was also in a Methadone program. At the beginning of the interview, he asked if I would write letters to his lawyers requesting leniency. He said that his recent burglary attempt was to "try to get money to buy enough drugs to bump myself off." He also mentioned that he had once tried to choke his supervisor at work because he "couldn't take the pressure." No charges had been made and he had seen a psychiatrist for six months for "depression." He also had a history of one previous suicide attempt.

He complained of nervousness and sleep difficulties, which improved upon treatment with low doses of Thorazine. Over the next few weeks, I saw him two or three times a week for supportive therapy and offered to teach him relaxation therapy. He chose instead to do his own form of relaxation and meditation, with good results. Changes in his mood appeared to be related to changes in his physical condition. When he was physically sicker, he became demoralized and despondent; when he improved physically the despondency lifted.

Periodically, he would ask for a letter of leniency. I replied that the letter could not be done while he was on the medical ward, but that I would transfer him to the forensic psychiatry ward if he felt that he was not emotionally fit to stand trial or that he had been emotionally ill when he commited the crime. Surprisingly, he declined this offer. When his medical condition stabilized, he was returned to jail.

COMPARISON WITH OTHER STUDIES

Bustamente and Ford (1981) reviewed the literature on psychiatric consultations and found that in general hospitals, the most common reasons for requesting psychiatric consultation are depression and suicidal ideation, diagnostic evaluation, management problems, behavioral problems, failure to find evidence of physical disease, and dispositional problems. These authors found that depression and organic brain syndromes were the most prevalent psychiatric diagnoses.

Dilley, et al (1985) reported on psychiatric consultation with 13 AIDS patients, 11 of whom were homosexual men and two who were bisexual men. Depression was the reason for the referral of 10 of these patients. Adjustment disorder with depressed mood was the most frequent psychiatric diagnosis reported.

In the present study, the three most frequent reasons for requesting psychiatric consultation were assessment of competency, suicidal behavior, and behavioral disturbances. These accounted for 57% of the consultation requests. With the exception of the high percentage (23%) of competency assessments, these results are similar to those reported by Bustamente and Ford (1981) and Dilley, et al (1985). In the other studies, however, assessment of competency was not specifically listed as a reason for requesting psychiatric consultation. In this study, depression and atypical psychosis (organic versus functional) were the most common diagnoses. This finding is similar to those of the other studies.

MANAGEMENT GUIDELINES FOR HOSPITALIZED PSYCHIATRIC PATIENTS WITH AIDS

1. Assessment should be done to identify the presenting problem, that is, the reason for the psychiatric consultation.
2. Any underlying psychiatric disorder should be diagnosed and treated. In particular, past psychiatric history should be documented and verified. This effort may include contacting the patient's family and previous psychiatric care providers, such as hospitals, clinics and therapists. Administration of psychotropic medications may need to be resumed. If necessary, patients should be seen for brief supportive psychotherapy while on the medical ward.

3. A mental status evaluation should be done, with particular attention to cognitive impairments. Are symptoms consistent with past psychiatric symptoms, or are they new? If new psychotic symptoms are present, then one should consider the possibility that they have an organic etiology and do an appropriate work-up for treatable or correctable etiologies. This may include such tests as lumbar puncture, EEG, and cranial CAT scan.

4. To treat behavioral disturbances, it may be necessary to give neuroleptics such as Haldol rapidly, in high doses, or both. Chronic psychiatric patients may be refractory to high-dose neuroleptic therapy. Patients with behavioral reactions secondary to organic brain syndromes may also need rapid tranquilization, restraints, and close observation.

5. The management of suicidal behavior should include frequent assessments, suicide precautions, and psychiatric hospitalization.

6. Family involvement is a crucial factor: patients can become depressed and even suicidal if their families are not supportive and refuse to take them home. Often, however, patients' physical illnesses are too severe for their families to care for them at home. When this is the case, patients who wish to go home may remain depressed. This is an area in which more work needs to be done.

REFERENCES

BUSTAMENTE, J. P. and C. V. FORD. 1981. "Characteristics of General Hospital Patients Referred for Psychiatric Consultation." *Journal of Clinical Psychiatry* 42:338-341.

DILLEY, J. W. et al. 1985. "Findings in Psychiatric Consultations with Patients with Acquired Immune Deficiency Syndrome." *American Journal of Psychiatry* 142:82-86.

GLICKMAN, L. S. 1980. *Psychiatric Consultation in the General Hospital.* New York: Marcel Decker.

HOLLAND, J. C. and S. TROSS. 1985. "The Psychosocial and Neuropsychiatric Sequelae of The Acquired Immunodeficiency Syndrome and Related Disorders." *Annals of Internal Medicine* 103:760-764.

LAMPKE, R. S. 1985. "Overview of AIDS Patients Seen in Psychiatric Consultation." Presented at Conference on Psychiatric Manifestations of AIDS, May 10, Brooklyn, New York.

WELLISCH, D. K. 1985. "UCLA Psychological Study of AIDS." *Frontiers of Radiation Therapy and Oncology* 19:155-158.

ADDITIONAL READING

NICHOLS, S. E. and D. G. OSTROW, eds. 1984. *Psychiatric Implications of Acquired Immune Deficiency Syndrome.* Washington, D. C.: American Psychiatric Press.

SILBERSTEIN, C. 1985. "Psychobiological Considerations in the Development of Acquired Immunodeficiency Syndrome." *Einstein Quarterly Journal of Biological Medicine* 3:136-143.

29

The Challenge of Providing Home Care for the Life-Threatened Psychiatric Patient

Jodie A. Emery

As our society recognizes the causes of mental disorders and develops better treatments for them, more and more patients are being returned to the community after hospitalization. This group includes psychiatric patients who have life-threatening illnesses. My job as a provider of home health care services is to assist these patients in adjusting as well as they can to life and death at home. This is a heavy responsibility even when patients are mentally healthy, but it is especially difficult when one is developing and delivering a plan of care for both the physical and emotional well-being of the psychiatric patient.

Setting up a care program has changed greatly in the past few years for all patients. With cost constraints, new and stringent regulations, and the development of diagnosis-related groups (DRGs), many patients are being brought home earlier and sicker, and to a situation in which fewer services are available. What used to be a skilled nursing case may only be eligible for "custodial" or aide-level care today. The challenge is not only to give the best possible services to each patient, but to do it in the amount of time allowed and at the lowest cost. This has led to a tremendous increase in the number of aide-level caregivers. Many of today's aide-level care providers come from different countries and cultures. In some of these countries it is still believed that illness, whether mental or physical, is a punishment or curse. Many of the aide-level personnel are uneducated and, through their cultures, may have acquired superstitions and various religious beliefs that affect their work. Therefore, there is much to be taught. We have to educate them, for example, to deal with the entire issue of death and dying in patients' homes. To educate this group to cope with the difficult problem of care and death of psychiatric patients requires extensive training and a great deal of support by the instructor. Effective caring requires knowledge, skill, and empathy. It is unreasonable to think that all personnel can effectively care for a dying patient, especially a psychiatric patient. Therefore after careful and in-depth screening, we begin the training process by educating each employee to use the same caring, consideration, and understanding they use with patients who will recover. The most fundamental advice is simply to relate to a dying patient with the best qualities we are able to bring to any caring patient–staff relationship.

We have learned that all people share certain basic needs. These needs must be met in order to function as human beings. Sometimes people are unable to meet their needs themselves and require help. We teach our caregivers that it is important to recognize what need they are trying to meet by their actions. Is it the need of the patient? Is it the need of the family? Is it the need of the caregiver? We want our staff to know that there is nothing wrong with fulfilling their own needs as they work, but that they must be alert not to do this at the expense of the patient.

Just as all people have similar basic needs, they also have differences. Patients who are ill or disabled have different needs, as do children and the aged. Patients who are mentally impaired react differently to their situations. We stress the importance of treating each patient appropriately, according to his particular needs.

Mentally healthy life-threatened patients can generally adapt to change, give and receive affection and love, tolerate stress to varying degrees, accept responsibility for their own feelings and actions, distinguish between reality and unreality, and form and keep relationships with others. This is not true of many psychiatric patients. In this latter group we deal with the same defense mechanisms that most people facing loss use, but with the psychiatric patients we must deal with them constantly. The most common mechanisms are: denial, depression, regression, repression, projection, rationalization, and aggression. The symptoms of mental impairment most often encountered are hallucinations, sleeplessness, fear, irritability, decreased memory, disorientation, forgetfulness, mood swings, and withdrawal.

Caring for these patients becomes complicated at times. Patients and aide-level caregivers become socially and emotionally intertwined. We stress to our staff that they will not always understand what is happening in the home, and we encourage them to discuss their feelings with other members of the health care team. If needed, we call in outside counseling experts to guide our caregivers as they provide their special services.

One of the most important parts of psychiatric care is to provide basic personal care and grooming and to pay careful attention to physical needs. We have found that the care of psychiatric life-threatened patients can be altered by attention to these details. For example, environmental factors that stimulate the senses — sight, touch, smell, taste, and hearing — are extremely important to the patients.

Most patients want to experience light, sound, and the movement of life around them. At the same time, we must be particularly sensitive to removing sounds that may be irritating or painful (e.g. alarm clocks, banging doors). We have found that comfort is provided by open shades or draperies, good lighting, and the use of light colors for bedspreads, clothing, and other such items. Patients' rooms should be well ventilated and arranged so that the patients can easily reach often-used items. Patients are encouraged to seek diversion and recreation by watching television or listening to the radio or records.

We recommend that patients be included in planning activities and that they do as much for themselves as possible. We encourage their efforts, and praise all of their successes. Our staff tries to instill the hope of realizing small, easily achieved goals, but without encouraging false hope. We try to relieve as many of patients' symptoms as possible and to provide good nutrition, rest, exercise, and good hygiene. Also try to offer patients intellectual stimulation, social contacts, diversions such as games and handiwork, and comforts such as gentle backrubs or sponge baths. Sometimes a caregiver simply sits and holds a patient's hand.

Our caregiver is often a patient's only constant companion. The doctor, therapist, and family rely on the caregiver's objective observations of the patient and the family. Caregivers must be extremely sensitive to the family's patterns of coping, must try to work within that pattern, and must be alert for problems in coping.

A caregiver enters a family to care for one of its members and becomes aware of how the family operates. Most of our patients live in some sort of family unit. It may be an extended family with several generations in the same house, a single-parent family, or a unit made up of friends who live together and regard themselves as a family. We care for our patients as best we can within the framework of the family situation. Employees may be sent to some families where they do not feel totally comfortable; they may be afraid and they may not understand what is happening. The family may have values and engage in actions that the caregiver personally disapproves of. It is the responsibility of the health care team to help our primary caregivers become comfortable with their feelings and understand why these feelings are natural. It is most important that our employees recognize and are honest about their reactions to patients and their families so that these responses do not interfere with providing good patient care.

This is not an easy process. Our caregivers must learn that the way patients cope with the home care situation often relates to recent events in their lives. A patient's psychiatric background may have caused important changes in the family, including financial difficulties, housing changes, role changes, and other significant events. Stress concentrated in a short time span has a cumulative effect on the ability to cope. If the family unit has experienced meaningful changes, the caregiver should be particularly sensitive to coping difficulties.

The care of a life-threatened psychiatric patient can disrupt normal family roles and force changes that affect the entire family. New ways of coping become necessary. The home health-care worker offers respite to family members who care for the patient on a regular basis and helps to minimize the role changes that occur. Family members who regularly care for the patient often need to vent their feelings and receive emotional support from someone. We educate our staff to encourage the family to live in a manner that is as close to their usual life style as possible.

In setting up care for life-threatened psychiatric patients, we aim for the following goals: (1) to promote patients' self-care and independence; (2) to make sure the patients are as safe and comfortable as possible; (3) to maintain patients' dignity and self respect; (4) to maintain stability in the home. In order to achieve these goals, we utilize a team approach that includes doctors, nurses, psychiatrists, social workers, clergy, and often volunteers, who assist our primary caregivers in providing total patient care. But our patients, regardless of their health status, rely on family and friends to be in contact with them — in short, to care. When patients have a life-threatening illness, they need family to help bolster their hope and to be their advocates. As Cousins (1979) asked, "If only in terms of ricochet effect on the patient, should the physician not treat the entire family?" All members of the health care team, but especially the primary caregivers, should work with the entire family. The family, as well as the patient, is a consumer of home health services. The role of the family in the patient-family relationship depends on the relationship that existed before the patient needed home health care.

In some circumstances, particularly when positive involvement is possible, family members need to be encouraged to participate, to be brought closer to the patient and to be involved in working with the home health-care team. In other instances, when intimacy only produces friction and hostility, distance between the patient and family is called for. Family members who visit once a week or once a month may spend "quality time" and have closer relationships with the patient than family members whose daily "stop-overs" are fraught with conflict and nagging.

Family needs or wishes can conflict with the needs of the patient. For example, family members may have problems in reacting to the patient, and their expressions reflect their uneasiness. They may visit at a time when the patient is agitated or too exhausted to enjoy company. Family members may, out of concern, go against the plan of care established for therapeutic purposes. The family expects certain actions from the patient and also the health care employee. A balance must be established that meets the patient's health needs, involves the family in the patient's care, and follows the health care team's policies and procedures. All parties involved will soon learn that the family's participation in the care of the patient can be advantageous to the patient, the family itself, and the primary caregiver. The family's ability and desire to assist with the patient's personal care gives the patient a sense of family warmth and support and gives the family a feeling of participation and usefulness.

Just as important is the support of family members by the health care team. This support is crucial in providing care for the dying patient. Frequently, it is family members who need assistance in communicating effectively and supportively with their loved one who is dying, and frequently it is family members who cause problems for themselves, the patient, and the primary caregiver because their feelings have not been worked through and they are extremely fatigued. Emotional support for the patient and family is a fundamental part of caring for the terminally ill psychiatric patient.

With the discomforts of dying, patients and family members may become very demanding; when the one who is dying is a psychiatric patient, the situation is intensified. Sometimes the home care employee becomes "caught in the middle" between the patient's and the family's anger and frustration. To counter this, we have our staff who are in this situation keep a diary. This allows them to verbalize their feelings and frustrations and also allows them to listen to others talk about how they have handled difficult situations. This has made a positive impact on our incidence of staff burnout.

Our concern is that we manage all patients' care in a way that ensures that the patients live until they die, that their families live with them as they are dying, and that their families continue to live afterward. "Dying with dignity" is an often-heard phrase. Dignity means worthiness. To dying patients, it means being able to stay in control as much as possible and to feel the loving support of important people in their lives. That gives them a sense of their own worth, so that they can approach death courageously and in a dignified way. As Kent (1983) has said:

> For after all, the manner of a person's dying is his last act both for himself and for those he loves, and it can be a heritage he leaves for the memory of those who come after him. Therefore, to be dignified throughout the last days of one's life is more than simply a question of style. It is a question of helping us all feel that the summing up at the end gives a particular kind of importance and majesty to the life that was led.

REFERENCES

COUSINS, N. 1979. *Anatomy of an Illness*. New York: W. W. Norton & Company.
KENT, M. 1983. *Concerning Death. A Practical Guide for Living*. New York: McGraw-Hill.

30

Reactions of Therapists to the Death of Elderly Patients in Psychotherapy

Theresa A. Ladero

In the natural course of events, elderly people are more apt to die than younger people, and may do so while in therapy. These deaths, with the resulting hurt to our therapeutic narcissism, as well as the stimulation of our fears regarding aging and death, may be behind the well-known avoidance of involvement in the psychotherapeutic treatment of the elderly. This chapter will explore the ways in which geriatric therapists deal with the deaths of their patients and the implications of their responses with respect to their practice. What therapists do can sometimes affect the quality or nature of patients' death and the reactions of the survivors.

REVIEW OF THE LITERATURE

A search of the literature reveals much about bereavement, but little about the bereavement of therapists, particularly in reaction to the death of the aged. Some studies have dealt with attitudes towards the elderly in general and with the reasons why individuals do not desire to treat or practice in the field of gero-psychiatry. Ford and Sbordone (1980), for example, found that mental health workers tended to view the elderly as having poorer prognoses than younger people. Kastenbaum (1963) declared that therapists fear the issues of death they might have to deal with in relation to the older patient. In addition, they rationalize that since the elderly are nearer to death, they are not worth the investment of great amounts of time. Finally, Kastenbaum noted that many therapists look down on the elderly as a low-status group.

Therapists sometimes resist working with the elderly on issues of countertransference. Poggi and Berland (1985) found that therapists working with the elderly tended to avoid sexual material, felt more comfortable being called "the boys," and tended to emphasize these patients' physical problems and avoid any psychological problems they presented.

The interrelationships between the attitudes of therapists and those of their elderly patients might also be relevant. As Feifel (1965) pointed out, there are differences among the aged regarding the idea of death. A patient who is fearful or uncomfortable with the idea of death may resort to the defenses of avoidance and denial. If his therapist has similar reactions, the two may form an unconscious collusion to stay away from looking at and preparing for death. On the other hand, the most effective geropsychiatric workers, according to Mutschler (1971), are those who have experienced and resolved their own losses, and who therefore are not as threatened as others by the topic.

After all, when a person is very ill and is going to die soon, a major part of the therapeutic task is to help that person toward an appropriate death. This task, which is part of what Erikson (1953) called the development task of "ego integrity" at the last stage of life, is behind the questions that prompted this essay.

THE SURVEY

As a gero-psychiatric nurse specialist and therapist in the gero-psychiatric clinic and consultation service at the Bronx Municipal Hospital Center in New York, I am a member of a geriatric team that includes a psychiatrist, who is also the director of the service, a senior psychologist, a certified social worker, and several psychiatric rehabilitation workers. In a systematic survey of 125 patients whom I treated from 1979 through 1984, I found that 22 of these patients, or 18%, had died while in treatment (mostly for depression). Such a large loss can exact a significant emotional toll, especially if the therapist is dedicated to the task of helping the troubled elderly and has established close, meaningful relationships with these patients.

Table 1 provides a description of the patients who died while in therapy. Several factors should be noted about them. Their age range was from 66 to 93 years; the mean age was 77.8 years. Fifty percent were females and 50% were males.

The fact that 95% of the sample were white reflects the large number of Jewish and Italian persons living in the area of the Bronx Municipal Hospital Center. The majority of the patients, 82%, were single.

Eighty-six percent of the group came to the clinic with a chief complaint of depression; only 14% presented with psychosis. The medical problems that resulted in death were the diseases common in this age group; 36% had cardiovascular disease, 36% died of stroke, 5% of pneumonia, and 18% of cancer; unfortunately, one male with a diagnosis of psychosis committed suicide.

TABLE 1

Characteristics of Patients who Died while in Therapy (n = 22)

	Number	%
Age		
66 - 74	7	32
75 - 84	11	50
85 - 93	4	18
Sex		
Male	11	50
Female	11	50
Race		
White	21	95
Non-white	1	5
Religion		
Roman Catholic	12	55
Jewish	9	40
Protestant	1	5
Marital Status		
Widowed or other	18	82
Married	4	18
Psychiatric Presentation		
Depression	19	86
Psychosis	3	14
Medical Problems		
Cardiovascular	8	36
Stroke	8	36
Cancer	4	18
Lung disease	2	10
Reactions of Therapist		
Avoidance	10	46
Guilt	6	27
Denial	6	27

CASE STUDIES

Mr. S., an 85-yeear-old white shoemaker, was referred to our clinic because he was suffering from stomach cancer and had refused surgery. Mr. S. expressed his feelings thus: "I am an old man. I have lived a full life. I know I have cancer and would rather take my chances than put myself or my family through unwanted suffering." He continued expressing the hope that the doctors would give him something for the pain. I respected his decision and accepted him as a patient for treatment.

During the three years that Mr. S. was in therapy, the focus of his treatment was on a life-review. He described his life as a full and happy one, filled with both physical and spiritual treasures. His two daughters, his remaining family, were devoted to him and wished Mr. S. to remain at home. I supported this decision.

The last time Mr. S. came to the clinic was three weeks before he died. He came to see me with his daughters and insisted on presenting me with a gift. He said he was glad he had gotten to know me and seemed at peace with himself. When he said goodbye, my reaction was one of sadness at the thought that I would probably never see him again.

I reacted to Mr. S.'s death with sadness, a feeling of helplessness, and avoidance, I closed his chart in haste and avoided any further contact with the family. This left me with a sense of incompleteness. Nevertheless, through this patient's accepting and serene attitude toward his own death, I recognized my avoidance and denial of my feelings as a defense.

In contrast, a sense of dissatisfaction predominated in my responses to Mrs. D., an 82-year-old white female suffering from severe cardiac problems. I treated her at her home, because she had previously undergone amputation of her right leg. She often said that she did not mind dying, but that she desperately wanted to fulfill her last wish. On my sixth visit, Mrs. D. was able to tell me that her daughter, her only child, had left home 35 years ago, and she had not seen her since. Mrs. D. wanted to see her daughter again before she died. I attempted to locate Mrs. D.'s daughter and, with the help of the social worker, finally managed to do so. I made a visit to Mrs. D.'s home in order to tell her the good news and found that she had died.

I felt devastated, frustrated, impotent, and guilty. Guilt was the most dominant reaction. I felt that I had failed this patient by not being able to grant her last wish. Three days later, Mrs. D.'s daughter phoned and stated that she wanted nothing to do with her mother. Because of my feelings of guilt, I attended Mrs. D.'s funeral. I also felt a sense of loss, and used the defense of denial in relation to the daughter's rejection.

In the case of Mrs. R., as with Mr. S., I felt a sense of satisfaction. Mrs. R. was an 88-year-old white female who came to the clinic explicitly looking for a kind counselor to whom she could confess her sins before she died. Mrs. R. felt that she could not do so with her two children or with anyone else she knew personally. I saw this patient for a total of six visits, during which she "confessed" her grave sins. The counseling consisted mainly of listening to and agreeing with this aged woman and emphatically conveying understanding of her suffering and need for privacy. At the end of the last visit, she thanked me and left.

After Mrs. R. died, I again experienced a wish for avoidance and denial. Nevertheless, I felt that I had helped fulfill this woman's need for completion, and good gestalt in her life. Mrs. R. had directed her therapy, and in recognizing her need to do so, I felt that I had helped her die in peace.

Mrs. O. was a 66-year-old woman whom I had been seeing for more than a year. When Mrs. O. developed cancer and it metastasized rapidly, I felt a sense of guilt, as though, perhaps, I should have been more vigilant. The patient died after six weeks in the hospital, and although I had visited frequently, denial and guilt were my main defenses when she died. I avoided contact with the family and felt a prevailing sense of incompleteness.

DISCUSSION

A survey of the 22 patients who had died while in therapy, of whom the four just described were a representative sample, pointed to four major ways in which I had dealt with the patients' death:

1. A process of gradual disengagement and diminution of sessions. This took place primarily with those who were ill and clearly had to terminate psychotherapy.
2. A close and intimate contact, which sometimes included attendance at the funeral services and the maintenance of contact with the patients' families.
3. Guilt, characterized by concern about whether or not I had been found wanting as a therapist or had contributed in some measure to the death.
4. To my distress, avoidance and denial were my most frequent reactions. They were also easy ones to justify, since the patients often became too sick to continue psychotherapy. One outcome of conducting the survey and writing this report is that I have become more open and self-confronting.

CONCLUSION

When patients die, no matter at what age, their therapists often must go through a mourning process. Some may think that it is easier to deal with the death of an elderly person than with the death of a younger one. Even if it is easier, it is by no means easy; and if it is easy, then we are often avoiding a necessary life task in ourselves. If therapists can face their own grief, the result is an increased ability to help patients and their surviving relatives to futher growth and personal maturity. What followed from my experiences and means of dealing with them is a sense of satisfaction in helping a person toward the opportunity to live a fuller life in the time remaining and to achieve an appropriate death.

As a result of this survey, my colleagues and I have instituted postmortem meetings regarding all patients who die while in therapy at the clinic. It is recommended that health workers in all areas dealing with geriatric patients conduct similar meetings in order to share their experiences with each other, to provide a meaningful termination with patients, and to secure closure in a worthwhile manner.

REFERENCES

ERIKSON, E. H. 1956. "The Problem of Ego Identity." *Journal of the American Psychoanalytical Association* 4:56-121.

FEIFEL, H. "Attitudes Toward Death." In H. Feifel, ed. *The Meaning of Death*. New York: McGraw-Hill.

FORD, C. and R. SBORDONE. 1980. "Attitudes of Psychiatrists Toward Elderly Patients." *American Journal of Psychiatry* 137:571-575.

KASTENBAUM, R. 1963. "The Reluctant Therapist." *Geriatrics* 18:296-301.

MUTSCHLER, P. 1971. "Factors Affecting Choice of an Preservation in Social Work in the Aged." *Gerontologist* 11:231-241.

POGGI, R. G. and D. I BERLAND. 1985. "The Therapist's Reaction to the Elderly." *Gerontologist* 25:508-512.

Subject Index